# Jane Hicks Gentry

# Jane Hicks Gentry

## *A Singer Among Singers*

Betty N. Smith

*Betty N. Smith* (signature)

With a Foreword by
Cecelia Conway

THE UNIVERSITY PRESS OF KENTUCKY

Publication of this volume was made possible in part by grants
from the E.O. Robinson Mountain Fund and the National
Endowment for the Humanities.

Scholarly publisher for the Commonwealth,
serving Bellarmine College, Berea College, Centre
College of Kentucky, Eastern Kentucky University,
The Filson Club Historical Society, Georgetown College,
Kentucky Historical Society, Kentucky State University,
Morehead State University, Murray State University,
Northern Kentucky University, Transylvania University,
University of Kentucky, University of Louisville,
and Western Kentucky University.

*Frontispiece* : Jane Gentry with her granddaughter Haladine,
Alfred's daughter, ca. 1922. They are seated beside the garden house
built by the German prisoners of war on the grounds of Sunnybank.

*Editorial and Sales Offices:* The University Press of Kentucky
663 South Limestone Street, Lexington, Kentucky 40508-4008

02  01  00  99  98      5  4  3  2  1


Library of Congress Cataloging-in-Publication Data

Smith, Betty N.
    Jane Hicks Gentry : a singer among singers / Betty N. Smith.
        p.    cm.
    Includes bibliographical references (p.    ), discography (p.    ) and index.
    ISBN 0-8131-0936-1 (alk. paper)
    1. Gentry, Jane Hicks, d. 1925.  2. Folk singers—Appalachian Region,
Southern—Biography.  3. Folk music—Appalachian Region, Southern.
4. Folk songs, English—Appalachian Region, Southern.  5. Jack tales
—Appalachian Region, Southern.  I. Title.
ML420.G34S65    1998
782.42162'13'0092—dc21
[B]                                                      97-31636

# Contents

Music heard early in life lays down a rich bed of memories against which you evaluate and absorb music encountered later. It is so with words and word patterns. Like music, the patterns of melody, rhythm and quality of voice become templates against which we judge the sweetness and justness of new patterns and rhythms; the patterns laid down in our memories create expectations and a hunger for fulfillment again. . . . In those early years all the seeds of love were planted. . . . Planting magic in the mind of a child.

—Robert MacNeil, "Wordstruck"

# Foreword

## Cecelia Conway

*Jane Hicks Gentry: A Singer Among Singers* is an engaging book. Betty Smith wishes that Gentry could have written the book herself; we are lucky that Smith has written it for us. Her energy, patience, and sensitivity may be akin to Gentry's own, and Smith's insights benefit from her own standing as a singer and musician.

In many ways, this book resembles some of those written by women about Appalachia during Gentry's lifetime—and the book she herself might have written had she not been too busy living to record her life. Smith's dedication to uncovering Gentry's life story is evident throughout. She has conducted extensive interviews with, and uncovered written records by, many of those who knew Gentry. The number of diverse and prestigious people moved by this mountain singer is exceptional, and Smith, in weaving their voices into her text, clearly shows how much sentiment is coming from them. The traditional anecdotes she introduces balance and deepen the tone of her story. She has done an admirable job of making important connections between Gentry's life experiences and her artistic expression.

Women readers and scholars of Appalachia will want to think carefully about the silences in Gentry's life that Smith has uncovered for us. What is the significance of the parts of Gentry's life story that remain understated or mysterious? What do these silences suggest about the greater hardships Jane lived with and the pain she endured but did not dwell upon or wish to express? What resonances and context do these silences provide for Gentry's own self-characterization: "I have learnt how to feel badly and keep cheerful." What do they say about her values and fears? Why were her songs omitted from the extensive *Frank C. Brown Collection of North Carolina Folklore*, and why has her full story remained obscure so long?

For her biography of Gentry, Smith has drawn together an impressive array of materials: Cecil Sharp's memories of collecting folksongs from Gentry, a novelist's essays about Gentry (even his lost novel on her life), important geographical and historical information about Hot Springs, extensive genealogical records, and the memories of widely scattered family members and friends. The biographical chapters lead the reader into those dealing with the many genres of Gentry's reportory, her Jack tales and varied songs--for me the most provocative portions of the book. Smith presents these diverse materials in a way that evokes the voice of Jane Gentry herself. In counterpointing family history with folklore, Smith has created a compelling portrait of an engaging and important folk artist.

# Preface

This book should have been written by Jane Gentry. With her quick wit and her lively rhetoric she would have told the story better than anyone else possibly could. But where would she have found the time to write it down? She was too busy living.

For more than twenty-five years Jane Hicks Gentry has enriched my life as I have gone about collecting every bit of information about her I could find. She is at the top of my list of people I would have liked to know. But, in a way, I do know her. I know her much better than many people I have known for years. There was about her an air of simplicity, a natural unaffected grace, and her face was lit with an engaging smile. She carried on conversation in simple but colorful language and showed evidence of a creative mind. I can just hear her saying, "My heart were floppin' like the wings of a skeered potteridge," or "My face got as hot as a smokin' griddle." There was never any doubt about what she meant even if you were from "off," as one esteemed Appalachian scholar would put it. She sang and told stories wherever she was and whatever the occasion—in her own kitchen or before the Ballad Society or for the schoolchildren. When I think of her, William Blake's poetic phrase comes to mind—I somehow believe she learned early in life to "catch joy on the wing." This is the Jane Gentry who has become real to me.

Unlike people who have many projects going and are afraid they will never finish them, Jane Gentry lived each day as though it were her last. Whatever she did, she did well. Her life was certainly not an easy one. Quite the contrary, anyone would have called it "hard." If there was a dark side of her life, it was that, in spite of her cheerful acceptance, most of her days were filled with backbreaking toil, and she had a painful back problem much of her life. Nola Jane, Jane's youngest child, massaged her mother's back with liniment at night, but in all of her recorded conversations about her life Jane did not speak of this. By the end of most of her days she must have been bone-tired, but what her children remembered about her was that she always sang as she went about her daily work. She enjoyed cooking and baking and she did them with great skill. Even people who didn't think they liked southern cooking enjoyed Jane and Maud's boardinghouse food. She was an extraordinary weaver and spinner. Her hands, although gnarled from years of constant use, were seldom idle, and she taught anyone who wanted to learn how to tat and knit. She even made pulled lace, which most people consider too time-consuming. She was a marvelous singer of songs and teller of tales, and this is what brought her to my attention.

In the late sixties I began using Jane's songs and those of her daughter Maud Long in my programs, classes, and workshops on ballads and Appalachian music. I was fortunate enough to own Cecil Sharp's *English Folk Songs from the Southern Appalachians,* where I found forty of Jane Gentry's songs. I also owned *The Frank C. Brown Collection of North Carolina Folklore* and was, and continue to be, puzzled by the absence of Gentry materials. I ordered all of Maud's Library of Congress recordings of ballads, songs, and Jack tales. I found fifteen of Jane's stories, collected by Isabel Gordon Carter, in a 1925 issue of the *Journal of American Folklore.* I was fascinated by this woman from the mountain county of Madison, which had more than its share of musicians and ballad singers. I knew many of them. I also knew quite a few ballads and songs. My father was a fine shape note singer and knew some good ballads. "Barbry Allen" was my grandmother's baby-rocking song, but this Mrs. Gentry had an incredible repertoire. In 1975 I included her ballad "The False Knight in the Road" on a recording titled *Songs Traditionally Sung in North Carolina* for Folk Legacy Records.

In 1985 two things happened that set me on a course of action that eventually led to this book. Terrell Crow, editor of the *Tar Heel Junior Historian,* asked me to write an article for a music issue. I submitted a list of possible subjects, and "Jane Gentry" was selected. I was encouraged to do more work on the subject. Not long afterward I heard from Michael Hill, researcher for the Division of Archives and History of the North Carolina Department of Cultural Resources, who said that a marker for Cecil Sharp was being considered and asked for my suggestions. My sentiment was that Sharp's contacts in North Carolina were primarily with John and Olive Dame Campbell and with the singers he met. There was already a marker for the Campbells at John C. Campbell Folk School at Brasstown, so I suggested that a marker be placed in Hot Springs. This would honor not only Sharp but also the singer who gave him more songs than any other informant in the southern mountains. I thought perhaps Maud Long's name might also appear on the marker, but it seems that one must be dead for twenty-five years before that can happen. And so the marker was placed in front of Sunnybank, Jane's last home, which was already on the National Register for Historic Places. It was dedicated on October 3, 1986, at the Bascom Lamar Lunsford Festival at Mars Hill College. Elizabeth Dotterer, Elmer Hall, and I felt that a local gathering to celebrate the marker would be appropriate. Over lunch at my home on Bluff Mountain the three of us planned the celebration.

I sent out invitations, and on a Sunday afternoon, October 18, we gathered in the parlor of Sunnybank. "Miss Peggy" Dotterer told stories; Daron Douglas, Maud's granddaughter, and I sang ballads, and everyone told stories about Grandmother Jane and Aunt Maud. Two granddaughters, Betty and Lalla Rolfe, who were on a camping trip, showed up not knowing that they would find family and friends gathered to honor their grandmother. The night before, I had a call from Jane's youngest daughter, Nola Jane Gentry Yrjana, in Alaska, who wanted to be there and who spoke for the family in expressing appreciation for the efforts to honor her mother, Cecil Sharp, and Maud Long. Elmer Hall, proprietor of Sunnybank—The Inn at Hot Springs, invited all those present to a delicious supper of soup, salad, and a savory brioche. It was a party Jane and Maud would have enjoyed.

I think it was Joe Hickerson who planted the idea for a book. I was in the Archive of Folk Song in the American Folklife Center at the Library of Congress.

I had written the article about Jane and was working on a paper to be read at the Appalachian Studies Conference when Joe said he thought that writing a book would be the only way to lay this project to rest.

It was during my first visit with Bill Moore in his store on Meadow Fork that he dubbed Jane "the most beautiful singer" and "a singer among singers." He was married to "Aunt Janie's" niece Susan Reese, and they named their son after Jane's father, Ransom Hicks. Moore knew everybody in the county because he had worked for the Madison County Tax Department. He had an extraordinarily good memory and was a fine storyteller. An equally good informant was Elizabeth Dotterer, generally known as "Miss Peggy." She was a good historian for Hot Springs, because she was a good observer and had a phenomenal memory. Much of the history she learned from her Grandmother Rumbough, who told her stories about the early days in Hot Springs. She rode her horse all through the area and always seemed to know what was going on. Miss Peggy was about the age of Nola Jane and had been in and out of the Gentry home. Maud was a good singer and I was a good singer, she would tell me, but Jane was out of the past, what she called "genuine." I miss those afternoons spent listening to her tell about life in Hot Springs when she was young.

In September 1990, I flew to Fairbanks and spent almost a week with Nola Jane. I had corresponded with her for several years and called her occasionally. One Sunday afternoon in January 1989 I heard the weather report for Fairbanks—51 degrees below zero. I called to ask how she and her husband, Bill Yrjana, both of whom were in their eighties, were faring. They were having trouble keeping the furnace hot enough and they were carrying hot Alpo and cooked cabbage to a dog team Bill was trying to raise. The next year she moved to the Pioneer Home in Fairbanks, one of the homes the state of Alaska maintains for its pioneers. I knew this change would be difficult for this independent, spunky woman, who had indeed been a pioneer, had taught Athabaskan Indian children, and had continued to tutor them after she retired. I felt an urgency to meet her. Everybody said she was like her mother. I checked into a motel in Fairbanks and walked over to visit her each day. She seemed happy to be talking about her family, and I was happy to be spending time with Jane Gentry's daughter.

Although she has been legally blind for ten years, I have carried on a lively correspondence with Jeannette Armstrong, daughter of Emily, the second oldest daughter, who moved to Alaska and then to Washington State, pioneering on Whidbey Island. I also visited Jeannette at her home in San Luis Obispo, California. It has been interesting to learn that Emily brought up her children in the same way she was brought up—telling them stories and singing them songs. Jeannette likes to tell about "reading in the dark." Emily would lie down with her at night after the lights were out and tell stories of her childhood back in North Carolina and recite Bible verses and poems.

In 1990 Eugene Hicks, grandson of Uncle Doc, Jane's brother, bought the hotel property and reopened the hot springs. I heard that Gene's uncle Nathan Hicks had a trailer parked on the property, and I went to look for him. A spry-looking fellow riding a bicycle in the campground turned out to be Uncle Nathan. He said he was named for Ray Hicks's father, although he is usually called by his nickname, " Uncle Gabe," and said he had been riding a bicycle for fifty years. In his late seventies and still going strong, he comes over from Marion in the warm months and helps with maintenance of the springs and soaks in the mineral water every day. He told me wonderful stories about Uncle Doc and the days on Meadow Fork.

Nola Jane sent me a copy of *Flashbacks to Dawn*. This book about the Asheville Normal School was written by Mary Kestler Clyde, Nola Jane's roommate at the normal school and at Duke University. Chapter 11 was titled "Gentle Jane's Recital" and was an account of Jane Gentry's chapel program in the fall of 1920. I visited Mrs. Clyde at a Presbyterian retirement home in Clearwater, Florida, and listened to more stories about the Gentrys.

Collectors of oral materials tend to tell us more about the songs and stories than about the singers and tellers of tales. We know more about the collectors than we do about the informants. I became even more aware of this when I found Jane's stories included in such collections as *A Harvest of World Folk Tales* (Viking Press) with credit given only to the collector, Isabel Gordon Carter. And yet, the most important person must always be the tradition bearer. Because Jane Gentry died about the time I was born, my research had to be done by seeking out family and acquaintances, by correspondence, and the written word. There were no diaries, only one letter, and that not in her handwriting. I heard at a scholarly meeting that she had a trunk full of broadsides and that she played instruments. I found no evidence of this, but I did find wonderful stories from many people. Some were stories heard as much as seventy-five years before. It was amazing to hear Eugenia Elliott tell of experiences when she was a student at Dorland Institute and Jane lived next door. Pat Roberts, ninety-one years old, looking twenty years younger, talked about having to get the voting booths set up for the Republican primary and in the next breath remembered what Jane Gentry told the students at the Asheville Normal School when Roberts was a student there. She had made such an impression that the stories were well remembered. Over the years, correspondence and conversations with Jane's grandchildren, great-grandchildren, nephews, neighbors, and friends have sent me searching for more family stories. On my numerous trips to Gentry Hardware, Jim and Dot Gentry have given me names, addresses, and stories as well. The more I heard, the more I came to realize that Jane Gentry was not just an exceptional singer and storyteller. She was a rare person. I continued to meet people who found Jane as fascinating as I did. It has been a remarkable experience.

Much could still be done. This is the age of "the story." Stories are being analyzed from every imaginable viewpoint, and when the Jack tales are mentioned Jane's name comes up. Her repertoire of both songs and stories will be of interest to people in various fields. Perhaps examination of Jane Gentry's life and music from a feminist perspective will be of interest to scholars. Her life was so full, her oral materials so rich and numerous that it would be overwhelming to try to analyze every facet at length. I would not want this quiet singer to become lost in the jargon.

I entered Jane in the North Carolina Women's History Project, for I felt that she was representative of women who have great talent and ability and who use their gifts in taking care of their families, being good neighbors, and enriching the lives of schoolchildren and anyone else with whom they have contact. She made use of her songs, ballads, and stories in everything she did. They were as natural to her as breathing. Her great faith, her capacity for happiness, and her "headful" of mountain lore carried her through hard times and improved the lives of those around her. Jane Gentry and Loyal Jones's *Appalachian Values* are perhaps two of the most important tools available to combat the negative stereotypes of Appalachian people.

There are a few studies in which we see the singers in their own environment—*Sang Branch Settlers* (Leonard Roberts), *Singing Family of the Cumberlands* (Jean Ritchie), *A Singer and Her Songs* (Almeda Riddle with Roger Abrahams), and *Never Without a Song* (Katharine D. Newman). The songs and stories are there, but they are there as a part of the life of the singer and teller of tales, the family, and the community. I would have you know Jane Gentry in the midst of her family, her mountain environment, and her encounters with the outside world.

This is the story of a woman whose life revolved around her family and an oral tradition of song and story. She was too busy to write about her life, but the songs and stories flowed from her lips as she went about her work. I feel compelled to tell about Jane Gentry. Listen with your heart to her sweet singing. Let her stories entertain you and her optimistic view of life warm you.

I have had help from many people, and most of them are mentioned in the text or the notes. I am especially grateful to Loyal Jones for his encouragement, for his wonderful way of really listening, and for his uncommon good sense. When he was head of the Appalachian Center at Berea College he was instrumental in my receiving a Mellon Fellowship which enabled me to get all of the songs and stories ready for the book. I am grateful to John Forbes for his patient transcription of the tunes and his willingness to make another and yet another almost insignificant change. To Richard Dillingham at Mars Hill College I am indebted for making available the hard copies of the Sharp manuscripts. My heartfelt thanks go to all the friends who have encouraged me in this endeavor, especially to Gordon McKinney, Judith McCulloh, Cecelia Conway, and Jan Davidson, all of whom thought this story should be told.

I wish to thank the staff at the Vaughn Williams Memorial Library in London for locating and allowing me to use the excerpts from Cecil Sharp's diary and the librarians and archivists at Berea College, Harvard University, the John C. Campbell Folk School, Mars Hill College, Rollins College, the Southern Collection at the University of North Carolina, St. Lawrence University, the University of Virginia, and Warren Wilson College, and Lucille Roberts at the Marshall Library. I am indebted to Tinha Anderson, Sharon Baker, Mary Kestler Clyde, Phyllis Davies, Daron Douglas, Jane Long Douglas, Frances Dunham, Eugenia Elliott, Maud Clay Gibbs, Eugene Hicks, Nathan Hicks, Harley Jolley, Nancy Lippard, Hazel Moore, Pat Roberts, Lalla and Betty Rolfe, Bobbie Shuping, Haladine Gentry Sink, and Ruth Smith. Thanks to my friend Muriel Miller Dressler for her poem "Mountain Sarvis."

Some of my informants were approaching ninety years of age and they have recently died—Bill Moore, Elizabeth Dotterer, and Nola Jane Gentry Yrjana—the ones who really knew Jane Gentry. Betty Rolfe and Bobbie Shuping, Mae's daughters, have also passed away. I am sorry that they will not see this story in print.

To my husband, Bill, I am eternally grateful for his enthusiastic interest in this project and for his support and help with whatever I asked—driving miles out of the way to visit Nola Jane's roommate, Mary Kestler Clyde; horsing the Explorer up an all but impassable road to a cemetery; taking pictures of just about everything; allowing a part of our vacation for a visit with Jeannette Armstrong; spending several afternoons in Bill Moore's store. He loved it, all except watching me fly off to Alaska without him and the hours I have spent at the computer. And now my children, Jan and Ed, Bill and Pam, and my grandchildren, Bradley, Jenny, and Monica, can not only listen to me tell about Jane Gentry, they can read about her.

Part I

# Meet Jane Hicks Gentry

Jane Gentry's gravestone, Oddfellows' Cemetery, Hot Springs.

# Chapter I

# An Introduction

Nearly all mountaineers are singers. Their untrained voices are of good
timbre, the women's being sweet and high and tremulous, and their
sense of pitch and tone and rhythm remarkably true.
                    —Emma Bell Miles, *The Spirit of the Mountains*

On October 6, 1987, an historical marker was erected by the state of North
Carolina in front of a house called Sunnybank in Hot Springs. It reads:

BALLADRY
English folklorist Cecil Sharp in 1916 collected ballads in the "Laurel
Country." Jane Gentry who supplied many of the songs lived here.

She was called "a singer among singers," and some said she was the most
beautiful singer they had ever heard. In Jane Gentry's world, ballads were a part of
everyday life. Among her own people in the mountains of western North Carolina
she was known as a singer, one of the best singers, but they made no distinction
between Jane the woman and Jane the singer. She had a tremendous repertoire of
oral materials—songs, ballads, tales, and riddles—but that was just one facet of
her life.

She was born in a remote part of the Appalachian Mountains and lived her
life there. She did not cultivate the appearance of an unpolished mountain woman
or try to impress those who sought her out; and she was sought after by collectors
of ballads and tales and by a writer who thought she was the happiest and most
wonderful person he had ever met. She came to her art forms by birthright, not
through any self-conscious attempt to do the popular thing. There is no evidence
that Jane Gentry ever earned a penny from exercising her musical and storytelling
talents. There was no market for her music in the early twentieth century, and
she gave it freely.

Jane Gentry lived life well in her sixty-two years. It was said that she lived
every day as though it were her last. This is the story of a woman who out of her
own genius composed a rich, full, and in many ways adventuresome life for a
woman of her day. In another time, in another place, she might have been successful at any number of pursuits, for whatever she did, she did with vigor and passion.
Those who came her way found her easy to talk to and ready to share her many

talents. In 1980, fifty-five years after Jane's death, her daughter Lalla told a gathering of grandchildren and great-grandchildren that she could still see her mother standing on the porch of Sunnybank with an apron on. She always wore an apron. "And I don't care if the Queen of Sheba would come back to life and come to see my mother, my mother would be able to greet her and make her welcome. An old washer woman or the president's wife would have gotten the same greeting. My mother was never at a loss," she said.

Cecil Sharp, the English folk song collector, went to see her many times and collected seventy songs and ballads, more than from any other person he encountered in his travels through the southern mountains. Forty of her songs were published in Sharp's *English Folk Songs from the Southern Appalachians.* Isabel Gordon Carter went to see her, and she told Carter at least fifteen Jack tales and what have come to be called "Grandfather Tales." These were published in the *Journal of American Folklore* in 1925. Hers are the earliest texts of the ballads, songs, and stories from the Hicks-Harmon family. She had learned them well, and she was the first of this now famous family to be discovered by collectors.

Jane was born in Watauga County in northwestern North Carolina, on December 18, 1863, during the Civil War, in the year Abraham Lincoln issued the Emancipation Proclamation. Her father, Ransom Merritt Hicks, was a farmer, a preacher, and a Federal soldier. Her mother Emoline (Emily) Harmon Hicks, was the daughter of Council Harmon. Jane grew up near her grandfather, "Old Counce," whose descendants have carried on a rich and lively heritage of Jack tales. She was twelve years old when Ransom Hicks moved his family to Madison County, which Manly Wade Wellman described as "probably the least known . . . most misunderstood and most interesting of all counties in North Carolina."[1] From any direction the traveler must enter Madison through a gap, some more hazardous than others at that time. It was a county already fertile with traditional music, a county that several decades later Bascom Lamar Lunsford called "the last stand of the natural people."

Jane Gentry was born in the Southern Appalachians when it was frontier country, a country inviting to hunters and farmers seeking a place to build a home and start a farm. It was a land of ancient trees, clear rushing waters, and game aplenty. Here, where the vegetation of the North and the South meet, were splendidly timbered forests, rich with more varieties of trees, wildflowers, and flowering shrubs than in all of Europe. For the blue haze that hangs heavily over the peaks of the mountains they were labeled Blue Ridge and Smoky Mountains. Jane lived all her life in a time and place when self-reliance, neighborliness, and pride of good craftsmanship were important characteristics to possess. It was important to be able to look after oneself and one's family, and it was necessary that neighbors help one another. Jane Gentry was a good neighbor, and in that role she made use of her store of tales and songs.

When she was almost sixteen years old she married Jasper Newton Gentry, a neighbor boy, whom she dearly loved. They were exceptional parents who reared nine children and moved their family to the town of Hot Springs in 1898 so that the children could get an education at Dorland Institute, a Presbyterian mission school. Jane was an outstanding cook who successfully ran a boardinghouse in Hot Springs, a town whose mineral springs and hotel made it a famous tourist attraction. She did all that was possible for her to do in her time and place.

Jane was a short, rather heavyset woman who walked stooped over. Some said her back trouble was the result of a fall from a horse in her youth; others thought it was congenital because her son Alfred walked the same way. Her hands were rough and gnarled from constant work, but it was her face, her smile, that drew people to her. She had an easy rapport with everyone she met, particularly with children, even city children. One of Jane's granddaughters said that the school-children looked forward to her coming on Fridays to tell stories and sing songs. Swaddling a child was not work for her. She knew how to do it with joy and would not have missed the experience. There are those who believe that she still looks after the babies who spend the night in Sunnybank, the beautiful old house that was her last home.

Jane told the writer Irving Bacheller how she felt about babies: "Good land, mister! when the las' baby walked out o' my arms an' I were shet of 'em forever I felt kindly cold an' lonesome an' was shamed to see folks; seemed as though my breast ought to be covered by a baby when anybody come to the door. Babies be sech good company. Ye don't git lonesome with 'em. Ye kin learn 'em real young to know when you're funnin' with 'em er teasin' er sorrowful. An' ye kin visit with 'em. Ye don't know what heaven is, honey, twil ye've held hit in yer arms years and years as I done."[2]

The Gentrys were hard workers. Everybody said so. They raised almost everything they ate, raised their own sheep, and Jane spun, wove, dyed, knitted, and sewed their clothes and household linens. Their children learned to work and always had chores. Sometimes Jane and Newt hoed corn after the children had been put to bed, and they were seen repairing the barn roof by moonlight. But in spite of the hard work and long hours, her children said their mother sang all the time and they always knew where she was for they could hear her singing. In the evening the family would gather around the fire for stories and songs, little hands busy, each with a shoe full of fleece out of which he or she must pick the briars and sticks. The child's own shoe was used because the amount the shoe held reflected the size of the child and the amount of fleece each could be expected to pick.

Jane's house had a warm feeling, and everyone who entered was included in whatever was going on at the time—peeling apples, stringing beans, shelling peas—while Jane told stories. It was said that you hardly noticed you were working. In fact, Maud Long, the Gentry daughter who carried on her mother's tradition of songs and stories and recorded them for the Library of Congress, said that the secret to getting so much done was that you didn't call it work.

Jane saw the same sun come up, followed the same cycle of seasons, felt the same pain and weariness that came with hard work and pioneer living as did every other woman on the frontier. She heard the same songs and the same stories that many people heard, but she cherished them and remembered them and all her life she included them in everything she did. It has been said that women on the frontier were the bearers of tradition, the repositories of tribal lore, while the men belonged to the young nation. The women reared their children and preserved family life while the adventurous men were hunting and exploring. It could not be said of Newt Gentry that he left all the work to Jane. He was known as a good helpmate, and they worked side by side. Jane Gentry was not only a tradition bearer in her own family, she kept the songs and stories alive by singing and telling them wherever she was. Jane said, "Sometimes the neighbors would send for me to get the blues tuk off 'em, an' I'd go an' pray with 'em, nurse the sick an' tell 'em stories an' cheer 'em up."[3]

It would be understandable if this woman with so many children, with so much to do, were able to handle only the problems of her own family, but Jane was unusually sensitive to those around her. She once sat across the table from a man whose wife had died recently. Jane did not know him, but she sensed his unhappiness. She said to him, "You're a man of troubles." Then he told her about the death of his wife. They talked about what it meant to lead a Christian life— "Not easy," she said, "but pleasant."[4] Bacheller spoke of "her great charity of spirit, her patient, deep humanity."[5]

Good craftsmanship produced good, useful household and farm necessities. Although these traits and skills were important to life, there is also evidence of a sense of beauty and artistic expression. Being poor does not imply that one is aesthetically poor. Jane was a weaver and spinner of note, and the coverlets she wove for the beds were not just warm, they were beautiful and are still beautiful today. She always wore an apron trimmed with tatting she had made. Artistic expression and self-reliance were evident in her ability to entertain herself and others with song and story.

In spite of critics such as Arnold Toynbee, who saw the Appalachian people as no better than barbarians,[6] and in spite of popular misconceptions gained from movies, comic strips, and fiction, for the most part these were resourceful people, practically self-supporting. Because they had little contact with so-called civilization, they were described as quaint, existing in a state of arrested development. Cecil Sharp replied to such a critic, "I should prefer to call it a case of arrested degeneration."[7] This Englishman found that though many were unlettered, they had an "easy, unaffected bearing and the unselfconscious manners of the well-bred." Though few could read and write, "they were good talkers and their talk showed that they had wisdom and knowledge."[8] Sharp visited Mrs. Gentry on many occasions, but never did he refer to her as "quaint," nor did he use any other such description. He did say that he had a "three hour seance" with her on a day when he took down a number of songs. Although she had almost no formal education, Jane could read and write and she and Newt wanted their children to go to school. It was unusual for the time, but Jane's father and his father before him could read.

Historical evidence tells us that there were people living in the mountains who were lazy and degenerate. They were described as such by some writers who implied that these were characteristics of mountain people. This "strange land" with its "peculiar people," phrases from the pens of writers, seem not so peculiar when we meet them one on one. That is not to say that all mountain women were like Jane Gentry. Of course not, but there must have been many who lived their lives as well as she did. Very little has been written about these women, very little that has come from the women themselves. Many could not write, and most, like Jane Gentry, did not have a minute in the day to write their memoirs. Perhaps it would not have occurred to her to do so. That is why it is important to tell her story.

It is important to tell Jane's story not just for what it tells us about mountain life before the roads were paved. We can learn much from Jane herself. She had a good sense of who she was and of the importance of what she knew. Though she had little formal education, she used her good mind and took advantage of the opportunities open to her. She was not intimidated by people who were better educated, by "city people" who spoke proper English; indeed, she seemed to enjoy meeting them, and many were very impressed with her. She sang and told her tales freely, considering that she should share these talents with other people. She did have some rather unusual experiences. Irving Bacheller, a famous writer of the day, came to Hot Springs for a vacation, and his meeting with Jane Gentry resulted in a novel, short stories, and magazine articles. He admired her, not so much for her ballads and tales as for her faith, her courage, and her capacity for happiness. He recorded their conversations, and it is from his writings that we know about Jane's early years. At his invitation she rode the train to New York for a visit with him and his wife. When the Ballad Society was formed in Asheville, Mrs. Gentry sang ballads for that first meeting and received a standing ovation. Professor Alphonso Smith, founder of the Virginia Folk-Lore Society, appeared on the program with her and called it a privilege to meet a lady "so rich in memory of so rare a type of literature."

Jane was called "the mountain friend of Dorland" by the Board of National Missions of the Presbyterian Church when it paid tribute to her in a leaflet printed after her death. She lived next door to the school, and all of her children attended Dorland Institute, later to become Dorland-Bell. She scrubbed floors, did washing, boarded teachers, and wove coverlets to pay tuition. But Jane was always there to lend a hand when she was needed. She shared stories and songs in chapel and in classes and was invited by the teachers to help entertain out-of-town guests. It was through this connection with the Presbyterians at Dorland Institute that Mrs. Gentry came to the attention of Cecil Sharp.

Jane had the courage of her convictions, and when she could not get anybody to do anything about a still that was "spilin' up the boys," she set out with Aunt Tildy to take care of the problem. But Jane is the storyteller and this is how she told it to Irving Bacheller:

> One evenin' a'ter meetin' I says to Aunt Tildy: "Will you take a walk with me in the morning?" I says.
> "Whar to?" says she.
> "Oh jist 'round an' 'round," says I.
> I went down next mornin' to her house. They were a big skift o' snow on the ground. I give her a stick an' I had one myself. We started out an' walked a little ways.
> Then I says: "Thar be a wild still up hur in the mount'ins. I want you to holp me hunt hit. I cain't git none o' my folks to holp me, so I'm ergoin' to try an' find hit."
> She ketched her breath. They cut up wild when they thought ary one were a'ter their stills. Onct they was a man come to take the senses (census) o' the people, and Henry Slimp druv him erway at the p'int o' a gun—they was so carritly (suspicious?) o' strangers.
> "Hain't ye skeered?" she whispers
> "Cain't no more'n kill us," says I. "But I reckon the Lord'll take keer o' us. . . . Them stills has got to be cut out o' hur and me and you has got to do hit."

We started up the mount'in—jist as steep as that, jist like that, so steep—but we could ketch erlong with our sticks on the trees an' bushes. An' it were the snowiest day I ever did see in my life. The fog froze on the timber twil hit were perfectly awful lookin' to be out.

I went ahead as I were the youngest; I went pullin' up the mount'in an' by and by we got to the top. We went on an' started down eround the mount'in. The walk were jist so narrer that we couldn't walk side by side, so we started Injun like. I guess I went a mile from thar and the snow most half a leg deep. Then we come to a dreadful la'r'l, hit's la'r'l an' ivy we call hit. I think you call hit la'r'l and rhodydendrum. (She had been living in Hot Springs for a few years when she met Bacheller and had met people from other areas who called the shrub rhododendron.) Thar were a lot o' big pine trees thar. Oh, how snowy 'twere out on that la'r'l trail—looked like you'd go down over your head.

We stopped to git our breaths and my heart were floppin' like wings of a skeered potteridge. 'Twere so still down thar. Bang! goes a rifle right nigh us and a bullet skittered through the bushes over our heads an' down come a lot o' snow on us like hit had tore into a feather bed. Seemed like my back had bruk in two in the middle. I knowed somebody were watchin' us. Aunt Tildy's face turned white like 'twere snowin' inside o' her.

"Skeered?" she whispers.

"Bawdacious!" I says. "Let's pray to God a minnit."

We done prayed in our hearts. I see Aunt Tildy's lips movin,' but they made nary bit o' noise no more than the wings o' a whippoorill.

"They shan't skeer me," I says, "I'm jist ergoin' right on. The Lord has told me to."

The bushes jist flipped up under our clothes and our stockin's an' dresses was all wet.

"Well," I says, "Now you take down this erway and I'll go up that erway."

So we went erbout twenty-five yards, I reckon, and come to a trail eround the mount'in. Hits jist as slick as glass. We dug erlong on that trail erbout half a mile eround the side o' the mount'in and I jist run into the still-house. I stepped back a step or tew. I thought somebody might be in thar and shoot us.

I stepped back and said, "Here 'tis, Aunt Tildy."

And thar 'twere, and we got home wet an' erbout half froze. No, he couldn't afford to kill us. And pap went for the revenoor officer, but when we got down thar the still were gone, and that were the windin' up o' hit.[9]

And that is how Jane Gentry became known as the "Revenoor Lady." Bacheller had great admiration for Mrs. Gentry, and although it is very difficult to capture speech, he diligently tried to reproduce her colorful, lively speech.

As with all of the family stories, however, each teller has variations not remembered in other accounts. After more than seventy years Eugenia Elliott, who was a student at Dorland Institute, remembered the story of the still. It took place, she said, about Christmas time. Mrs. Gentry knew there was a still, and she worried that the local boys would get drunk and somebody would get hurt or killed. She put on her bonnet and shawl and with a friend started out to ask the operator of the still to close down during the holidays. As they came in sight of the still she saw a man coming out. He was carrying a rope. "Are we gonna be hung?" she asked herself. He didn't speak and neither did she. They went on to the still, and she begged the man who ran the still not to sell whiskey during Christmas. He agreed to shut it down.[10]

Either variant of the story is believable in view of what we know about Jane Gentry. Both tellers were recalling a story told years before, Bacheller with the help of notes, Eugenia Elliott with her excellent memory. Both heard the story from a storyteller who never told a story the same way twice.

Perhaps it would have been incomprehensible to Jane Gentry that we would be interested in her today. The durability of the oral literature she treasured—and she did treasure it—would have pleased her.

Chapter 2

# The Hickses
# and the Harmons

Unless we know where we came from, something about the road we traveled as a people, how can we know who we are and where we're going?

—Lena Penland Purkey, *Home in Madison County*

Although Cecil Sharp and Isabel Gordon Carter published Jane Gentry's oral materials, they told us very little about her. It is not unusual that the singer or storyteller is known by name only while the song or story receives attention as an important piece of oral literature. Sharp and his assistant, Maud Karpeles, spoke in general terms of the people of the Appalachian communities where the collecting was done, and Sharp admired their natural good manners and the musical environment in which they lived. He was much impressed with the quality and the quantity of Jane's songs. Carter spoke of Jane's great ability as a storyteller. It is important that we know about her, more about her family, and how and from whom she learned the songs and stories.

Several conditions had to exist for Jane to become such a repository of oral materials and for her to feel comfortable sharing them with other people. She had to hear the songs and stories and commit them to memory, and she had to live where she would be heard, where there were opportunities to sing and tell stories. Born into a family with a tradition of singing and storytelling, she grew up in a time and place in which these activities were a part of everyday life. There was time for stories and songs. This was an accepted means of entertaining oneself and one's family and friends. She also had to have the courage of her conviction that what she knew was important. Although many family members knew some of the songs and stories, Jane Gentry was a gifted singer and teller of tales, as well as one who recognized their usefulness and the importance of carrying on the tradition. The traditions of singing and storytelling existed in both the fraternal and the maternal sides of her family. Both the Hickses and the Harmons were among the early settlers in Watauga County. But which family brought with them the songs and stories?

# Ancestry of Jane Hicks Gentry

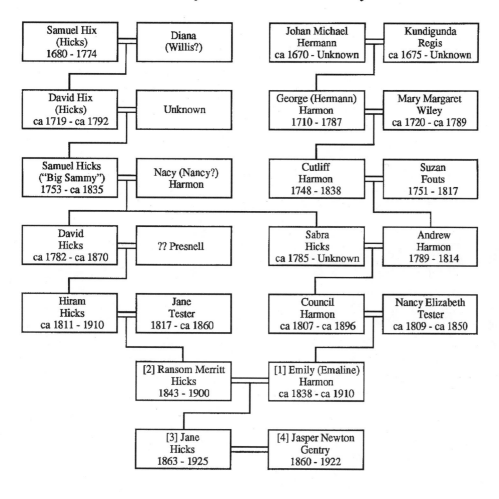

# The Hicks Family

The Hicks family has its roots in England. According to the records of the London Company, the first Hicks (Hix), William, came to the Virginia colony of Jamestown in 1618. There were others who settled in New England, some arriving on the first ship to follow the *Mayflower*. The first member of the Watauga line of the Hicks family appears to have arrived in Virginia in 1637. Samuel Hix came as an indentured servant to a plantation at the mouth of the Rappahannock River in lower Chesapeake Bay. The earliest record of the Watauga River Hicks line in family tradition is 1680, the year Samuel's grandson, also named Samuel, was born in Gloucester County. By 1717 this Samuel had settled in Henrico County (now Goochland), Virginia. Documents show that Samuel was a planter and that he purchased the land he lived on in 1726—sixty-nine acres on Tuckahoe Creek in Henrico County—for £50 sterling. A family legend suggests that he was married to Diana, whose surname may have been Willis. In 1764 the family moved to Granville County, North Carolina. Samuel's son David was the first to settle on the Watauga River. David settled first in Orange County (later Caswell County) in the early 1760s, then moved to Surry County (now Stokes County) and in 1776 or 1777 settled on the Watauga River.[1]

## David Hix

The first United States census in 1790 showed that several members of the Hix family had settled in the Appalachian Mountains—in Burke, Wilkes, and Ashe Counties. By 1777 David had staked out his claim to three hundred acres in what is now known as Valle Crucis. The earliest written record of his being in the Watauga area is in the 1778 tax records for Washington County. The names of David and his son, David Jr. appear. He did not obtain title to his Valle Crucis land until 1791, when he received a state grant.

David Hix was known to have had two sons, Samuel and David, and four daughters, Dinah or Diana, Sarah, Catherine, and an unnamed daughter who married William Asher. There is no record of his wife. For reasons of safety David Hix built a second residence near what is now Banner Elk. This was called the "Improvement" and referred to as a camp. The family tells many stories about David Hix, and he has been confused with his son Samuel in some histories. He was said to have been a Tory who hid out in his "Improvement" during the Revolutionary War.

Even after the war he hid out, coming home at dark for his supplies. His five boys were mischievous, and they manufactured a pistol out of a buck's horn which they fired by applying a live coal to the touchhole. When their father returned from the house carrying his rations, they would fire it and frighten him so much that he would drop everything and flee to his concealed camp in the mountains.[2]

This story is attributed to the first Hix who came to Watauga, and John Preston Arthur's *History of Western North Carolina* gives his name as Samuel. Another story in oral tradition is that he sold his holdings to Benjamin Ward for "a rifle, a dog, and a sheepskin."[3] Oral history is colorful if not always accurate, and in a family of storytellers it is not surprising that there is a generous supply of stories about ancestors from several generations back. This story suggests that David Hix may have had as many as five sons.

### Samuel Hix (Hicks) ("Big Sammy")

One of David's sons, Samuel, known as "Big Sammy," was born in 1753 in Goochland County, Virginia. Some histories say that Samuel came to the Watauga area in 1779 or 1780. His name does not appear on any records until 1783, when he was paid for militia service against the Chickamauga Indians. Since the state of North Carolina did not have cash to pay its soldiers, Revolutionary War vouchers were issued. Those issued to Samuel were signed by John Sevier, the most prominent militia commander at that time.[4]

According to the Hicks family history, Samuel and his wife, Sarah, whose last name is unknown, had nine children: five sons, David, Goulder, Samuel ("Little Sammy"), Harmon, and William, and four daughters, Sabra, Sallie, Fanny, and Elizabeth. A World Family Tree genealogy, however, shows Samuel married to Nacy (Nancy?) Harmon, daughter of Samuel Harmon. Both histories show daughter Sallie (Sarah) married to Barnabas (Barney) Oakes. Samuel Hix is believed to be the grandfather from whom Council Harmon learned the Jack tales and songs.

### Sabra Hix (Hicks) Harmon

Sabra, the oldest daughter of Samuel, was born about 1785. Sabra married Andrew Harmon, son of Cutliff Harmon, in 1806 or 1807. It was to this union that Council Harmon was born in 1807. With Council Harmon's generation the exchange of first names between the Hickses and the Harmons began to take place, names such as Andrew, Mathias, Carroll, Goulder, and David.

## The Harmon Family

In Arthur's *History of Watauga County*, Valle Crucis is called the "Valley of Cousins" because of the kinship among many of the inhabitants. Cutliff Harmon came into the valley of Cove Creek in 1791. He came from Randolph County, North Carolina, and bought 522 acres from James Gwyn for £300, the deed bearing the date August 6, 1791. Other families arrived at about the same time with the names of Egger, Smith, Councill, Horton, Mast, and Tester. The intermarriage of these families with those who were already there—Hicks, Asher, Ward, Dugger, Holzclaw, Heatley, Baird, Linville, Whittenton, and Dyer—created a community of closely related families.

The Harmons were Germans who came to America about 1726. Johan and Kundigunda Hermann lived along the Danube River in Württemberg on the southern border of Germany. Their oldest son, Heinrich Adam Hermann (Harman), his wife, Louisa Katrina Mathias, their first child, Adam, and Heinrich's six brothers, Jacob, Valentine, Mathias, George, Daniel, and John left Germany in the mid-

1720s. They sailed aboard the ship *Charlotte* for America. When the ship stopped on the Isle of Man to take on supplies, Louisa gave birth to her second child, Henry. They arrived in Philadelphia County in 1726, where they stayed for eight or ten years. All of the brothers except Mathias moved on to Maryland, where George met and married an American-born woman, Mary Margaret Wiley, in 1744.

From Maryland, the Hermann brothers, their wives, and children journeyed down the Shenandoah Valley to Strasburg, Virginia. About 1748 Adam Harmon and others, Drapers among them, went west "to grow up with the country." They established the first settlement west of the great Allegheny divide—the first on the waters of New River. The name given to this settlement was Draper's Meadows. On July 8, 1755, a party of Shawnees from beyond the Ohio River attacked the settlement and killed, wounded, or captured everyone there at the time. Among the six prisoners were Mary Draper Ingles and her two sons. The Indians marched the captives beyond the Ohio, where Mary was separated from her sons. Mary Ingles escaped near Big Bone Lick (now in Kentucky) and followed streams for forty days until she reached the home of Adam Harmon just west of Draper's Meadows.[5]

In 1787 Adam and his son Captain Mathias Harmon founded Harmon's Station, the first fort in the Big Sandy Valley. Adam and his sons were known to be explorers and long hunters. In the art of woodcraft and Indian warfare Mathias was said to have no equal. In the fall of 1787, while the men from Harmon's Station were on a hunting trip, a band of Cherokees and Shawnees attacked the home of Jennie Wiley. They had mistaken her home for that of Mathias Harmon whose cabin was about a mile away. He had driven off an Indian attack a few days before. Three of her children and her brother were killed, and she and her baby were taken prisoner. It was the next day before Mathias and his band of hunters returned home and began the search for Jennie Wiley. They failed to find her, but after eleven months in captivity she escaped and reached Harmon's Station just ahead of her captors.[6]

### George Harmon

George, like his brothers, fought in the Indian wars. He traveled on south to Rowan County (now Randolph County), North Carolina. In his will in Randolph County, August 20, 1786, George gave his wife, Mary Margaret, one-half of his plantation and named his sons George, Cutliff, Mathias, and Phillip. His daughters were Elizabeth (Elie) and Katherine.

### Cutliff Harmon

Cutliff Harmon was born to George and Mary Margaret Harmon in 1748 in Rowan County (Randolph). He was married to Suzan Fouts. The Harmon (Hermann) and Fouts (Phautz) families had been friends and neighbors for many years, settling in the same counties in Pennsylvania and North Carolina. It was after his marriage that Cutliff became employed by Daniel Boone, the frontiersman, and a Colonel Robinson to transport goods from the Yadkin Valley in North Carolina to Sycamore Shoals near Elizabethton, Tennessee and from the mountains of Western North Carolina to the State of Franklin (now East Tennessee). On one of these trips Cutliff passed through Wilkes County (later Ashe County and now Watauga County). He liked the mountain country so well that he bought land on Cove Creek. Present U.S. Highway 321, the route from Boone to Elizabethton, Tennessee, runs through Cove Creek.

Cutliff brought his wife and seven children, Mary, Catherine, Nancy, Elizabeth, Mathias, Andrew, and Susan, to what is now Sugar Grove around 1791. Three children were born to the couple after the move to Cove Creek—Rebecca, Eli, and Rachel. There is a high rock west of Boone at the mouth of Phillips Branch that was called Shupe's Rockhouse, from a family that once lived there. The story is told that Cutliff Harmon settled under this rock and lived there with his wife and children while he built a home for them. The rockhouse was a "beautiful and lovely chamber midway in the face of the cliff 100 feet high—entered by a descending stairway of three natural stone steps." It has since been called Harmon Rockhouse. It is believed that this was the birthplace of the first white child born in the area.[7] Tall sycamore trees now hide the entrance to the rockhouse for most of the year. When Highway 321 was constructed, the course of the Watauga River was changed so that when the trees shed their leaves the rockhouse is visible from the intersection of Highway 321 and Phillips Branch Road. Cutliff's neighbors along the Watauga River were Benjamin Ward Sr., a Revolutionary War veteran, and David Hix. Cutliff's wife, Suzan, died in 1817 and he married Elizabeth Parker in 1825. He lived to the age of ninety.

The Harmons carved out a niche in the histories of Virginia, Eastern Kentucky, and Western North Carolina. They were famous as frontiersmen, explorers, hunters, and Indian fighters. A book was devoted to the founding of Harmon Station. An outdoor drama in Radford, Virginia, portrayed the kidnapping of Mary Draper Ingles. But they were not known as singers or storytellers. Apparently the Hicks family was the wellspring of the oral materials handed down in this family.

### Andrew Harmon

Andrew Harmon was born in Rowan (Randolph) County, February 5, 1789, Cutliff and Suzan's sixth child. For several generations the Harmons and the Hickses were close neighbors but the alliance between the two families began with the marriage of Sabra, daughter of Samuel Hix (Hicks), and Andrew Harmon, son of Cutliff Harmon. Andrew Harmon was killed by a falling tree on May 16, 1814, when he was only twenty-five years old. He was cutting a tree near what is now Sugar Grove on land owned by his father-in-law, Samuel Hix. As the tree began to fall, Andrew's shoestring got caught and kept him from moving away. He was working alone, and it was late that night when Sabra and the children found him.[8]

### Council Harmon

After Andrew Harmon's death Sabra was left with four young children, Council, eight, Goulder, six, Mathias, four, and Rachel, nearly three. Cutliff Harmon deeded sixty-four acres of land to Sabra's children in 1814 for their "better maintenance and preparement." Sabra may have moved back to her father's home, for Council told his children that he grew up in the household with Samuel Hicks II, known as "Little Sammy," who was about fourteen years old when Andrew died. He said that he learned from both Samuels the songs and Jack tales for which he later became noted.[9]

In 1820 Andrew's sister Elizabeth died. Her husband, Duke Ward, and Sabra were married around 1822. Records show that Duke Ward made land entries in the county of Rhea, Hiawassee District, Tennessee, on May 25, 1824, for two tracts of land, one of 160 acres and one of 80 acres. The 80-acre certificate was transferred to Robert Elder on December 27, 1824, and the certificate on the 160 acres was transferred to John Bailey on February 15, 1825. The next record of Duke and Sabra Ward is found in the 1830 census of Clinton, Illinois.[10] The Hicks family history suggests that they stayed on the Watauga River until about 1830, when they moved to Clinton. Sabra took her daughter Rachel with her, and local tradition has it that she left Council and Goulder in the care of Andrew's sister Susan Harmon Mast, and her husband, John Mast. If the departure date is accurate, however, they would have been young men at that time. There is no further trace of Mathias in Watauga County. Duke Ward was known as a great wrestler who had not met his match in the mountains of North Carolina. After moving to Illinois, he became a champion wrestler, but not long after the move he was killed in a wrestling match. It was said that he was thrown from the ring and his neck was broken in the fall.

Sabra gave her stepson and nephew Amos Ward power of attorney and sent him back to Watauga County to dispose of and divide her properties and possessions on Cove Creek. Amos, like his father, was not easily provoked but well able to defend himself. It seems that Amos walked into a bar in Chicago and encountered a bully who whipped every man who came into the place. The bully knocked Amos's tall hat from his head with a billy stick and Amos grabbed him by the hair of his head and proceeded to give him the beating of his life. He pitched him out of the bar and became known as the little man who whipped the bully of Chicago.[11]

The Gentry family Bible gives Council's birthplace and that of his wife as Peorido (Peoria?), Illinois. Rebecca Teaster is the name given his wife in this same Bible. This information is at odds with the family history. There is no evidence that Sabra went to Illinois until after her second marriage, and oral history has it that Council did not go with her. It is believed that Sabra never returned to North Carolina.

Council Harmon married Nancy Elizabeth (Betsy) Tester, daughter of Samuel Tester and Mary Elizabeth Daniels, in 1826. Both the Harmon and Hicks family histories support this information. The Tester family had come to the Watauga from South Carolina in 1791. This was the only Tester family living in the area at the time, and they did not have a daughter named Rebecca. Of the union of Council and Betsy there were thirteen children: Louisa Jane (Eliza), Susannah (Susan), Lucinda, Rev. Andrew J. (Andy), Eli George Washington, Ellen, Emoline (Emily), Cyrena (Rene), Rebecca (Becky), Goulder Monroe (Coon), Sabra, William Riley, and Sarah Anne Cameline. A second marriage to Cecelia (Celia) Ward Watson produced six children: Alice, Council (Counce), Julia Ann, Cordelia (Dill), McKeller (Kell), and Adeline (or Adalade).

Council Harmon settled on Big Ridge, Beech Creek, Beech Mountain, and Buckeye during various periods of his life. He was a farmer all his working life. "Old Counce" was certainly the kind of man about whom unforgettable tales are told. The tales he told have been perpetuated through several different family lines, but the tales about him have lived on as well. Every person who spoke of him painted the picture of a warm, kindly, fun-loving man—the greatest story-teller of them all and the first to gain a reputation as such.

Goulder Harmon, Council's brother, and his wife, Rebecca, were very resourceful people. The description of their lifestyle tells in some detail how families managed in pioneer times. They lived near Council on Big Ridge, Beech Creek, Beech Mountain, and Buckeye. This area was rich with ginseng ("sang"), and one could enter a tract of land and pay for it in dried ginseng roots at the rate of about twelve and one-half cents per acre. Goulder made churns out of deerskins that had been cleaned and sewn at all the openings except the mouth. Rebecca would pour in milk or soured cream and shake the bag back and forth until she had butter and buttermilk.

Rebecca raised flax and wove it into cloth, bed ticks, and rope. She and Goulder had a cane mill and made maple syrup and sugar. During the winter they saved ashes from green wood. In March, before the weather got too warm, Rebecca would make soap from the ashes or she would make gut soap from the intestines of animals. They raised sheep and cattle. About the first of April, Goulder would take his young cattle to Beech Mountain to graze. In the fall he would bring them back and sell them. The milk cows wore bells and were kept closer to home.

Goulder's three-room house was made of hewn logs and had glass windows. The kitchen was a lean-to about twelve by twenty feet. There was one bed in the kitchen, four in the living room, and three upstairs to accommodate their family of eleven children. Rebecca had her loom upstairs, where she also dried apples and kept cider and vinegar. After forty-seven years of marriage, Rebecca died, and Goulder married Polly Flannery, who had six children of her own. Goulder could read and write, and we assume that Council could also, for they grew up together.[12]

### Emoline (Emily) Harmon

Emoline (Emily), the seventh child born to Council and Betsy Harmon, about 1838, was the mother of Jane Gentry. The family Bible gives her birthdate as December 29, 1835, which does not agree with family history and with the 1910 census, which shows her to be seventy-two years of age. Emily Harmon was married first to Carroll Hicks, son of Samuel II ("Little Sammy"). The 1860 census shows Emily and Carroll living in the Mountain Home District of Watauga County. They had one child, Rachel, one year old. If Rachel lived, she would have been four or five years old when Emily married Ransom Hicks, but there is no further record of her and no oral history about her. Carroll Hicks was killed in 1862 while on duty with the 58th North Carolina Infantry Regiment at Cumberland Gap, Tennessee. Emily applied for death benefits from the Confederate government in early 1863 as Carroll's widow. In 1863 she married Ransom Merritt Hicks, son of Hiram and grandson of David Hix.

### David Hix (Hicks)

David Hix was born in Valle Crucis about 1782, the oldest son of Samuel and Sarah Hix, a brother to Sabra Hix. It is believed that he served in the War of 1812 and fought in the Battle of New Orleans. His name does not appear in the War of 1812 records, but the records are incomplete. He married a Miss Presnell (first name unknown) and established a home in Avery County, in all probability near what is now Banner Elk. The following account appeared in a history of Avery County:

> David Hix, who had been with General Andrew Jackson at the Battle of New Orleans, moved near the Big Falls of Elk, in what is now the Cranberry settlement. It was he, it seems, whom the first ghosts followed into what is now Avery County, for he often complained that they "pestered him lots." He used to think "they mought 'av been the ghosts of the bloomin' Henglish" whom he helped slay in that belated battle, for one particular ghost always carried a bale of cotton with bullet holes in it. Hix hunted, fished, killed poisonous snakes and wild animals, brewed homemade medicines when members of his family were ailing. When his beard and hair became too long, he trimmed them with his hunting knife, with which he picked his teeth and trimmed his toenails. He tanned hides, made shoes for his family, and often pounded chestnuts and acorns into a coarse meal for bread to be eaten with the wild meat which he obtained from the wilderness. At bedtime, his wife shook the "kivers," pillows, and skins for any snakes that might have hidden among them since the previous night. This was called "snakin" the beds. Scores of women who followed their men into the mountains or were born here, did the same thing, for it was an easy matter for copperheads and rattlers to slither through the cracks of floors and walls and hide in the semi-darkness of the windowless cabins. A crude sundial on the outside and hacked notches about the doors helped to measure time on sunny days. But David Hix could calculate almost the exact time whenever he looked at the sun and stars.[13]

In 1821 David Hix married Susannah Asher. In the 1840 census his children were listed as Hiram and John Wesley by his first marriage and Adam, David, Sally, Millery, Margarite, Tempa, Daniel, and Luvenia by his marriage to Susannah Asher.

### Hiram Hix (Hicks)

It is the oldest son of David Hix, Hiram, born between 1811 and 1814, who is of interest, for he was the father of Ransom and Jane's paternal grandfather. According to family history, Hiram married Jane Tester in 1834, although his marriage bond was signed by his cousin Samuel Hicks ("Little Sammy") in 1830. No explanation is given for this discrepancy. At that time Hiram could read and write, but "Little Sammy" could not so he made his mark on the marriage bond with an "X." Hiram and Jennie produced two sets of twins, John and Mary, born in

1838, and Ransom and Margaret, born in 1842. Other children were Melissa, Eli, Charlotte, Rhoda, Zachariah, Julia, Center, Jim J., Copelin (Cope), and Emily. Census records seem to indicate that sometime before 1870 Hiram remarried and left his children in the care of his son Eli, still in his early twenties, and a housekeeper by the name of Mary Mathews. He set up housekeeping with his new wife, Elizabeth, and lived nearby. It is possible that there is some confusion about Hiram's children. Some may have been grandchildren.

It is interesting that his descendants have little recollection of Hiram Hicks. No children were named after him and he is seldom recognized among his great grandchildren. The few recollections of Hiram that remain were handed down through collateral families and by other lines of the Hicks family.[14]

Arthur gave the following account of Hiram Hix:

Just before the Civil War, how long no one now knows, Noah Mast, claiming that he had loaned Hiram Hix a crosscut saw, sued him for its recovery. Hix had some affliction of the eye-lids, rendering it necessary that he should prop them open with his fingers in order to see. He and his wife lived under a big cliff near the mouth of Cove Creek, called the Harmon Rock-House. [The same rock under which the Cutliff Harmon family lived while they were building their cabin.] This cliff projected out a considerable distance and the open space was enclosed with boards and other timbers, thus affording some degree of comfort even in winter, the smoke going out of a flue built against the side of the cliff. Here Hix kept a boat and charged a nickel to put passengers across the river. He also built a sort of cantilever bridge, the first in the world, most probably, using two firm rocks which extended into the stream, thus forming a narrow channel at that point. Based upon these immovable rocks were two long logs, hewn flat on the upper surface, one projecting from each bank toward the other, but not meeting above mid-stream by several feet—too wide a gap to be jumped by ordinary folk. The shore ends of these logs were weighted to the ground by huge stones piled on them. Hix kept a thick and broad plank which was just long enough to bridge this gap between the projecting ends of the two logs. Upon the payment of five cents, Hix would place this board in position and the foot-passenger could then pass over dry-shod. This was a "cantilever" because he claimed he couldn't leave her in position. Whether the revenue from his boat and board was sufficient to pay his lawyers in the suit Mast had brought against him for that crosscut saw or not, Hix managed to keep it in court until he won it, thus throwing Mast in the costs, which is a very undesirable place to be thrown. This was one of the first suits to be tried in the new town of Boone, and a boy who heard one of the lawyers ask a witness what there was that was "peculiar" about that saw, was so struck by the word "peculiar" that he remembers it to this day, when he is an old man."[15]

Although it has been suggested that Hiram's descendants did not remember him, the stories still circulate about him. Marshall Ward, a descendant of Council Harmon and a well-known storyteller, described Hiram as a "big man, perhaps as tall as 6 feet, 6 inches, with an irascible nature." As did other members of his family and his ancestors, Hiram loved to hunt. According to Marshall Ward, one time Hiram found a bee tree. He cut it down, but he had nothing in which to carry the honey, so he told his wife, Mandy, to take off her dress. He put the honey on it and tied it to a pole. He carried one end and she the other and when the honey dripped through the dress, he scurried back to wipe it up.[16]

### Ransom Hicks

Ransom Merritt Hicks was born in Watauga County on December 13, 1843, at Watauga Falls. In 1863 he married Emily Harmon Hicks, daughter of Council and Betsy Harmon. According to census records, Ransom could read and write. There were few, if any, schools in the area and it seems likely that Hiram taught him since it appears that Hiram could read. There is a story in tradition that Hiram lived in Virginia at one time. Perhaps it was there that he learned to read and in turn taught his two sons, Ransom and John.[17]

According to family oral history, Ransom Hicks was a minister and a Federal soldier.[18] He carried the mail between Boone and Lenoir. One account says that he rode a mule, but his great-grandson Eugene Hicks says that he was a lover of horses and always owned a good horse. He thinks he would have been riding a horse. He relates a story from Civil War times about Yankee soldiers whose horses were tired commandeering Ransom's horse. He protested that he was carrying the United States mail and needed his horse, so they left him an old nag. That night Ransom slipped into the Yankee camp and recovered his horse but left the old nag so he would not be accused of horse-stealing.[19]

During the Civil War Ransom did not enlist in the company in which his brother and cousins did so his sympathies apparently did not lie with the South. The Hickses, like many of their neighbors, were not known to have deep feelings about the war one way or another. This was a region of fiercely independent settlers and few slaves. Some sided with the South, some with the North, and others remained neutral. In 1862, D Company of the Fifty-eighth North Carolina Infantry Regiment was organized and called itself the North Carolina Partisan Rangers. Seven members of the Hicks family joined the company, among them John, Ransom's older brother, and four of Little Sammy's sons—Andrew, Levi, Patterson, and Carroll, Emily's first husband. Carroll and Patterson were killed in a powderhouse explosion at Cumberland Gap in 1862. John, Andrew, and Levi deserted and hid out until the war was over. John and Andrew were not court-martialed. Levi was charged with desertion in absentia but could not be located. They all had families, and when they saw what war was like, they must have lost any fervor they had and simply went home. In this family one would expect war stories to be included in the repertoires of some of its members. Although the war did generate violent feelings in the mountains and families were divided by the diversity of sympathies, the stories about the Hicks boys are not judgmental. In recounting the story of the desertion of another family member of D Company, the teller would begin, "When ol' Tice left the army down there in Georgia an' decided to come home."[20]

It was of the union of Ransom Hicks and Emily Harmon that Jane Hicks Gentry was born. Until she was twelve years old she lived in the midst of this large family of storytellers and ballad singers. She told Isabel Gordon Carter that she learned the "Jack, Will, and Tom" tales when she was a child from her grandfather, Council Harmon, who learned them from his mother, Sabra Hix. She said: "They're the oldest stories that ever been in existence, I reckon. Old Grandpop aluz told us—we'd hire him to tell us. Law, he could tell 'em."[21]

Carter mistakenly gave Jane's birthplace as Randolph County. This suggests that Jane knew her family history, as most of the Hickses and Harmons do. Carter probably misunderstood which generation lived in Randolph County. Jane did not mention her grandfather Hiram, but "Old Counce" was the center of her world, as he was for all the children in the family. Miles Ward, another grandchild, said: "Ever when I'd see Old Counce a-coming, I'd run to meet him so I could walk with him back to the house. Then he'd sit and take me up on his lap, and I'd ask him right off for a Jack Tale. He'd tell me one, too; never did fail me. He loved to tell about Jack."[22]

It was not unusual for the children to ask their grandfather to tell stories. Parents were busy with daily chores. Council Harmon was certainly an extraordinary teller of tales and must have recognized the fact that children are the best audience for stories. Council never lost his childish love of fun. He did like to have a good time and children are quick to see this. The following description of "Old Counce" in the Harmon Genealogy comes from family stories:

> Council was a tall, slim man who spoke with a long drawl, was lively and funny, and was a great storyteller. He was a harmless man, never meddling in other people's business or bothering anyone. It was "Counce" who first told the well-known Jack tales, and he delighted to tell them to children. According to Council's grandson, the late Roby Monroe Ward, Council once said that he learned the tales from one of his grandfathers who had learned them from the early settlers of the United States. . . . Council was a good and devoted . . . member of his church, but he could not resist music. Whenever anybody began picking a banjo, Council would hit the floor and start dancing, even if he was in church. When he was seventy years old he could still clog, buckdance, and run reels. He also loved to make music himself and to sing. Every time he got involved in such activities, someone would tell on him and the preacher would get after him the next Sunday. Council delighted in worldly things and this brought much concern to the church. He was constantly being brought before the church as he loved a nip at the bottle. The church would send him word to come whenever he was needing to be brought before the congregation, and he would come forward and "mit" and "fess" (his own words for admitting and confessing his sins). The church would then restore him to fellowship, but in a short while he had to be called again.[23]

In a family with more than its share of memorable characters, Council Harmon is the one most often mentioned. It is remarkable that after so many years he is still remembered fondly by family members and written about often by folklorists and others interested in storytelling.

Chapter 3

# From Watauga to Madison

The heritage of the past is the seed that brings forth the harvest of the future.
> —Inscription on the National Archives building, Washington, D.C.

In about the year 1875 several Watauga County families moved to Madison County, North Carolina. This rugged, mountainous county played its part in the westward movement. The main traffic route from the coast to the Midwest went through Madison County. As early as 1795 a wagon traveled from South Carolina to Knoxville, Tennessee, through Warm Springs (later Hot Springs) and Paint Rock at the Tennessee state line. In time drovers by the hundreds and thousands drove their stock along this road through Madison County to Charleston and other points south and east.[1]

It is doubtful that these Watauga families were a part of the westward movement. They moved to a remote cove about forty miles northwest of Asheville and about fifteen miles from Warm Springs—Hickses, Harmons, Rowlands, and Stricklands. Ransom and Emily Hicks were among them. Jane told Irving Bacheller that they went first to "Aunt Elly's." Emily's sister Ellen and her husband, Mike Rowland, had come to Madison County a year or two before. The Hickses and the Harmons settled on Meadow Fork and the Rowlands on Little Creek. Another of Emily's sisters, Cyrena (Rene), who was married to William Rowland, settled on Little Creek. Mike Rowland bought land as early as 1873 and his brother, William, in 1874. Ransom bought his first farm in September 1876. Ransom signed his name. Emily made her mark and Ransom signed for her—"Emly." Ransom continued to buy land until 1891, all of it from the Davises, Allen and John, who were their neighbors.

The 1880 census listed Council Harmon as a member of Michael Rowland's household. He is not listed in Watauga County in 1880 although his second wife, Cecelia, and some of their children are. It is possible that he came with the other members of the family, or he may have come later for a visit. His occupation is listed as mill operator, which might suggest a prolonged visit. He may have been helping out at Ransom's mill. He must not have been gone for a very long time because his grandchildren in Watauga remembered him in his seventies, and his absence is not noted in family histories and stories. Monroe Ward said: "Seventy years old, he could clog and buckdance just as good as a boy sixteen."[2] It does mean that his grandchildren in Madison County spent some time with this grand old man. Council would have been about seventy-three in 1880, and it is clear that he returned to Watauga County before he died. According to the Harmon family history he lived with his daughter Cameline Ward after he quit farming. Cameline's son Monroe learned the Jack tales from his grandfather during the time he lived with them. He died around 1896 and was the second person to be buried in the Zion Hill Cemetery in Sugar Grove.

Jane told of the journey to their new home on the Meadow Fork of Spring Creek: "I were twelve when pappy moved from Watauga into Madison County. Tuk everythin' in a big covered wagon. Me an' my brother drove the cows an' milked 'em into stone jugs. When evenin' come we'd stop where they were water an' boil some corn meal an' have a milk an' mush supper an' then pappy would play on his fiddle."[3] When they arrived at Aunt Ellie's, Newt Gentry, a long, gawky fellow about fifteen years old, was there to help them unload.

No one seems to know why after four generations on the Watauga River these families chose to settle in an area similar to the one they had left. It was well after the Civil War, but the bitterness that resulted from neighbor fighting neighbor, the feuding and the raiding, lasted for years. Perhaps they wanted to get a new start far away from the painful memories. But it was an ordeal to move whole families through rugged mountains. They came from high, rough mountains into mountains not quite so high but a valley so remote as to make one wonder how they knew it was there. What route did they take? Perhaps they followed what is now Route 19E and 19 south from Valle Crucis to Shull's Mills on a road that crossed the North Toe River, then on to Burnsville. Keeping to the low ground, they must have traveled a road that generally followed the course of Ivy Creek to the Buncombe Turnpike. For fifty years the Turnpike had been the highway connecting North Carolina to other southern states, and in all probability they took this road to Warm Springs, crossing both the Laurel River and the French Broad. If they did go through Warm Springs, they probably moved from there along Spring Creek gorge on what is now state road 209 to Meadow Fork. Their journey took them by Grandfather Mountain in whose shadow they had grown up. Could they see the Black Mountains in the distance where Mount Mitchell rose, almost a thousand feet taller? They were at home among ancient forests of oaks and chestnuts, hickories, poplars, and walnuts, the hillsides thick with rhododendron, which they called laurel.

Crossing into Madison County the landscape was much the same. They must have stopped in Marshall, the county seat, a narrow little town with the French Broad River running through its middle, the town rising up steeply on either bank. Following the river, the turnpike would take them through the "wild beauty of the gorge" with its rugged cliffs overhanging the road, "fringed with ferns and mosses." There were chestnut trees and walnut trees ten feet in diameter.[4]

It must have taken two or three weeks to make this journey, which today can be driven easily in less than three hours. Much depended on the river crossings. A year or so before this little band came through, all of the bridges in this part of the country had been washed away by floods. In the years after the Civil War there was little money to build roads and bridges and the politics of the area

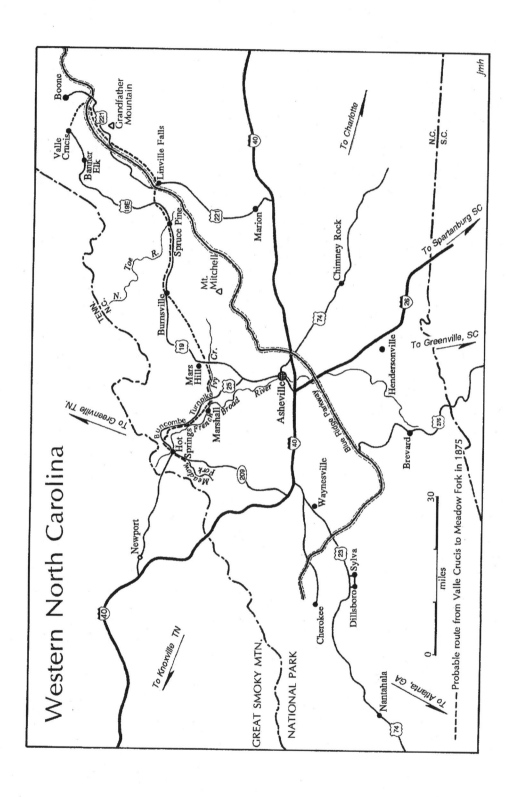

Western North Carolina

was not conducive to getting such things done. If the water was not too high, the Laurel River could be forded. The alternative was to wait for the river to go down or to be ferried across by Wash Farnsworth, a Negro who ran a stand on the bank of the Laurel. He had cabins where drivers could stay the night and a dugout canoe on which he could ferry wagons across the river.[5] It is likely that they had to be ferried across the French Broad at Warm Springs.

If they were looking for work, they might have gone to the mica mines near Spruce Pine or the iron mines at Cranberry. There were weaving and cotton mills as close as Elkin. But they chose to continue the life they knew. They were independent souls who worked for themselves, not for other men. A man did not have to hire on extra hands when help was needed, and there were times when help was needed—for barn or house raisings, cornhuskings, molasses making. His neighbor would come to help out and he helped his neighbor in return. And so they set out to pioneer all over again, to clear land and build homes with homemade tools.

Ransom settled his family on the Meadow Fork of Spring Creek. The land lying on either side of the stream is flat and fertile and stretches for almost ten miles of good farmland. To this day it supports lush stands of tobacco, corn, and cabbage. It was attractive to those seeking homesteads. There was plenty of good water and streams teeming with fish. Meadow Fork begins its journey at an elevation of almost four thousand feet in the Maple Springs-Brushy Ridge area near the Tennessee line. It flows north until it joins Spring Creek at the juncture of North Carolina Route 209. Along the way it is joined by Spring Branch, East Fork, Little Creek, Long Branch, Panther Branch, and Roaring Fork. When it reaches Spring Creek it is a full-fledged mountain trout stream, and today is so designated by the North Carolina Wildlife Commission. This lovely fertile valley was protected by wooded hills with game in abundance to provide meat. The new settlers must have heard good things about it from those who had come to Spring Creek before them. It is considered today to be a place with an ideal climate, but they would not have known that. The post office address of the Hicks family was Lynch, North Carolina, located near where Long Branch comes into Meadow Fork. This post office was later designated as Joe and presently is Hot Springs.

The Hicks family came to a county still hurting from its own Civil War wounds —a county, like Watauga, where families and communities were divided, where the Shelton Laurel massacre of 1863 left the legacy of "Bloody Madison," which persists to this day. Confederate soldiers captured and murdered thirteen prisoners ranging in age from thirteen to fifty-nine years whom they suspected of being Unionist guerrillas.[6] This happened on the other side of the county from Meadow Fork, but perhaps they did not know of that either.

Ransom Hicks was known to be a good and honorable man who wanted to help everybody. He ran a mill and was arrested when he ground meal for blockaders who made illicit whiskey. Of course, like all of his neighbors he was of necessity a farmer, but he was also called to be a preacher. Bill Moore said that his stepfather was making whiskey when Preacher Hicks came by his farm. Ransom saw what was going on, much to the chagrin of his stepfather, but the preacher's comment was, "I'm not hunting for stills today. I'm looking for a notary public."[7]

Ransom and Emily had five children, not a large family for that day. Emily had already had one child of which there is no record beyond the age of one year.

Perhaps she died and Emily was left alone after the death of her first husband. The Hicks family history names Ransom as the father of a son, William, born to Fannie Hicks in 1864. The basis for this belief is that descendants remember Great-Grandma Fannie, but little more than the name of Great-Grandpa Ransom.[8] Oral tradition has it that the only person who could have given this information refused to talk about it. Jane was Ransom and Emily's first child, born in 1863, and John Riley came along a year and a half later on May 2, 1865. Mary was born September 12, 1871, Margaret Elizabeth in 1872, and William Ransom, always known as "Doc," on March 15, 1875. This youngest child was born about the time the Hicks family came to Madison County.

Jane told Irving Bacheller about her early years: "My pappy were a minister, name of Ransom Hicks. Mammy were always peckin' me over the head with a stick. She were turrible ill and cross, pore woman! I were that foundered with the peckin' that I declar'd that I never would whup ef God sent me childern. You'll whup as much into 'em as you whup out o' 'em."[9] Life was not easy for Emily. The move had been an adventure for the men, but it was an ordeal for women trying to take care of the children, especially one as young as William. Her days were completely taken up with her immediate family. She had left behind that big extended family with more than its share of music makers, singers, and storytellers. Her sisters were not so very far away, but she seldom got away from the home place. If a trip was made to the store or to Marshall, it would be made by Ransom. Travel was difficult, and it took several days to go to the county seat and back.

When asked if she had a hard life, Jane answered: "Twere like a three-legged cat's. They didn't shoe me till I were nine yur old. I used to walk miles and miles bar'foot in the snow."[10] *The Madison County Record*, the newspaper published in Marshall, seemed to confirm the notion that life was not easy in Madison County: "Some folks say that Madison County folks are hard as nails, rough as pig iron, balky as mules, and tough as shoe leather. Well, son, they've got to be hard and tough, for that's the way life is in these here hills. Hard as nails."[11] It is amazing that Jane grew up to be such a gentle, caring person. She was tough in the sense that she could withstand whatever hardships came her way, but hardship never made her bitter or bad-tempered. She seemed to be of the same temperament as her grandfather, Council, who was gentle and fun-loving.

These pioneers were generally people without voices. There was no time to write down what was happening. The days were filled with hard work, struggling to get land cleared, crops in, a home place livable. The children fed stock, milked cows, washed dishes, filled the water bucket, filled the woodbox with firewood, split rails, built fences, grubbed new ground, picked and strung beans, weeded the garden, and did whatever needed doing according to their age and size. They generally had enough to eat, such as it was. Jane learned early to "make do or do without," and she never knew any other way of life than to work hard to meet the needs of those she loved. As long as she lived, even after she moved to town, she still followed this way of life.

Jane had "dyspepsey" when she was growing up, "a poor, yeller-lookin' thing." Her mother thought it was because she did not use tobacco like everyone else in the family. The opinion was that if she used tobacco she would be strong like the other children. "Down thar all the girls spit amber 'fore they was ten yur old but me." Even after she married she got sick, and the advice was the same, but she said, "No, I be too nice a womern to use that filthy stuff. I tried but I got as sick as an ol' buzzard."[12]

There was very little formal education to be had. Jane recalled: "I learnt myself to read so's I could read the Bible a little bit, and that winter they built a log schoolhouse and I went to school for two weeks. We studied the Bible and the old blue-back spellin' book, and I got so I could spell powerful good for a mountin' girl. I could jist wade right through the whole crowd, all but Shed (Newt) Gentry— nobody could spell like him."[13] It was true. At spelling bees Jane could outspell almost anybody, and she remained a good speller all her life. She would spell and pronounce each syllable, for example in—com—pre—hen—si—bi—li—ty.[14] Ransom's father had been able to read and had taught his sons to read. In all probability Ransom saw that his children learned to read, for according to family history Emily could not read.

But Emily knew things that she would not have learned from reading about them. She knew the ballads she had heard all her life. As she sat at her loom she sang softly to herself, "Jack went a-sailing with trouble on his mind, to leave his native country and his darling dear behind." This was the most peaceful time of the day, and the old songs spoke to her in ways she could not communicate to anyone, not even to Ransom. "Come in, come in, my two little babes, And eat and drink with me."

We do not know what happened to her firstborn child, but we can be sure Emily remembered it every day of her life. She sang as she went about her chores, while she hoed the garden and peeled vegetables. She never sat her children down and taught them the songs, but the children heard them and remembered them and passed them on to their children in much the same way.

In the evening when the supper dishes were done, Emily would join the family around the fire. On some evenings she drew her spinning wheel to her for she could spin while her mind was busy with other pursuits. Then the stories and songs and riddles would begin. It had always been this way in Emily's own home. It is probable that both Ransom and Emily knew the stories for they both came from the same people. Jane gave her mother credit for the songs and ballads, but Emily carried the stories also for Jane mentioned learning a witch story from her mother. Doc's grandchildren remember well the stories told at bedtime. It is conceivable that Jane and John Riley, the oldest of the children, took turns at telling the stories for they had heard them all their lives, long before they came to Meadow Fork.

For lives filled with chores that must be done over and over, for limbs weary from strenuous labor, for minds hungry for things to make dreams of, the stories brought a measure of excitement at first, but as the evening wore on little bodies relaxed and heads began to nod. The fire died down and the children were sent off to bed, some of them carried, still begging for one more story. The coals would be covered over with ashes to have a start for the fire in the morning. Matches were scarce, and there would be no breakfast until the hearth fire was burning.

When she was almost sixteen years old Jane Hicks married Jasper Newton Gentry (also known as Newton Jasper Gentry). Newt, as he was called, was the son of Joseph and Martha Horton Gentry, who had come from Alexander County and were living on Spring Creek. Jane told Bacheller about her courtship:

I never talked to no boy much. Onct, when a boy came an' asked me to go to meetin' with him I had a dish o' coffee to grind up an' I were so skeered I swallowed a button an' what I done with the coffee I never did know, never twill this. Onct, when I went to a neighbor's an' borried a gourd o' soap I seed a boy runnin' to ketch up with me. I run like a skeered b'ar an' kep out o' his way. I were so 'shamed o' that gourd o' soap. He couldn't 'a' ketched me if he'd been a horse. There were a neighbor's boy, John (Newt) Gentry, and often he'd come an' holp me with my work. He weren't purty—just a big mount'in huger. But my! I did love him. He were so good to me.[15]

Perhaps he wasn't "purty," but Jasper Newton Gentry was a rugged, handsome man who in later years wore a trim mustache.

One winter day when she was fifteen, she went to a neighbor's to get her mother's spinning wheel. She was carrying it home through the snow when she saw Newt Gentry coming. She was so ashamed to have him see her carrying a spinning wheel that she tried to hide it by the fence. He hurried to her side and found her crying. He said he would carry the wheel.

"Then he leaned against the fence an' tuk my hand," she went on.
"'Do you 'member what I said the other day?' he asked.
"'No, I don't 'member.' says I. 'What did you say?'
"'That I were goin' to get married an' go over to Marshall an' take up some land,' says he. 'Jane, I just want you to go with me. Will you?'
"'Course I will,'" says I.
"I got married an' left my mammy who were always peckin' me over the head with a stick. Nex' day we tuk a honeymoon walk of twenty five mile to Marshall. 'Twere rainin' when we got there late in the evenin' an' we were wet so our shoes sucked."[16]

Their parents were not in favor of the marriage. Newt's mother said she was "nothin' but a child."

Madison County records show that N.J. Gentry, age nineteen, and Jennie Hix, age nineteen, were married, date of issue, November 15, 1879; date of marriage, November 19, 1880. There seems to be a mistake in either the marriage date or the issue date, and Jane was not yet nineteen years old. The family Bible gives the marriage date as November 19, 1879. She would have been sixteen in December.

John [Newt] asked me, "Be you happy?"
"Only one thing could make me ary bit happier," I says.
"What's that?" he says. "A weddin' ring."
"You can have it, honey," says he, an he done bought hit that night.

She pointed to her ring, now worn to a thin thread of gold.[17] Newt had seventy dollars in his pocket that day. "I never see so much money in all my life—never," she said.

Lord o' mercy, we didn't need no more riches than we had—nary bit! We was so happy we didn't feel as heavy as a feather, but the village o' Marshall skeered us—so many people an' things to look at. Made our eyes and ears sore.

    Pappy hired some land and we got out. He went to work buildin' a pole cabin. Jist little logs twere made of. You could 'a' picked a dog up by the tail and throwed him out o' the chimley, hit were so low and big. I could set my chair in the hearth and look out the top o' hit. We lived thar three yur and cl'ared the ground and made tobacker. We had one old bed, back in a corner, and hit had jist one leg on hit.

    When Pappy went erway, ef I heard ary un comin' I flew under the bed and hid thar twil he were gone. One baby were born thar the second yur one night when I were alone. Pappy had gone for a neighbor woman.[18]

All of Jane's brothers and sisters married and settled on Meadow Fork. John Riley, Jane's oldest brother, married Mary Keener on January 19, 1884. They had five children—Emma Matilda, Zachariah (Zachary) Harmon, Bessie Mae, Dayton (Datis), and Hester. Mary's first marriage was to Ambrose Norris and her second to Taylor Vaughn. Margaret Elizabeth married Marion F. Reese on February 7, 1895. Their daughter, Susan, was the wife of William (Bill) Moore. William Ransom (Doc) married Harriett Reese, a sister of Marion Reese, Margaret's husband. They had ten children—Bailey, Etis, Roscoe, Arvin, Hawley, Nathan, Roy, Margaret, Marion, and Rebecca Emily.

    Preacher Hicks helped found a new church on Meadow Fork now known as Keenerville Christian Church. He was the first pastor, and Jane Gentry became the singing leader. This church from the beginning has had no creed except the Bible. The members say that they are not the only Christians, but they are Christians only. They have never been affiliated with any established denomination. The old history of the church has been lost, but the members have not forgotten that Jesse Keener donated the land for it. This was also the site of Keener School, and the old school building is still standing on the property. Maud Gentry Long credited her grandfather with being one reason all of Jane's children learned the Bible and the right way to live.

    The 1900 census showed Ransom at sixty-two years of age living with his son William Ransom (Doc) Hicks and his daughter-in-law Harriett. This was the year Ransom died. The 1910 census showed Emily, seventy-two years of age, living with William and Harriett, along with John Riley and Zachariah, John's son. Mary, John's wife, was taken to Broughton State Hospital in Morganton around 1907, where she later died. Jane Gentry told Bacheller that she raised some of her brother's children, and perhaps she did take the younger children while Zachariah lived with Uncle Doc and later with Doc's son Etis.

    On February 27, 1900, Emily Gentry, the second oldest daughter, was teaching school in a remote mountain cove when she had one of several extrasensory perception (ESP) experiences. In each case she had a premonition of death or an overwhelming feeling that someone was in danger. She dreamed one night of a white horse and on the saddle was written: "Father is dead." She closed school and left for home, for she dearly loved her father. It was a two-day walk, and when she arrived home she learned that it was her grandfather Ransom who was dead.

While he was riding his horse in the mountains, a violent storm erupted with thunder and lightning. He had taken shelter in an abandoned building. The horse reared in fright at the noise and flashing light and kicked down the building, killing them both.[19] Three weeks before his death, Preacher Hicks had picked out his burial place in the cemetery at Keenersville Christian Church, and he was the first person buried there.

Chapter 4

# Plantin' and Hoein' on Meadow Fork

Children are a poor man's riches.

—English Proverb

After their November 1879 wedding, Newt and Jane settled in to married life near Marshall. Growing up as the oldest girl in the family had prepared Jane well for her role as wife and mother. She had looked forward to having children of her own, and a year later their first baby, Lydia Nora, was born. Her birth was registered at Marshall. By the time Martha Emily, their second child, was born in 1882, Newt and Jane had moved back to Meadow Fork. Her birth was registered at Lynch on Meadow Fork, as were those of their next six children, Mary Magdalene, Alfred Chanay, Allie Mae, Lillie Bertha Maud, Roy Stevens, and Lalla Marvin. Nola Jane, the youngest, was born after the family moved to Hot Springs.

On August 16, 1886, Newt bought land from Andre Cushing and built a home for his family. It was a fine house for its time and place and was located just up the road from Ransom's church. This house is still standing, unoccupied, and is known as the Lawson Suttles place. Built of wood siding and painted yellow, it was at one time the only painted house in the area.

Their lifestyle could be described as rugged and hard, and they certainly worked hard. They made, raised, or hunted for almost everything they ate and wore and used. They were dependent on the sun and the rain to guarantee a yield from their crops. Living among majestic mountains, surrounded by towering hickory and chestnut trees, they spent much of their time out of doors, breathed fresh, clean air, and drank clean water. This life was typical for most families in rural Madison County at that time.

In the spring of the year it is still possible to find a hillside abloom with trillium, and if you go beyond the paved road the woods are aquiver with the white blossoms of "sarvis" (serviceberry) trees. You may even find a lush patch of mayapple or wake robins and, if you search diligently, white violets. The "mountain sarvis" blooms early in the spring, generally in March, but it has been known to bloom in February. In extremely cold winters the wispy white blossoms may

wait until April to make their appearance. They grow even in the higher eleva-
tions, and they are the first blossoms to be seen after the long winter, often blos-
soming out while the snow is still on the ground, white on white. Mountain people
knew that when the "sarvis" bloomed it would not be long before the circuit-
riding preacher would come through and hold services—preaching, conducting
weddings, and holding funerals for the ones who had died during the winter. West
Virginia poet Muriel Miller Dressler expressed well the significance of the "sarvis"
to mountain people:

> I trust the Lord and if I had a doubt,
> It would leave me when I see the sarvis brave
> Its way through winter's ice and snow, and it
> Pleasures me to know it's by her grave.
> Then, John, I think of us and our long sleep.
> There's room for us to rest beside our kin.
> I know when Gabriel blows his horn, we'll answer,
> And with the saints of God, go marchin' in.
> The preacher man will ride the circuit soon,
> Go, John, see if the sarvis is in bloom.[1]

Later the flame azalea and laurel and rhododendron set the woods afire
with color. Much of Pisgah Forest has been clear-cut, but one can still imagine
what it must have been like before the turn of the century.

Jane spoke of the early days on Meadow Fork: "Often in plantin' or hoein'
time, Pappy an' me u'd work all night together in the cove—'bout the only chanct
we had to visit like we used to done. We'd have our suppers at midnight, an' go
back an' scratch eround on the mount'in an' talk 'twil daylight come an' the babies 'gun to holler fer breakfast. Nex' day I'd be kindly tard—I would. Sometimes
I lay down on the bed 'twil I'd see some little feller come in with holes in his
breeches. Then I'd clomb out, an' pray an' go to work ag'in."[2]

Newt and Jane were endowed with the strength and fiber of their pioneer
ancestors. They endured hardship without complaint and wrested a livelihood out
of the mountain ground. They focused on their strong points, not their weak ones.
Jane never used her bent back as an excuse, but she did use love of her children as
a reason to work hard. It probably never occurred to them to question the direction of their lives. They were true to their instincts and used the talents and
strengths they had to the fullest. They lived among people who, as Cecil Sharp
said, were not "on the make," so keeping up with neighbors was not an issue.
They had a true sense of the value of things, and their relationships with their
neighbors ran deep and were marked by sympathetic attitudes.

In 1933 Warren Wilson wrote of the standard of living found among mountain people: "They live a life as happy as others. They have attained. They are
wise. They pray; they understand God. They know the great thoughts; in fact,
their way of thinking is the more dignified because it concerns itself less with
trifles. There is less of disguise and hypocrisy in their life."[3]

Those early years must have prepared Jane for almost anything.

I just saved every feather an' put 'em away in a poke that hung by the fireplace. Never seed no money. Saved everything else er I reckon we'd 'a' starved. All summer I'd kindly scratch up the sunlight an' save hit for the dark days. Hit come handy when the childern got the measles an' I got hit too. Holped me when Maggie got the tyford fever. I 'member I had to give her a teaspoonful o' milk every five minutes. When I'd go to sleep in the night the spoon would drop out o' my hand an' wake me up an' tell me to get up an' tend to my work.[4]

Emily told her daughter Jeannette of the days when Jane would take a sack of corn and ride a horse to the next valley to a mill to have the corn ground; the children would listen for her singing, for they could hear her well before she reached home. Jane herself spoke of this: "When we needed hit, I'd leave the babies with pappy, an' go off to the mill with half a bushel o' corn two an' a half miles an' back. Kindly enjoyed hit on a purty day—hit were so still an' nice in the woods. Rested me. Pappy would watch the babies an' scratch eround with his hoe. They missed me dreadful when I got gone, an' the babies would holler lonesome—pappy said—and oh how I loved to get back!"[5]

Jane Long Douglas, daughter of Maud Gentry Long, in commenting on a description of the lives of her mother and her grandmother as being "hard," said that neither one of them would have wanted to be portrayed in that way. Whatever life presented was to be dealt with. She spoke of her mother as always being "on top" and "exuding hope."[6] When Irving Bacheller met Jane Gentry for the first time, he said that her form was bent with toil, but "her voice and countenance had a singular sweetness and gentleness. She greeted us with a cheerful smile and a merry word. We sat with her and as she sewed she told us the amazing story of her life in the mountains. We saw her often and always in her voice and look and manner was the unmistakable note of happiness."[7] By most people's standards, Jane's life was not easy, but there is not a trace of self-pity in remembrances of her. She said to Bacheller, "I've learnt how to feel badly and keep cheerful."

Jane believed in doing whatever it took to make life more bearable. To people who were ill she must have been as welcome as a breath of fresh air. They would come for her when they were sick. "I'd find 'em crowded into a little room, around some un burnin' up with fever, moanin' and wringin' their hands and skeerin' the sick un, and breathin' up the air. I'd drive 'em all out o' the house, an' open the door an' windows an' when the sick were half dead I've pulled 'em up the slant, with just air an' nourishment an' cheerful talk."[8] She would offer a cool cloth for a forehead, a sponge bath, clean sheets, all the while preparing broth and assigning tasks to the children. She would send the children to the spring for fresh water and set them to dusting and cleaning, perhaps preparing vegetables, and they would feel useful and important. Her children always knew that they all had responsibilities, no matter what their ages. There was little hope of getting a doctor right away. Someone would have to go for miles to get word to him, so her neighbors knew that they could call on Jane, who seemed to know how to "take hold" and bring relief to the sick. Croup, flu, injuries, all afflictions that would send people to the doctor or the emergency room today were treated with herbs and plants, for everything they needed grew all around them. The courage and wisdom it took to treat the sick came from experience, common sense, and insight, and the recipes for age-old remedies came from earlier generations.

Once a neighbor's child developed a pain in her hip. For several months she was not able to walk and had to be lifted and turned. In time her hip " bu'sted." The pain was intense and she could not lie still. The doctor brought another doctor, and they held a consultation. The diagnosis was that some kind of worm was eating up the marrow in her bones. They gave the family no hope. The little girl asked for a winter-john apple, and Jane asked the doctor if it would hurt the child. The doctor said to give her anything she wanted for she could not live. Jane scraped a bite of apple and promised more if it agreed with her. They cooked a chicken, and the family was prepared to let her eat the whole chicken if she wanted it. Jane fed her gradually. The little girl had faith that if everyone prayed for her she would recover. All the people who could or would pray were sent for. Some fed her and turned her, but somebody was praying for her all the time. Jane said, "We prayed an' prayed an' prayed twil our tongues was slick, but I reckon the chicken an' the little winter-john apple prayed the best of any of us. An' she begun to get better from that time."[9]

She never lost a child, but with nine children there were times of suffering and distress. Jane would have agreed with Helen Keller that "although the world is full of suffering, it is also full of the overcoming of it." She recalled: "One day my littlest were clombin' a log fence an' pulled the top log down on him an' smashed his leg just below the hip. Oh, what a night I had! Gritted my teeth together an' held the little feller in my arms an' he yellin' like a painter 'gin the doctor would come. Tuk fourteen hours to git him thar, but he done tinkered that leg an' saved hit."[10]

Accidents did happen. The boys were chopping wood one day. Alfred was wielding the ax when Roy saw a curl of wood. Curly shavings make good playthings, and Roy grabbed for it. The ax hit Roy in the head. Jane wrapped his head and nursed him, and he recovered. When asked if she had ever been sick, she said:

Twice I were sick—measles and rheumatiz—but I kep right on with the work. The rheumatiz come like rain out a clear sky.

Onct I had been hoppin' eround in the field all day gittin' in the wheat. A'ter supper I set down and quilted twil erbout midnight and went to bed, and when I got inter bed I tuk a ketch in my hip. Oh-h-h-oh! hit seemed like lightnin' and thunder were runnin' through my j'ints. Pappy arned [ironed] erway with a hot arn on them pains twil he eased 'em, but twere five months that I walked nary step. I never lost a day's work. They'd holp me out o' bed in the mornin,' and I'd cyard and sew and cook and weave and wash. They drug me from the table to the stove and back again.

Then she laughed as she remembered something that happened during that painful time.

A young heifer come in that never had bin milked. Everybody tried to milk that wild cow but couldn't, so I asked pap to drag me out to her and he drug me close ernough so as I could git holt o' her teat with my hand. I begun milkin' her into a half-gallon cup. She'd kick, and I'd dodge a little, so she wouldn't hit the cup. Pap, he says to me: "Don't you dodge that erway and she'll stop kickin'."

So I didn't dodge next time she kicked. Pap were standin' out beyond her. Zip went the wild cow's foot. That cup jist sailed right up in the air twil hit got even with pap's face, then hit swung side-erways and jist lammed him right ercross the nose, and the milk rained all over him.

And she laughed heartily again.[11]

When winter closed in and darkness deepened and snow lay on the ground waiting for more to come, life became harder to bear. Old-timers speak of winters in their youth as having been colder than winters today. Snows came more often, were much heavier, and stayed longer. Temperatures were generally lower. Nathan Hicks remembered how cold the winters were and how it snowed all winter. Uncle Doc, his father, carried the mail on horseback, and he told of seeing trees on Bluff Mountain that would freeze and "bust."[12] Especially in winter these people, called "Golden Rule Neighbors" by Judge Felix Alley, became mindful of their neighbors who might not be so fortunate. They lived by the code that everyone within their reach was a neighbor and might need their assistance. These were strong, sturdy, self-reliant men and women who carved out the mountain empire from rugged wilderness, but they were also folks with social and friendly habits.[13]

Conversations about weather bring to mind years when there were crippling blizzards, when rivers froze over, a frozen world where the sun did not shine for days and when it did, it looked thin and pale. Winter in the mountains was a silent time, a season of long nights, a time for staying inside near the fire, a time for spinning and weaving and piecing quilts, a time for repairing shoes and harnesses. Wind whistled around the cabin and food simmered in a kettle hung over the fire or in a cast iron pot with live coals heaped on and round it. There were some problems they did not have—trees falling on power lines, cars not starting. With a good supply of wood, food laid back, kerosene lamps, hand-loomed clothes, and long underwear, the Gentrys and their neighbors were generally prepared for low temperatures, ice, and snow. It is not surprising that family ties were strong for all the members depended on each other. At times, however, there must have been almost too much togetherness. It was impossible to get away from one another in those small cabins and impossible to get away from themselves, except for the times when stories were told and ballads were sung and everyone was transported into another world.

Today most people would worry if they did not have a book or a recording or the television to take up leisure time. The Gentrys were not afraid to rely on their own resources. Their heads were full of stories. They did not need instruments to make music, but if they wanted them they would make them as Uncle Doc did. They used their voices to sing and they knew enough songs that they never tired of them. The children learned in their early years to use their imagination. Stories and ballads elicited images, and each listener created his own drama.

In the fall the whole Gentry family was busy preparing for winter—cutting and hauling wood, bringing in the cattle and sheep, digging and storing potatoes, gathering pumpkins, drying fruit, and cooking apple butter in a big iron pot. Late fall, about Thanksgiving, if cold weather had set in and the flies were gone, it was time for killing hogs and curing hams and shoulders, smoking and stuffing sausage, and canning souse meat and liver mush to be opened on winter days.

The Gentrys were very fond of leather britches. They were one of the few green vegetables they could look forward to in the winter. They began to prepare them when the cornfield beans came in. Jane's cookbook gave directions for preparing "leather britchy beans" as follows: Wash green beans. Snip off both stem and tip ends. String together in two-foot lengths (using string from flour sacks). Hang in the sun to dry. (The green will turn brown and wrinkled.) Take off string and store in half-gallon glass canning jars. When ready to cook, break into bite-size lengths. Use salt pork for seasoning.[14]

Emily told her daughter Jeannette about her growing-up years on Meadow Fork.

> There were so many varied skills to be learned but there was nothing tiresome or monotonous. The caring for sheep, the carding, spinning, weaving, sewing, patching, darning, gardening, gathering, preserving for winter, the wild bounty of fruit and nuts to be harvested, always a baby to care for; a friend or neighbor needing help. Every day was filled to the brim and ran over into the evenings when the Jack tales brought everyone concentrating on a special task—like shelling peas or stringing "leather britches," or husking corn. . . . According to Mother, Jane Gentry made living fun—never at a loss for things to be done. . . . Mother's growing-up years were very happy—no hint of it having been hard."[15]

This had always been a land where you made the best of what you had, where every member of the family had numerous tasks and skills. Newt was not just a farmer but a blacksmith, a tanner, and a cobbler. Jane was a spinner, weaver, knitter, and dyer in addition to doing all the chores required to feed a family. Everybody worked in the fields and in the garden.

Uncle Doc, Jane's brother, could do almost anything. If he didn't have a tool he made one. He lost an eye when he bent over while pulling corn and a cornstalk punctured his eye. But he did not allow himself to be handicapped by this unfortunate accident. His people thought that all of the strength of the bad eye went into the good eye. He was an expert rifle shot. He could get ten or fifteen robins out of flock and pop the breasts out for a pie. Doc made guns and bored holes through steel by hand using a long bow and arrow-like tool. He caned chairs with white oak splits. Uncle Doc was a wheelwright who made wheels out of black gum, spinning wheels, and even wooden bicycles for his children. He once made a long wagon that would carry nine children and "fly down hills." The mothers "hollered" when it turned over and skinned up the children so he had to shorten it. He caught groundhogs and made banjo heads of the hides. He made bullwhips out of cut saplings, stripped the bark back, and braided it, with a popper of dogwood on the end. Like his father and grandfather before him, Uncle Doc could read and taught his sons to read. Like his father and grandfather, he was a mail carrier. He carried the mail out of Till Stamey's store on Meadow Fork.[16] Uncle Doc and his boys played banjos and guitars and sang. It was a lifelong practice that when his sons would get together they always played music.

"The Baby in the Briarpatch" is a Gentry family story that has been included in published works by Irving Bacheller and Mary Kestler Clyde and that has been carried along in oral tradition by many members of the family. The versions are very different, as one would expect for a story that has been perpetuated orally. This is the story as told by Betty Rolfe, whose mother, Mae, was the Gentrys' fifth child. The story was told to her by her aunt Maud Long. Mrs. Rolfe and her two young sons lived with Aunt Maud in Sunnybank for several years.

> Grandmother and the two oldest, and I think it was Lalla [Jeannette thinks the baby was her mother, Emily, and Mary Kestler Clyde calls the baby "Joe"] who was in the cradle had gone out to hoe corn in the field. And she had cut a birch bark—where the men had been cutting wood, and you know how they split the bark off the wood so it won't rot. Then they can use it for barns and houses and whatever needed building. Grandmother had gone to the field to hoe corn and she put the baby in the bark; laid it down with its blanket and put it under the shade of a tree. And she went off and started hoeing corn. She told the two girls to look after the baby. And they got to playing and got a little off from the baby. The sun came out and it got hot and Grandmother worked right on until it came time to stop for lunch. She went back to get lunch and feed the children. In the meantime the sun had come in under the tree and closed up the birch bark and the baby got restless and started squirming around in there and when that happened it started rolling down the mountainside. They couldn't find the baby anywhere, so they didn't know what had happened to the baby. So they ran and got Grandfather and everybody started looking. They had searched all over for quite a long time—four or five kids looking by that time—scattered all over looking. Finally one of them looked down in a briar patch— quite a long way down the mountain they saw this little log, and sure enough the baby was inside and almost closed up tight by the time they got to it—but not a scratch on her. And that's the tale Aunt Maud told me.[17]

When she was a student at Dorland Institute, Eugenia Elliott heard Jane tell the story. She remembered one element not mentioned by anyone else. It seems that Jane's father had threatened to take her children away if she did not take better care of them. He was referring to her practice of taking them to the field while she worked. When the baby was missing, she thought her father had come and gotten the baby. Jane had a reputation for being an unusually good mother. Perhaps Jane, the storyteller, was embroidering her story. She was blessed with a sense of humor that came through in her stories, or perhaps it was her father's sense of humor. It was a frightening experience, if indeed the baby in her bark cradle rolled through a burning trash pile, as Jane herself told the story.[18]

From the trees, shrubs, wildflowers, and herbs that flourished around their home, the Gentrys gathered roots, bark, and plants to be used for medicinal purposes, for tea, for seasoning, and for dyes. Ginger, spicewood, peppermint, and sassafras for tea, cherry bark for coughs and bronchial irritations, dogwood root for toothache, blackberries and elderberries for jelly and wine, wild greens—lamb's-quarters, dandelion, and watercress—all were free for the gathering. Ginseng grew wild and could be sold or traded. There were companies in East Tennessee, Western North Carolina, and Virginia with representatives who traveled a circuit of country stores bartering for roots and herbs collected nearby.[19]

In the fall of the year when the berries dropped off the ginseng plants hidden away deep in the woods, the Gentry children collected the roots. One morning after they had finished their customary tasks, the three oldest girls, Nora, Emily, and Maggie, took their sacks and went to gather ginseng, or "sang," as it was called. They had climbed a mile or so over the hill when they heard what sounded like a lost person calling "yoo hoo." Emily knew what it was like to be lost. She remembered being lost with her father and having to spend the night in the woods and the terror of sleeping on the ground where there might be copperheads. She also remembered coming to a farm house in the morning where they were given a breakfast of cornbread, green onions, and buttermilk. The girls began answering the call as it came closer. They climbed on stumps and logs, trying to catch a glimpse of the caller. Suddenly they realized that it was not a person but a "painter" (panther). Nora took charge. She had her two younger sisters run down the mountain toward home ahead of her. Each one would drop something at intervals—a sack, a sunbonnet, an apron. The "painter" was catching up, but each time it began to gather speed it would stop and sniff a dropped object and then begin to run again. The girls were screaming as they neared home, and Uncle Doc heard them. With his one good eye he took aim and shot the panther as it leaped up on the rock wall. The girls dropped exhausted on the porch.[20]

In 1894, when Emily was twelve years old, she had a pet sheep which she had raised from a lamb. Some neighbor boys captured the lamb and held it struggling over an open well. They probably meant no real harm, but it slipped from their hands and drowned before it could be rescued. Of course, Emily grieved for her lost sheep and her parents tried to comfort her. Her father sheared the sheep and her mother helped her to dye and spin the fleece. She wove her first coverlet in a Whig Rose pattern.[21]

The colors of the coverlet are red, shaded from pale pink to red, probably dyed with madder, and what appears to be very dark brown, perhaps dyed with black walnut shells. The colors are still bright. It is woven twenty ends per inch in the warp. There are two thirty-nine-inch panels sewn together. The center seam is matched at one end and becomes more and more crooked. This is typical of the way seams were done at that time. The coverlet is in very good condition for its age. A few threads are broken at one end of the seam edge, both warp and weft, and the other end is mended with bright red cotton thread. A narrow hem is turned under and neatly whipped. During Jeannette's childhood the coverlet was used in many ways—as a coverlet, as a room divider draped in a doorway, and as a library table cover. It was her mother's "magic carpet," which took her back home to the mountains of North Carolina.[22] The coverlet now is in the care of Jeannette's granddaughter Dawna Davies.

The daughter of a preacher, Jane Gentry knew her Bible. She learned to read so that she could read the Bible. On Sunday everyone put on their "Sunday best" and walked to church. "Sunday mornin's in the summer I'd be up early an' milk an' git breakfast an' the children ready. Then we'd leg hit off three mile to Sunday School. Got home in time for dinner. The sun would be hot on the little uns comin' back. We'd have to pick up the littlest an' carry 'em 'gin we got home. If I were 'lone I'd be totin' three to onct part o' the way."[23]

Sometimes after church the minister and visitors would come to dinner. One warm summer Sunday dinner was delayed, but the flies were troublesome so Emily was given the job of chasing them away. She must have been about seven years old. Tiring soon of the wearisome task and looking about for help, she remembered her garden friend who was a good fly catcher. It was just a few steps to the garden where she gathered up the big toad and planted him in the center of the table. He made chasing flies much more interesting—until someone spotted him. Both the toad and Emily were relieved of their jobs.[24]

Jane Gentry, like most women of her day, was always ready for company, not disturbed by extra people for a meal. Even strangers were welcome for where else would they go for food and lodging? And strangers were welcome for the news and conversation they brought. The preacher was invited to someone's home during the warm months when they could hold services. Extra mouths involved only cooking a little more of what they had, and Jane was generous with her good cooking.

Newt Gentry raised a tobacco crop every year, and the boys, Alfred and Roy, helped their father. Madison County was and is still tobacco-growing country, and burley tobacco for pipes is still the cash crop for most farmers. They began in the spring with seedbeds, and it would be late fall before they would know whether their hard work had paid off. Mr. Gentry and the boys took the tobacco in a wagon to sell at the warehouse in Marshall. Newt would buy the boys lunch in town. They teased Alfred because he thought his first banana was a sweet potato. They didn't see many bananas in those days in Marshall and probably none in Meadow Fork. Newt taught the girls to help with the gardening. All the girls learned how to set out plants and put in seeds. Nola Jane said, "That was our greatest pleasure to assist him [her father] with planting vegetables and watching them grow."[25]

Chapter 5

# Moving to Town

A good wife that sings well is the best musical instrument.
—Mother Goose

"I would leave them as they are and not meddle. They are happy, contented, and live simply and healthily, and I am not at all sure that any of us can introduce them to anything better than this," Cecil Sharp wrote to Mrs. James Storrow, a devoted supporter who assisted him during his stay in America and was his hostess at her home in Lincoln, Massachusetts, in 1916. He had met teachers in the mission schools whom he admired, but he had questions about what they were teaching. He thought that the people they had come to improve were in some aspects more "cultivated" than some of the instructors.[1] Sharp was not alone in his opinion. John C. Campbell said: "Those who know mountain people know that illiteracy is not necessarily synonymous with ignorance, and that an ability to pass written or oral tests is after all an inadequate measure of knowledge. If we accept as a definition of education, adaptation of life to environment, many a Highlander would compare favorably with some of the college graduates who have come into his community to educate him." He suggested that the difference is that the illiterate person learns by experience rather than by the accumulated experiences of others.[2] The lifestyle of the Gentrys fit Sharp's description—simple and healthy. But as was typical of many other mountain parents, they wanted education for their children. Sharp did believe that they should be taught to read and write, but the Gentrys had more in mind.

There was a Presbyterian mission school, Dorland Institute, in Hot Springs, a village about fifteen miles from Meadow Fork. By the late 1880s northern churches had "discovered" the southern mountains and were sending missionaries to "improve the social and moral condition" of the people and to establish schools and churches. There were already churches in the mountains. By 1860 there were more churches per capita in the mountains than in any other part of North Carolina. After the Civil War northern churches with southern counterparts believed that ministers who had supported the Confederate cause were unfit to preach and teach. Northern Protestant denominations that were not represented there saw the region as "unchurched." Missionaries were sent, not to serve individuals, but rather to "serve the mountain people as a people." This attitude set them apart as "different." What Henry Shapiro calls "otherness" seemed to be a problem.[3] The Presbyterians wanted to bring mountain people in line with greater America—educated and "Christianized."[4]

In 1898 the Gentrys moved the family to Hot Springs so that all of their children could attend school eight months of the year instead of the three or four months afforded by the county school near their Meadow Fork home. Lalla was born that year, and Roy was three years old. Had they lived out their lives on Meadow Fork, it is doubtful that we would have heard of Jane Gentry. It was through the Presbyterian teachers at Hot Springs that she met both Irving Bacheller and Cecil Sharp.

The town of Hot Springs is located in a fertile valley on the French Broad River, six miles east of the Tennessee border. It is surrounded by the high crests of the Pisgah and Unaka Mountains and is bounded by Pisgah National Forest. Spring Creek flows out of the mountains, through laurel-banked cliffs into the town, and empties into the French Broad in the middle of town, at the sight of the hot mineral springs. In the Gentrys' time there was a swinging bridge over Spring Creek for foot traffic.

The French Broad River, which the Indians called Tahkiostie, flows northwest from Transylvania County in North Carolina to Knoxville, Tennessee, where it joins with the Holston River to become the Tennessee River. Along the way it is sometimes wide and peaceful; at other times it passes through narrow gorges and becomes rapid and rough. Just before the river reaches Hot Springs, it narrows at Deep Water, where trains cross on a trestle. Legend has it that the river is ninety feet deep here and covers an engine and tender sent to the bottom in a train wreck. As it approaches Hot Springs, the river widens and the mountains give way to make room for the little town of Hot Springs.

Hot Springs is still a small town of about seven hundred people. The Appalachian Trail runs down the main street. River rafters and canoeists put in at Barnard and end their trips in Hot Springs. Its history has been colorful and its legends persist- Indian legends about Paint Rock, Lover's Leap, and the fish monster called dakwa. It is a town whose people still know how to live simply and how to make do or do without, for the town has been for some years in an economic slump since the tourists stopped coming to the big hotel that was there when the Gentrys moved to Hot Springs. Since Uncle Doc's grandson Eugene Hicks bought the hotel property and reopened the springs in 1990, however, there have been signs of an upswing in the local economy and tourists have begun to rediscover Hot Springs.

It would be hard to imagine a more striking contrast than that between the remote cove where neighbors might be miles apart and the resort town with an elegant hotel surrounded by green, shaded lawns and peopled with those who came for the gay social life and for the curative benefits of the springs. A guest at the hotel described it as having an "air of do-nothing gayety which pervades such places."[5] The industrious Gentrys would not have considered such an "air" appropriate for their way of life and, indeed, it did have little effect on local people. As one writer noted, "About the only natives who got inside were the hired help."[6]

Large pools of mineral water bubble up along the banks of the French Broad River, as well as in the river itself. They range in temperature from 98 to 102 degrees Fahrenheit. These warm springs made the town famous as a resort area as early as 1800. The Cherokees believed in the curative powers of the water and had made pilgrimages to the springs for centuries. The springs were discovered by two settlers, Thomas Morgan and Henry Reynolds, in 1778. They stumbled on the springs while hunting for their horses, which had been stolen by the Indians.[7] By the next year people were coming to the springs seeking cures for their ailments. The settlement was called Warm Springs. James Patton bought the springs in 1831 and built a magnificent hotel on the Buncombe Turnpike, which connected Greenville, South Carolina, with Greeneville, Tennessee. The turnpike, completed in 1827, joined at Saluda Gap with South Carolina's road to Charleston, continued on to Asheville, then stretched along the French Broad River to Warm Springs and at Paint Rock joined a Tennessee road.[8]

Patton's fine two-story hotel had a wide, pillared piazza facing the river. It could accommodate 250 people and had a dining room, a bar, parlors, and a ballroom. There were half a dozen cottages for guests and stables for their horses. The accommodations were lavish, and there were musicales, balls, and outings to Paint Rock and other points of interest, as well as deer hunts for the gentlemen. The hotel burned in 1838, but John Patton built an even grander establishment. It was brick with thirteen pillars to symbolize the thirteen original colonies and had dining accommodations for 500 guests. In 1844 Zebulon Vance, a future governor of North Carolina, left Washington College in Tennessee when his father died and came home to help his family. He went to work as a desk clerk at the Warm Springs Hotel.

After the death of James Patton in 1862, James Henry Rumbough, a stage operator from Greeneville, Tennessee, bought the Warm Springs Hotel. He had joined the Confederate army and moved his family to Warm Springs, believing that they would be safer there. While Rumbough was away during the war, his wife, Carrie, a resourceful woman, poured kerosene on the bridge over the French Broad River and burned it as Federal soldiers approached the hotel at Warm Springs. Colonel Rumbough came back from the Civil War and started a new stage service from Greeneville, Tennessee, to Greenville, South Carolina. The springs were enclosed and equipped with dressing rooms. In 1883 the hotel was called the Hot and Warm Springs Hotel. A hot spring of 117 degrees had been discovered, while others tested out at 102 to 104 degrees. The waters were believed to cure gout, rheumatism, dyspepsia, torpid liver, paralysis, neuralgia, and other diseases and afflictions. There was a resident physician, and the rates were $2.50 per day for room and board or $40.00 to $60.00 per month.

Hot Springs was by this time accessible by railroad from Tennessee and North Carolina.[9] The Western North Carolina Division of the Richmond and Danville Railroad had been completed through the town in 1882, and in time six passenger trains stopped every day on the run from Asheville to Knoxville. There was a railroad depot and a telegraph office. Sometimes as many as one hundred people would get off the train. Some would stay at the hotel, others would stay in boardinghouses, and still others would line up with buckets to get mineral water from the springs.[10]

But again in 1884 the hotel burned, and Colonel Rumbough sold the property to a group of New York investors, the Southern Improvement Company. During the 1890s the the town's name was changed to Hot Springs and the Mountain Park Hotel was constructed. It was equipped with elevators, bowling alleys, tennis courts, and a golf course, reputed to be the first one in North Carolina. The hotel was heated with steam. But the Southern Improvement Company had over-extended its credit, and Colonel Rumbough bought back the hotel property.

When the Gentrys moved to the town, it was called Hot Springs and the hotel was called the Mountain Park. It was a thriving community much like tourist towns today. The local people had little to do with the hotel except for those who worked there or supplied vegetables, fruit, or meat for the dining room. In the summer of 1882 more than forty people were working for the hotel. Farmers in the area filled such orders as seven sheep (643 pounds) for $16.07, 253 chickens for $42.37, 67 pounds of pork for $6.70, 25 1/2 pounds of butter for $4.24, 47 ducks for $7.05, 10 1/2 dozen eggs for $1.57, 3 beeves (2,100 pounds) for $52.50, and 3 bushels of apples for $1.50.[11]

The Dorland Institute had been organized in 1886 by the Reverend Luke Dorland and his wife, Juliette, who chose Hot Springs as a place to retire. After the Civil War the Freedman's Committee of the Presbyterian Church, USA, commissioned the Reverend Dorland to find a location for a school for Negro girls. This venture became Scotia Seminary in Cabarrus County, North Carolina, and it began in the Dorland home, just as Dorland Institute did in 1886. Dorland Institute began with his neighbors' children meeting around the dining room table. With some help from the Presbyterian Board of Home Missions for books and equipment, Rev. Dorland built a two-story school at his own expense.[12] In 1918 it become Dorland-Bell School with an accredited high school.

Because the Presbyterians set very high standards for the education of their ministers, many frontier communities found themselves without spiritual leaders. The Baptists and Methodists, whose preachers were not required to have seminary training, increased in numbers. There were two fields in which the Presbyterians excelled, however—education and health services. Between 1887 and 1909 they maintained eighteen schools and one hospital in Madison County.[13] The first of these mission schools was Dorland Institute, which stated as its purpose "to help girls from remote mountain districts who are not within reach of a good school; to lead those to a vision of the possibilities of a rich, happy life in the country; to send back into mountain homes young women who will know how to make healthy, happy Christian homes. . . . Our main interest is in the girl who will have no schooling after she leaves here."[14]

The county schools started in late August or early September and let out at harvest time, when all hands were needed on the farm. Winter weather made it almost impossible for schools to stay open. In time, nearby Spring Creek became a community of industrious, community-minded people who built schools and churches. Spring Creek Seminary, a high school, opened in 1895 and by 1906 had a term of seven months.

Nora, the oldest Gentry child, was the first in the family to enroll in Dorland Institute, encouraged by Julia Phillips, a teacher in the school, who sought out students "away back in the sticks," as Mrs. Gentry said. When she was old enough, Emily and her father made a two-day journey with a wagonload of apples to pay as tuition and enrolled her in the farm-mission school. Perhaps Nora and Emily were lonely and homesick at first, but Emily's children remember their mother describing her experience at Dorland Institute as "the opening of a wondrous door." In addition to the academic curriculum and Bible study, students learned housekeeping skills, sewing, and gardening. Because of their experience as the oldest children in a large family, Nora and Emily breezed through the classes in the domestic arts, and their skills gave them a way to earn tuition, room, and board. In the eighth grade students were introduced to algebra and Latin, and they graduated after completing the eighth grade.[15] Nora attended until 1895, the year she married. Emily graduated about 1897. All nine children attended Dorland-Bell Institute, and eight of them graduated. Mrs. Gentry did laundry, cleaned faculty rooms, and wove coverlets while Newt raised vegetables and apples to pay tuition for the children. When they were able to get a house big enough, they ran a boardinghouse, taking in teachers as well as tourists.

To maintain schools, churches, and hospitals these "fotched on" teachers and preachers had to appeal to northern congregations for support. Pat Roberts, who attended Asheville Normal School, another Presbyterian institution, told of those days when northern people would speak at chapel. "We always knew whether they had money or not by the way Dr. Calfee prayed. If he prayed for 'these poor underprivileged mountain girls,' we whispered, 'He's rich.'" A film was made to send up north that featured two girls. One lived in a log cabin and was "dull." She was shown in far-away shots, carrying water and doing other chores. The other girl was more appealing and was filmed in close-up shots. The film "disclosed" that the school had made a lady of her. The girls who were working their way through school often worked for faculty members, cleaning rooms and making beds. Roberts remarked: "We earned our education, but I don't think I could have gotten along without it."[16]

There is little doubt that the Gentrys felt that they could not have gotten along without Dorland Institute. As an alumna, Maud joined the ranks of the fund-raisers and wrote: "The friends of this school are investing their money not at 4 or 6 per cent but in the lives of the womanhood of our mountains."[17]

Emily's first job was teaching school back in a mountain cove, boarding around with the families of her students. One family took their children out of school and when asked why, they said: "Do you know what Emmy is teaching the children? That the earth is round and anybody knows that if that were so there would be no water in the well in the morning."[18]

The moves, first across the mountains to Madison County and then to the town of Hot Springs, were difficult for Jane. Mountain people are known to have a great sense of place and are reluctant to leave their homes. Making this move must have seemed to Jane and Newt the only way they could get good schooling for their children. For the first year or two the family moved back to Meadow Fork for the summer months to raise their crops but returned when school opened. With babies as well as school-age children this was no small chore, but apparently Jane Gentry accepted her situation wherever she was with practical good humor. When asked how she managed to educate her children she said: "I learnt 'em to read and write and use figgers, and I learnt 'em to be honest and fear God, and then I sent 'em down to the mission school and worked nights weavin' to pay the sixty dollars a yur, and God helped me. The boys seen how hard I worked, and they worked too.[19]

No modern mother could be more involved with her children's school than was Jane Gentry. She was not a prominent woman in town or even in the church. She was a quiet, busy woman—at home. But she had strong ties to Dorland because her children were there. From the time she moved to Hot Springs until her death, she made herself available to Dorland-Bell. For many years she lived next door to the school. There was much coming and going. Jane borrowed from the school kitchen and the school borrowed from her.

During the years she ran a boardinghouse, students worked for her from time to time, helping with cleaning, laundry, and preparing vegetables. Of course, Jane was a source of stories and ballads and songs, which she shared with students and visitors. At socials and programs Mrs. Gentry would entertain, often on holidays. Eugenia Elliott said that "when there was fiddle and banjo music Jane would dance—just do a few steps, not in a group. She would just get up and dance alone. It was like she couldn't sit still when there was music."[20] Old Counce would have understood.

To the teachers who came from the North and had little experience in mountain living, she offered her practical know-how as well as her good humor. She was called "the mountain friend of Dorland" by the Presbyterian Board of Missions when it paid tribute to her in a leaflet printed after her death. People who knew her said she never lost her mountain ways or her mountain speech and yet she was at home among the teachers and others who came to Dorland. Of course, she was aware that she did not talk like the teachers. Elizabeth Dotterer ("Miss Peggy"), granddaughter of James and Carrie Rumbough, grew up around her grandfather's hotel. Her phenomenal memory and her keen powers of observation made her a natural historian for Hot Springs. She remarked that Jane would hesitate at times when she used "hit" or "haint." But her speech was colorful and musical. Whatever it was that made her unique had nothing to do with education and little to do with association unless we go back along family lines—back to Council Harmon. Outsiders who expected all mountain people to fit the stereotype must have been puzzled by this humble, quiet woman with her sharp wit and her storehouse of knowledge.

The Gentry family had always lived up a "holler," far from any town, living off the land, resourceful and self-sufficient. In town they continued to raise most of what they ate. Everybody had gardens. They kept cows, chickens, and pigs for milk, butter, eggs, and meat. Newt Gentry had a little grocery store. He rented a piece of land about two miles out of town on the Newport highway where he raised vegetables. He fixed up his wagon with large hampers to carry sweet potatoes, Irish potatoes, corn, lettuce and other vegetables. The produce was transported to the store by horse and wagon. Nola Jane was always at her father's side, and Alfred was old enough to be good help. Nola Jane was given the job of putting on the brakes when the horses got too spry and tried to run too fast. But Newt Gentry was too generous in issuing credit to his customers and eventually went broke. Of course, he continued to farm and supply the food for the family and the boardinghouse table.

There were conveniences in Hot Springs that had not been available on Meadow Fork. Pete Lawson delivered ice to an icebox on the back porch, using large tongs. Once when he was delivering ice during a storm, lightning struck and he could not let go of the tongs.[21] The tree-lined streets in Hot Springs were not paved, and they were either dusty or muddy but all right for horses and wagons. Life centered around the trains. Few people went to Asheville by road. The Carolina Special, No. 27 and No. 28, went to Asheville in the morning and came back in the evening. About noon No. 12 went to Asheville, and No. 11 came from Asheville in the afternoon. The local train No. 101 came from Knoxville in the evening and No. 102 went to Tennessee in the morning. Wednesday was "dollar day." People who had business in Asheville tried to wait until Wednesday so they could go and return for a dollar. When the mail train, No. 11, was due, everybody who could get away went to the station, then followed the mail to the post office.

Michael O'Connor, Southern Railway train engineer on the Carolina Special, was known to everyone who rode the trains or lived near the tracks. He had a green engine with shamrocks on the side for "his Irish blood." No one could blow a whistle like O'Connor. In fact, he had a brass whistle made especially for him which sounded different from all others. People knew he was coming long before his train reached the station and went down to the tracks to wave at Mike. The girls knew they were growing up when he doffed his cap to them. Some people said they would "shiver with dread as the lonesome tones came through the air." Sick people tried to wait for Mike's train because he drove so "easy" and made sure that a cot in the baggage car would not get jerked around.[22] It was about 1920 before anyone owned a car in Hot Springs.

Although the life at the hotel had little to do with the townspeople, some people were a part of both worlds. James Henry ("Harry") Hill, Colonel Rumbough's grandson, was a dancer, singer, and comedian who entertained at the hotel, but he was a plumber by trade, and he would come to Dorland Institute to work on the plumbing. While he was there he would entertain the girls in the kitchen with songs and rhymes such as this one:

> There was a girl in our city,
> With another face she'd be pretty,
> But as it is when I look at her frizzy
> My heart bubbles over with pity.[23]

The years in Hot Springs were energetic ones for the Gentry family, seeing nine children through school. But then, when had life not been energetic? Everybody was assigned work, and when each child entered school he or she was given work to do there to help with tuition. Nola Jane concluded that it did her good to learn to work hard while she was growing up. The spinning and weaving continued, and some of the girls took up these tasks. Newt was good at keeping things in working order, handy at mending. He helped with the milking and always there were children around to carry the milk and do the churning. The older girls were expected to make the beds and keep the house clean, especially after their home became a boardinghouse.

With so many children as well as a constant stream of boarders and visitors, many stories were added to the family repertoire. One such story concerns Roy, who shared a room with Alfred. It seems that Roy crept in late one night and crawled into bed in the dark. He awoke early and felt the long hair of a guest who had gotten into the wrong room. He slipped out of bed, and as far as anyone knows, the young woman never knew he had been there.

Jane Gentry kept a hospitable house, boarding teachers and welcoming visitors warmly. A night's lodging and a meal cost less than fifty cents (James Gentry said thirty to forty cents), and this included feed for the lodger's horses. Miss Peggy was a contemporary of Nola Jane and spent a great deal of time in the Gentry home. "When I think of her I always think of 'busyness.' She wove, spun, tatted, knit, crocheted, and she was always teaching other people to do these things. I would go there and before I knew it I was peeling apples, shelling peas. . . . And she would sing and tell stories while we worked. There was a kind of atmosphere in her house. It seemed natural for her to sing and tell stories. I was fascinated by her."[24] Her hands were always busy, and she kept everybody else's hands busy. The people who lived in the Gentry boardinghouse, including the teachers, helped out. Few women of her day found time to make pulled lace. This was a skill some women might have known, but there was little time for such intricate handwork. But Mrs. Gentry did find time for it.[25] Even her aprons reflected her love of beautiful things, always trimmed with tatting or crocheted work. For Jane Gentry, making beautiful things made life more pleasant, just as her songs and stories did. They were not performances; they were just a natural part of everyday living. They were also a practical way to keep the children, and anyone else who happened to be present, busy.

Mrs. Gentry was usually the disciplinarian, but neither Newt nor Jane resorted to whipping. She is remembered as a mother who did not scold much. She talked gently and got things done that way.[26] There was one occasion on which Nola Jane expected to be punished. She found her mother weaving at the loom with tears running down her cheeks. It was unusual to find her mother in low spirits, and she wanted to know why. Jane said that she was worried about Lalla. Lalla, the next to youngest daughter, was very beautiful; in fact, people still describe her as looking like a movie star. Her mother felt that she might be attracting the young men away from other girls and she did not want her to take advantage of people. There was one young man in particular she was concerned about, a Baptist preacher at a church where Lalla played the organ and piano. So Nola Jane wrote a letter to the young man telling him that Lalla was already engaged and was going to be married and not to come around anymore. She signed her mother's and Maud's names. When the mail came and she saw a letter from the young man, she ran and hid behind the hog pen. Jane and Maud were angry, as angry as Nola Jane had ever seen them, but she did not get a spanking.[27]

When World War I broke out, the word came by newspaper on the first train from Asheville. The Mountain Park Hotel became an internment camp for some two thousand officers and crews of German commercial ships seized by the United States government. According to the *News Record*, the only newspaper published in Madison County, in 1918 there were about forty German families living in Hot Springs. The women and children were not guarded and lived in boardinghouses. Mrs. Gentry kept some of them in her boardinghouse. There was no feeling of ill will, and the German women, some of whom were good seamstresses, visited the women in the town. The German prisoners were industrious and spent a great deal of time building a village of scraps—wood, Prince Albert tobacco tins, and so on—chalets, a church, a merry-go-round, and shops. On Sunday afternoons the thirty-five-member German Imperial Band gave concerts. Years later people still talked about hearing "The Blue Danube Waltz."

Business was good in Hot Springs as well as in the surrounding county. The population of the town had quadrupled. Newt Gentry and other farmers from Hot Springs to Spring Creek to Meadow Fork raised vegetables and brought them to sell, including wagonloads of cabbage, for the Germans loved sauerkraut. Bill Moore said that the German women, who spoke no English, would climb aboard his wagon and choose their vegetables. He spoke no German, but they understood each other well enough to do business. He drove his wagon into the basement of the hotel to deliver vegetables, a basement so large he could turn his wagon and team of horses around.[28] Alfred and Roy worked as guards at the hotel.

But this was also a time of watching troop trains pass through town and of seeing the boys from Hot Springs go away to war. The usual groups of people waited for the mail train to see who got letters from their sons. They were there to sympathize when letters did not come. Alfred was called up for military service, but the war was over before he was inducted. Roy, who had already been in the army, was not called up.

One of the German wives had a collie dog; some said she was staying in Mrs. Gentry's boardinghouse. The dog carried notes from the woman to her husband. Miss Peggy remembered seeing the dog with the note in its mouth on the day before the first and only prisoner escaped. She said the woman was placed under house arrest in her room and that you could hear her screaming all over town. Miss Peggy thought the woman may have lived in Sunnybank but was not sure whether the Gentrys lived there at the time.[29] After the escape the military was brought in to guard the prisoners. The armistice brought a kind of madness that resulted in the German village being blown up. The celebrants planted dynamite around the buildings and destroyed most of them, even the beautiful little church made of Prince Albert tobacco cans. There are people in town who still treasure photographs of the fantastic "village."

In January 1920 the Mountain Park Hotel burned to the ground. It would not be the last hotel in Hot Springs, but there would not be another as grand as the Mountain Park. The year Mrs. Gentry died, the property was bought by Bessie Safford, daughter of James Rumbough. Her first marriage was to Andrew Johnson Jr. of Greeneville, Tennessee, son of the president. She built the Hot Springs Inn, but by 1930 she had given the hotel to the Catholic church. In 1976 the inn met the fate of all the other hotels; it burned to the ground.

Newt Gentry was a "true blue Republican." He brought up his children to be the same. There were many discussions and arguments over the subject. Mrs. Gentry just grinned and enjoyed the discussions and continued with whatever handwork she had in her lap. There were few families in Hot Springs who were Democrats at that time. In fact, Bill Moore, who was active in politics and served as county tax collector at one time, said that there were seven thousand Republicans and eight hundred Democrats in Madison County. Moore ran a store on Meadow Fork and was married to Jane's niece Susan Reese. He wore a belt inscribed "Mr. Democrat." Newt pinned a large Republican pin on Nola Jane's sweater when she started to school one morning, and the few Democrats made her life "pretty tough" and threatened to beat her up on the way home from school. She solved this problem by pretending to be sick, and the teacher allowed her to go home early. When Alfred became mayor of Hot Springs, he refused to change the town clock, as well as his own watch, at what he considered President Franklin Roosevelt's direction. Nola Jane, who lived in Alaska for many years, called herself a "stalwart independent."[30]

The Gentry family lived in several houses in Hot Springs, including a house up on Mountain Heights overlooking the town, which was later run as a boardinghouse by the Lance sisters, and one down by the river, which was flooded. One of

Maud's vivid memories was of her mother driving a horse and buggy across the bridge over the flooding French Broad River.[31] In 1910 Newt bought a house on Spring Street on the banks of Spring Creek. Nola Jane was about eight years old. The house caught fire in the night and burned. It was so badly damaged that they could not live there after the fire. It started about three o'clock in the morning. Their dog, J.W., a poodle, barked so violently that he woke the family and Nola Jane credited him with saving their lives. "Our father put the dog in my arms and in my outing gown, he told me to go ring the Baptist Church bell (an outside bell) for fire helpers. I was so excited I could hardly turn the large bell. Although I wanted to stay with my parents, Mother sent me to school the next day."[32] Until they could find another home, their good friends the Tom Frisby family took them in. In 1911 they bought the house on the banks of the French Broad River which was flooded in 1916. Their final home was Sunnybank.

County records show that in 1919 the Gentrys bought the home in which they would live out their days. There is some speculation that they lived there before that date. Some people believe Cecil Sharp called on Jane there. Some believe they lived there during World War I. But the fact that Cecil Sharp had to cross the river when he called on Jane in 1916 suggests otherwise. His accommodations were on the town side of the French Broad River.

On June 28, 1919, the deed to Sunnybank was transferred from B.I. and Ida Nicholson to J.N. Gentry and wife, Jane, (three-quarters undivided interest), and Maud Gentry (one-quarter undivided interest). Sunnybank, a lovely old house, now known as the Inn at Hot Springs, is on the National Register for Historic Places. It is owned and operated by Elmer O. Hall. The house was built in 1875 by Charles Merrit and sold in 1886 to Colonel and Mrs. Rumbough, who called the house Rosmond. It changed hands again in 1894, when it was used as a summer home, and again in 1912, when it was first opened to the public as a boarding-house by James E. Rector. It was sold again in 1912 to B.I. Nicholson, about whom little is known, and purchased from him by the Gentrys, who renamed the house "Sunnybank." Without a clue as to the origin of this name, one might speculate that perhaps Mrs. Gentry knew the old English carol with the lines: "As I sat on a sunny bank, a sunny bank, a sunny bank, / As I sat on a sunny bank on Christmas Day in the morning."

Uncle Doc and his family left Meadow Fork and moved to Marion in 1920. The textile mills recruited large families, especially those with boys. Children went to work at age fourteen until a law was passed that made sixteen the minimum age. Some of Doc's older children had already moved to Marion. It was a dry summer, and crops had failed. They came to Hot Springs and spent the night at Alfred's house and caught the train the next morning. Harriett, Doc's wife, had been listening to the train whistle for years but had never seen a train until the day she left Madison County. Jane's brother John and his son Zachariah moved with them, but John died in Marion the following year. Old ways die hard for families who have learned to do everything for themselves, including making their own tools. During the Depression one of Doc's sons, Bailey, was night watchman at Clinchfield Mill. He raised sheep in the mill yard to keep down the grass and sheared them there in the yard. Bill Moore bought Doc's farm for $1,000, and the apple trees Doc ordered from Sears mail order are still there behind Meadow Fork Baptist Church.

Chapter 6

# The Writer Meets
# the Storyteller

Happiness is not a reward—it is a consequence.
—Robert Green Ingersoll

This is not the first book written about Jane Gentry. Irving Bacheller (1859-1950), a famous writer of novels and short stories and Sunday editor of the *New York World* under Joseph Pulitzer, wrote a novel in 1916 titled "The Tower of a Hundred Bells." It was a tale of the mountains of western North Carolina in a valley in which he spent three winters.

An account of a meeting that led the author to Jane Gentry was written up in a quarterly report to the Women's Board of Missions of the Presbyterian Church USA in April 1914. Carrie B. Pond, a Dorland Institute teacher, described a typical day at the school, and these reports went out to missionary groups, some of which might be possible donors. To protect students and parents their names were not given in these reports. Just a single initial or, as in the following case, a substitute name was used:

> Come with us to a missionary meeting after school. We are meeting with Mrs. Graham [Gentry]. She and "Pappy" moved here from way up Spring Creek some years back to get "school chances," seeing as they "wasn't rich in much but children." Eight of the nine have come to the school.
>
> In Mrs. Graham's [Gentry's] hospitable living room we find women of varying degrees of culture. Mrs. Irving Bacheller, wife of [the author of] *Keeping up with Lizzie* and *D'ri and I*; Mrs. Childs, wife of the Asheville Normal School President; our minister's wife; a few Dorland teachers; several busy mothers and housewives, and even dear old Mrs. Beck who can't read but loves to come. The topic is Japan and the meeting is a "live" one, social, too, over its cup of cocoa and bit of cake."[1]

Anna Bacheller came away from this meeting very impressed with Mrs. Gentry. She told her husband that she had met the most wonderful human being, an unlettered mountain woman who kept a boardinghouse. He went to see her next day. This is how he described his first visit:

> I could hear voices as I came near the house and chiefly those of young children laughing as if at play. Then I heard the kindly voice of Mrs. Gentry. She sat on her little verandah sewing with a number of small children grouped around her. She was amusing them as she worked.
>
> "Go on with your story telling," I pleaded. "I am a child myself as young as any of these."
>
> "I were tellin' some mount'n stories," she answered. "It mout be they'd tickle ye. So if you'll be one o' the young uns, set down thar an' I'll scratch around an' see what I kin fetch out o' my ol' brains."
>
> I took the chair she offered and sat down with a girl of four on my lap while Mrs. Gentry opened a mine of old mountain folk lore which delighted me.
>
> "Well here comes:
>
> Eight humly, bumly bees,
> Seven humpity, crumpity no horn cows,
> Six hicketty, ficketty, custards,
> Five bob-tail, bald-face, skewball nags,
> Four colly birds,
> Two ducks and an ol' fat rooster.
>
> "Now we'll have a riddle tellin':
>
> As I walked out an' in I spied
> The livin' an' the dead.
> Six flew an' seven fled
> An' thar were one that limped and cried.
>
> "I reckon you cain't guess that. Hit's a potteridge's nest in a horse's skull."
>
> "Tell us a tale," said a small boy.
>
> "A tale! a tale!" the others echoed.
>
> "A tale! Well I declar! I reckon I'll have to tell you the tale o' . . . ."[2]

The riddle Mrs. Gentry told that day was recorded in 1923 by Isabel Gordon Carter:

> As I walked out the inn
> I spied the living in the dead.
> Six of them flew
> And seven of them fled
> If you can guess this riddle
> You can kill me dead.

A woman walked out and saw the skull of a dead horse and in it a partridge had hatched thirteen eggs. Six of the birds could fly and the others could not.[3]

Bacheller said that when he was there "her fingers were knotted, her form bent with human service although she was only fifty four years of age. . . . The natives of the village had good things to say of her and there was a note of respect in their tone more convincing even than their words. . . . On the whole she was the most remarkable human being I have every known."[4]

Bacheller was a prolific and successful writer. His novel *Eben Holden*, published in July 1900, was called "the most popular book in America" and hailed by some as the long-looked-for "American novel." Although some critics said it was not a great book, it outsold *The Wonderful Wizard of Oz*, *To Have and To Hold*, and other popular books of that year and held its own with Winston Churchill's *The Crisis*.[5] By April 1901, 250,000 copies had been sold. Nearly a quarter of a century after publication 3,000 copies were sold in one year.[6] William Dean Howells wrote: "I have read *Eben Holden* with great joy in its truth and freshness. You have got into your book a kind of life not in literature before, and you have got it there simply and frankly. It is as pure as water and as good as bread."[7]

Bacheller and his wife had come to Hot Springs for a rest. For many years Bacheller had been interested in the pursuit of happiness. He considered Abraham Lincoln, in spite of his great sorrows, to have been a profoundly happy man. President Lincoln's philosophy was that "most people are about as happy as they make up their minds to be." He thought Oliver Wendell Holmes had learned the secret of happiness because he had found the task he loved and had given his strength to it. John Burroughs, who knew birds and beasts and trees and flowers, said that he had discovered the secret of happiness—work, with either hands or head. Although Bacheller greatly admired him, he felt that Burroughs could believe in nothing beyond the reach of his senses and he perceived a dissatisfaction. After interviews with Mark Twain; Andrew Carnegie, a man rich in friends and treasure; Hetty Green, the richest woman in the world; and others, he decided that Jane Gentry was the happiest person he had ever met. He had not encountered anyone who had known such hardship, who worked so hard, and yet, who always had an aura of happiness. He felt this even when she was telling him about her experiences growing up and rearing a family on Meadow Fork. He seemed to have found a woman who had found the happiness that eluded his wealthy friends. He asked people who knew her if she was always gentle and good-natured, and they assured him that she was. He wanted to know more about her.

The Bachellers invited Mrs. Gentry to visit them in their Greenwich, Connecticut, home which they called Thrushwood. Bacheller described it as being as beautiful as his taste and means would allow. It was approached through a small forest and looked out on the shining waters of a quiet bay leading to the sea and beyond to the distant shore of Long Island Sound.[8] Jane had never traveled, had never ridden on a train, had never ridden in a car. Maud was teaching school in Raleigh at the time, but when school was out she came home to run the boardinghouse and her mother went to New York. Bacheller sent her a train ticket, and she took her first train ride. She was met at the station and driven to the Bacheller home by a chauffeur. This was her first ride in a car. There she told Bacheller more stories and he tried to unravel the mystery of how she came to be as she was.

Jane enjoyed telling stories of her trip to New York. Pat Roberts, at age ninety-one, still remembered hearing about the trip when she was a student at

Asheville Normal School. Jane talked of the big fine house the Bachellers lived in and of the chauffeur who came to get her and take her there. The maid came to her room and offered to unpack her bags. Mrs. Gentry told her that she had packed the bag to get there and she could unpack it. Sometime later the maid came to help her dress for dinner. Jane explained that she was dressed, that she had brought only one other dress, and she would wear the one she had on.[9]

During her stay with the Bachellers the writer decided that he would hire a stenographer to record his conversations with Jane. One young man applying for the job was asked if he thought he could do this. He answered that "no woman's tongue is quicker than my ability to capture it." At that, Jane's eyes began to twinkle and she recited one of her riddles—as fast as she could say it, as was her way with riddles:

> As I went around my willy-go whackum,
> There I spied ol Bow Backum.
> I went home after Tom Tackum,
> To run Bow Backum out of my willy-go-whackum.

The young man threw up his hands and left.[10]

Jane often told schoolchildren about her trip to New York. She was taken out to fine restaurants, and she related how Bacheller left a fifty-cent tip under her plate for the waiter. "I squeezed that silver piece hard before I left it there," she would say.[11] After all, it only cost fifty cents to spend the night and have a meal in her boardinghouse. Bill Moore remembered that she took a boat trip, and this must have been a great adventure for a woman who had lived all her life surrounded by high mountains.

She made quite a hit with children she met through the Bachellers. She would tell stories and riddles and sing songs, one after another. After each one, the children would sing out, "Tell us another one." When she grew tired or hoarse, she would tell them that her tongue was slick, or she would pretend that she had lost her voice. Just as Jane had done with her own children, she would give them something else to do—she would hand them a book to look at or start a picture on a pad for them to finish. In time, her voice would return.[12] These city children were as fascinated as mountain children had been.

One of the stories told by a granddaughter about the trip to New York is that Mrs. Gentry sang one evening on the *Metropolitan Opera Hour* a program of old English ballads. The one that brought down the house was "The Cherry Tree Carol," and she was said to have received a standing ovation.[13] This story has not been confirmed, but Jeannette Armstrong remembers her mother telling about it. Maud's daughter Jane and her granddaughter Daron are musicians with classical training, and they did not hear the story from Maud. It seems likely that she would have wanted them to know about this experience. Nevertheless, it is interesting that such a story has been perpetuated—that people who knew this mountain singer believed that she could charm sophisticated operagoers. She certainly charmed every other audience that we know about. Although Bacheller did not write about her singing, it is entirely possible that he did introduce her to such a group and it is possible that she sang ballads. He wrote a short story that was published in *Collier's* in October 1915 entitled "Left Behind" in which he introduces a mountain grandmother to a "gay company of men and women in evening dress." He began his introduction: "I have come here to tell you of certain great women whose labor and fortitude have made America, and I must begin by mentioning the most heroic woman I have ever known. She has the strength of a man in her heart and sinews, the beauty of a saint in her face, the courage of a hero, the faith of a prophet in her soul. Yet she has been the tenderest of mothers. I can think of nothing save the miracles of old, so wonderful as her accomplishments. . . . I want you all to see her and give her the honor due a great woman."[14] The short story is based on Bacheller's conversations with Jane Gentry, and in view of his other writings about her, he might well have introduced her in this way.

This material almost surely appeared in "Tower of a Hundred Bells." In April 1917 the book was finished, two copies awaiting delivery, one to his publisher and one to his safe. With this undertaking off his mind, he went with friends to New Jersey for a game of golf with the governor. He returned to find his home in flames, the book destroyed as well as notes and first drafts. The shock of the fire caused his wife's health to fail, and he did not attempt to rewrite the book. He described its hero as having a remarkable voice with which he could imitate all the beasts and birds of the mountain country. The heroine was based on Jane Gentry about whom he said, "I think she was the greatest person I have known. This I write with no hesitation, because of her faith, her kindness, her charity, her cheerfulness in the midst of misfortunes that might well have utterly broken the spirit."[15]

Sometime later he discovered notes from his conversations with Mrs. Gentry. He thought they were too good to be lost for they gave some notion of the "truth and vividness" of the novel. From these notes he wrote short stories, "My Lost Novel" in 1938 and "The Quest for Happiness" in 1926, as well as an article for *American Magazine,* "The Happiest Person I Ever Knew" in 1924. "Left Behind" was published in *Collier's* in 1915 soon after Jane's visit to New York. The two articles were published before her death, but it is not known whether she read them. Considering the affection the author and his wife felt for Jane, they may well have sent her copies. The house fire and the flood destroyed most of the Gentry family's paper materials.

Irving Bacheller was certainly a romantic writer, but many of his reviewers thought well of him. The *London Times* reviewer wrote: "Mr. Bacheller is admirable alike in his scenes of peace and war . . . eloquently poetical . . . grimly humorous. . . . Nor does anything in Crane's *Red Badge of Courage* bring home to us more forcibly the horrors of war." A reviewer described his poetry as "marked by virility, simplicity of manner, and genuine strength and feeling."[16] Bacheller was also a newspaper writer, and the stories about Mrs. Gentry were written for the popular market. He was not doing serious research; he was writing about a person he genuinely liked and respected, whom he considered unique and worthy of attention.

To understand Bacheller's great respect for Jane Gentry it is helpful to look at the man himself. According to one interpreter, he had a real appreciation of the simple things of life as well as a genuine feeling for "the beauty of moral excellence."[17] He had faith in the virtues of the rural life of his young years and a distrust in the vices of the city, where he spent most of his adult life. The secret of his popularity did not lie in his adaptability to contemporary literary taste. He was an American of the old school, and he always wrote from that point of view.

His writing style was simple and economical, his sentence structure and diction simple. *Eben Holden* may not have been a great book, but it was a veritable anthology of North Country folklore, and folklore was always of interest to him.[18]

Hamlin Garland wrote in a letter to his friend Charles Merrill: "He had a melodious tenor voice and when he lifted it in one the ballads which his people had brought over the mountains from 'Vaermont,' I listened with respect."[19] Because of this common interest and talent, no doubt Bacheller and Mrs. Gentry sang ballads for each other.

In 1884 Bacheller founded the first newspaper syndicate in America, through which he was responsible for publishing works by Rudyard Kipling, Mark Twain, Conan Doyle, Eugene Field, and others. After he had made the rounds of the "great magazines," Stephen Crane brought *Red Badge of Courage* to Bacheller. It was a besmudged handwritten copy of about fifty thousand words. Bacheller and his wife, Anna, read it to each other. Bacheller bought the serial rights. It was condensed and appeared in the *Philadelphia Press* December 3-8, 1894. It was an immediate success.[20]

We have no way of knowing how well Bacheller was able to convert Mrs. Gentry's dialect into print. He certainly took time and put a great deal of effort into writing it. Nola Jane, who was eleven years old at the time, said that Bacheller came to their home many times and made recordings.[21] There is some evidence of his fictionalizing and using names that are different from the family names, but he did this when he wrote of his own life and family. Lacking his notes, he may have tried to recall information that had been destroyed in the fire. The dialect from one story to another is much the same. On June 17, 1942, he wrote a letter to Maud:

Dear Maud Gentry Long,

I do thank you heartily for your kind letter. My wife and I fell in love with your mother who, I think, was the most remarkable woman we had known. I have never seen one of a more sublime faith. My beloved wife passed away in April, 1924. It was a sore loss. I do hope the two have met in heaven. I married her friend and schoolmate and here I am near 83 strong and still at work. I wrote a book largely about your mother and her mountain life which was destroyed by a fire that burned my home in 1917.
  Sincerely,
  Irving Bacheller[22]

# Chapter 7

# Old Counce, Jane, and the Jack Tales

These traditions are not good because they are old. It's the other way
around.

—Richard Chase

In Jane Gentry's day, storytelling was not taught. Old Counce planted the
seed. He simply told the stories as they had been told to him, and the children
listened. The stories were shaped by the social group in which they thrived, as
were the children. The family and the community passed judgment on the content of the stories just as they shaped the personalities of the children and conveyed their rituals, customs, and traditions. To be a member of a community is to
share its myths. The stories and the songs were Jane's cultural inheritance. She
met ghosts of past generations while she was cradled safely on her grandfather's
lap. Thus her young life was shaped by a family and a community in which singing songs and telling stories were as natural as breathing. She did not go to school,
but a great deal of learning took place in an informal way. Unconsciously, while
they were having a good time, Jane and her siblings and cousins learned songs and
riddles and stories. The knowledge gained stayed with them. The stories helped
them to make connections with the world around them. Their grandfather in his
role as storyteller conveyed ageless truths and timeless wisdom.

There has been much speculation about the source of Council Harmon's
Jack tales. He said that he learned them from his grandfather. There is some evidence that after his father's death he lived for periods of time with his grandfather
Samuel Hicks ("Big Sammy") and his uncle "Little Sammy," who was about seven
years older than Council. Little Sammy's descendants have described him as "mu-
sically talented and a natural entertainer. He liked to tell ghost stories and Jack
tales. He played the banjo and possibly other instruments, including the dulcimer.
He loved dances, social occasions, and celebrations. He was friendly, gregarious
and outgoing."[1] According to the Hicks family history, Council told his children
that he learned the tales and songs from both Samuels.

Many of the tales told by Old Counce were called Jack tales. That Jack is the British name for the hero in the tales prompts us to look to the English grandfather rather than the German one. Had Council learned them from Cutliff Harmon, his German grandfather, perhaps the hero would have been called Hans. Although the stories were known in England, Scotland, Germany, France, and Ireland, all of the family accounts point toward England as the source. And in this family of storytellers everyone has a story to tell about where the family came from.

Family tradition in every case attributes the tales to the English grandfather. Jane Gentry told Isabel Gordon Carter, a sociologist who collected the Jack tales from her, that she learned the stories when she was a child from her grandfather, who learned them from his mother. Stanley Hicks, instrument maker and storyteller, traced his lineage back to his "great-grandfather, David Hicks, who arrived from England in 1760, settling first in Wilkes County and then moving to Valle Crucis in Watauga County."[2] Stanley, born in 1911, learned the tales from his father, Roby Hicks and his paternal grandfather, Samuel Hicks III. As a teenager he also learned instrument making from his father and his grandfather.

According to Ray Hicks, "the classic American storyteller" and certainly the best-known current teller of Jack tales, the Hickses apparently came to North Carolina from Virginia; "before that, the old Hickses come from England." He told Thomas Burton: "Now my first related people lived down the mountain there what they call Valle Crucis today, in North Carolina; and they swapped that big bottom land at that time for a hog rifle and a hound dog and a sheep hide. And come up here, on up here a piece higher on the mountain; and then my great-grandpa Sam come on up in here what they call Spice Creek today and entered 500 acres at that time."[3]

Ray is the son of Nathan. His grandfather was Ben, son of Samuel Hicks III and Rebecca Harmon. Samuel's grandfather was Little Sammy, and Rebecca was the daughter of Council Harmon. Becky and her family made molasses using a horse-drawn cane mill to crush the cane. Becky was feeding cane into the mill when her arm got caught. Her arm was amputated between the elbow and the wrist. It was said that she rigged a leather strap to her arm and hoed and did her housework while her husband went off hunting most of the time. She was reputed to be very wise with a great knowledge of herbs and remedies.[4] Buna Hicks, wife of Roby, another of Rebecca's sons, reported that she learned many of her songs from her mother-in-law.

In 1930 Mr. and Mrs. Mellinger Henry were collecting traditional songs from Samuel Harmon of Cades Cove, Blount County, Tennessee. This Samuel was one of Council's grandsons, son of Goulder "Coon" Harmon. "Uncle Sam" could sing all night and never repeat a song, and when he recorded "I Loved a Lass" for Mrs. Henry, he told her that he had learned the song from his grandfather, who was born in England. Several of his Jack tales were recorded by Herbert Halpert. Both Samuel and his wife, Pollyanna, were raised in Big Sammy's household for Pollyanna's mother was Big Sammy's second wife. Uncle Sam's family left Valle Crucis before 1880, settling first in the Grandfather community near Linville and then in Cade's Cove shortly after 1880.

Nola Jane Gentry Yrjana, Jane Gentry's youngest daughter, had this to say about the source of her mother's songs and stories: "I am certain that my ancestors came from England and Scotland. Our mother spoke more of English history than of Scottish."[5] Although there is some confusion in the minds of the family members about which ancestors came from England and when they came, there is no question but that the family has passed down the belief that the tales and songs came from their English forefathers.

The Jack tales are American versions of European fairy tales referred to as "Marchen." These are tales involving a succession of motifs or episodes, moving in an unreal world and filled with the marvelous.[6] The hero, Jack, is young and poor or at some other disadvantage. In some tales he has two brothers, Will and Tom, who are older than Jack. In many stories he has no parents, no family, but he always comes out all right in the end. As Jane Gentry put it, "So Jack he come out the right end of the horn." And he did, even if he had to use magic to do it. Jack is sometimes called a "trickster," much like Brer Rabbit in African American tradition. Richard Chase's *Jack Tales* is perhaps the best-known collection, but the tales have been collected in other areas where oral tradition remained strong. Chase was interested in folk songs, and in 1935 Marshall Ward, a teacher and great-grandson of Council Harmon, brought the tales to his attention. He thought the tales were probably known only on Beech Mountain by descendants of Council Harmon. Then he saw an issue of the *Journal of American Folklore* with fifteen Jack tales told by Mrs. Jane Gentry of Hot Springs, North Carolina. From her daughter Maud Long he learned that she also was a descendant of Old Counce. Wherever he turned, the trail seemed to lead him back to Beech Mountain.

At one time the tales were known over most of the new frontier. They were a natural form of entertainment for people who had little contact with people outside their families and the settlement around them and little reading material for those who could read. But in the nineteenth century towns grew and people were not completely dependent upon the family for recreation. In the Southern Appalachians the tradition continued.

In 1947 Maud Long recorded for the Library of Congress about seven and a half hours of ballads, songs, and tales she had learned from her mother. She introduced the Jack tales as follows:

> I cannot remember when I heard the Jack, Will, and Tom tales for the first time. For we grew up on them like we did the mountain air and the lovely old ballads that my mother used to sing to us.
>
> But the occasion for the tales is a very vivid memory: It would be on a long, winter evening when, after supper, all of us were gathered before the big open fire, my mother taking care of the baby or else the baby was in the cradle very near to mother. And she would be sewing or carding. My father would be mending someone's shoes or maybe a bit of harness. The older girls were helping with the carding or the sewing. And all of us little ones would either have a lapful or a basket full of wool out of which we must pick all the burrs and the Spanish needles and bits of briars and dirt against the next day's carding. For my mother wove all of this wool that had been shorn from the backs of our own sheep—raised there on the farm that was in the heart of the Great Smoky Mountains in North Carolina—into linsey-woolsey, for hers and our dresses, or into blue jeans for my father's and brother's suits, or into blankets to keep us warm, or into the beautiful patterned coverlets, to

say nothing of all the socks and stockings and mitts and hoods that it took for a large family of nine children. And so she needed every bit of wool that she could get ready.

And to keep our eyes open and our hearts merry, my mother would tell these marvelous tales—the Jack, Will, and Tom tales.[7]

When Carter came to inquire about the Jack tales, Mrs. Gentry could not believe she was serious. She had always told the stories to entertain the children. She also loved to tell stories while chores were being done, to the point that it was said that visitors didn't notice that their hands were busy doing whatever task was at hand. Richard Chase related that one practical application of the tales was "keeping the kids on the job" for such tasks as stringing beans for canning or threading them to make leather britches. In this rural culture it was necessary that everyone, even young children, share the load of work. The stories and the songs helped to relieve the boredom of monotonous work.

Jack is, of course, no longer English. His adventures have become localized, but not entirely. They are a marvelous blend of old and new. There are giants and "municorns" (unicorns), but there are also ash cakes and banty hens. Kings live not in castles but in houses, and queens smoke pipes. Jack does not exclaim "my word," he says "bedads," and he has the manners of a southern mountain boy, kind to the people he meets. "Jack the Giant Killer" and "Jack and the Beanstalk" are widely known to generations of children, but they are only the tip of the iceberg. The giant in Mrs. Gentry's story had china bells fastened to the bed cords and said "fi foo fiddledly fun." Jack and his brothers, Will and Tom, become involved with Old Bluebeard, with the Fox, with Hardy Hardback, with the Northwest Wind, with the Calf Skin (or the Heifer Hide, as Maud Long called one of her favorite stories), just to mention a few.

The stories are fanciful and foolish and full of images that may seem farfetched, bizarre, or even grotesque. But they are nourishment for the imagination because they arise out of Jack's dreams and ambitions. He may start out in poor circumstances. "They uz a little old boy long time ago, didn't have no mammy or poppy, just growed up in the hog weeds, and he didn't even know his name, but everybody called him Jack" ("Old Stiff Dick"). There is nothing extraordinary about Jack; in fact, he is an ordinary boy who returns to being an ordinary boy, though perhaps a bit richer, when the adventure is over. "And they was married and they uz rich when I left there."

It has been pointed out that though Jack is an ordinary Appalachian farm boy from a poor family, he is a nonconformist. When his father is dividing his fortune among his sons, Jack asks for only the old pet fox. He strikes out on his own to make his way in the world or to take care of some apparent need. He takes on giants and witches and "everything from an elephant to an ant." It takes courage, but he uses his imagination, and his wits, and he is always successful. This cannot be said of his brothers, Tom and Will. C. Paige Gutierrez raised the question of Council Harmon's influence on the personality of Jack. Harmon was a nonconformist, and he certainly influenced the storytellers in his family. When he was seventy years old he was still dancing and calling dances even though that got him in trouble with the church. He was about seventy when he made his way across the mountains to Madison County, where some of his children had settled.

Was he attracted to the tales because he saw himself in Jack or did he impose his own personality on Jack?[8]

The adventures often include magic, as in "Hardy Hardback," when Jack stirs a stick in the spring until it turns to wine, or a woman who has been "witched into a cat" turns back into a pretty woman because Jack carries out the task required. Irving Bacheller asked Jane Gentry if she believed in witches, and her reply was, "Don't guess I do—not big—but they's some that do. I always allowed hit didn't do no harm. Used to be a man name of Jacksbo Hame. He said the way to know if you be a witch doctor is to go out on the mount'in at sunrise an' shoot nine times at the sun. If ye be a doctor right a'ter the las' shot blood'll flow out o' yer gun bar'l." Then she told him a witch story, "Sop, Doll, Sop," that her "mammy used to tell."

Onct they were a boy name o' Jack, an' he were dreadful worritty an' pore. This little boy he had no mammy an' pappy, an' were real tard o' livin,' an' so he thought he would har [hire] to the miller to 'tend his mill. That were a way o' dying, everybody said. He went over to the miller's house an' he says: "I want to har to you to 'tend to your mill for you."

"Well, I'll tell you, Jack, every miller that I har jist lives one night."

"Well, bedads, I'd jist as soon be dead as erlive, so I believe I'll take the job," says Jack.

The man har'd him, give him some meat an' some coffee, an' told him he would find cookin' tools down to the mill.

So Jack went down to the old log-mill. He cooked his supper, set down by his fry'n pan on the floor, broke him a piece of bread an' begun to sop hit into his pan o' fat. Were great big cracks in the mill-house—'twere jist a pole crib—an' the moon were a-shinin' through 'em purty an' bright. All of a sudden-like it got as dark as a dungeon, an' the cracks looked like they was filled up with coals o' fire. Jack blowed a blaze to see what had darkened the house so. When he did he seed all them cracks jist packed full o' cats. Every one o' them were black but one. This were an old tabby cat, an' the old tabby cat jumped right down by his fry'n-pan, reached hits paw over into the sop an' says: "Sop-doll-sop."

Jack says: "If you put your paw in that ergin I'll whack hit off."

She reached her paw in ergin and says: "Sop-doll-sop."

Then they were a quick swimmish o' cats! Ev'ry one o' them jumped right down on to the floor an' stood with their ha'r riz, lookin' at him.

She reached her paw in ergin an' he whacked hit off, an' when he whacked hit turned to a womern's hand with a ring on one finger. 'Twere a grand, purty ring. He picked that hand up an' couldn't take the ring off hit so he stuck the hand in his pocket. Every one o' the cats jist jumped right out through the cracks, like streaks o' black lightnin'.

An' soon as the cats had gone erway, that womern's hand 'gun to jump eround in his pocket, like a chicken with the head cut off o' hit, and he tried to throw hit out but hit hung on to the cloth, and he were skeered, so hollered and yelled and run up to the miller's house. Soon as he got out o' the mill that hand dod [died] and lay still as a rag in his pocket. The miller heard him and come out. Jack showed him the womern's hand an' told him 'bout the cats.

The miller said: "That's my wife's hand. She's sick this mornin'. I'll take this hand an' go see what she has to say."

He went in whar his wife lay in bed, and he says to her: "Sarah, let me see your left hand."

She poked him out her right hand.

He says: "Sarah, let me see your left hand."

She begun cryin' and says: "Hit's gone."

He says: "Yes, hur hit is. Sarah, you're a witch, and you're the one that's killed my millers. Now if you'll tell me who every one o' the rest o' them witches is, an' let me have them all burned, then they shan't burn you."

So he had the rest o' the witches burned and that made their friends all mad, but he wouldn't let them burn his wife, 'count o' his promise; but he let them hang her. And that put an end to a good many witches in these hur parts.[9]

Because Jack is an ordinary boy, we learn a great deal about the lifestyle of the person who tells the story. Mrs. Gentry would explain: "In them days they didn't never come up to the house and ring the door bell, they always hollered, 'Hello.' So Jack hollered, 'Hello.'" The old lady says, "What'll ye have for supper, Jack?" and we learn what people ate every day—turnips, potatoes, pumpkin, meat and bread, mush and milk. But a feast consisted of such things as baked pig, stuffed goose, roast chicken, pies, and cake. When the preacher comes they put the mush and milk away and cook chicken and make coffee.

Ever the teacher, Jane would explain as she did when she used the word "tomihawk" (or tomihatchet) in "Jack the Giant Killer." "That's a thing like a hatchet 'cept it has two heads to it. They used it in olden times. Indians use hit to scalp with." Maud called it a "tomihatchet." In the same story Jane used the word "ad-ver-tise-ment" which meant "Put up a board or hew out the side of a tree and write what he want to." Jack swapped his calf skin for the "chist" (chest) and five hundred guineas. Jane said, "My mammy always told that a five dollar bill was as much as a guinea."

Although the language of the tales is colorful and localized, it is not difficult to get into the spirit of the story. When Carter was taking down Mrs. Gentry's stories she thought that the speech was in a state of change. Jane might say "was" or "uz," "climb" or "clomb," "get" or "git," "it" or "hit." Sometimes two forms of a word would appear in the same sentence. Carter saw Mrs. Gentry after she had been living in Hot Springs for over twenty years and had been exposed to the idiom of people from other areas.

"Little Dicky Wigbun" (Little Dicky Whigburn) is a cante-fable, a combination of song and story, known in central, eastern, and southern Europe. The German form is "Der Alte Hildebrand." In this story Mrs. Gentry spoke of "clear apsul rum" as well as "clear apful rum." She said that her grandfather had used both terms.

Oh, Little Dicky Wigbun
To London he's gone
To buy me a bottle of Clear Apful Rum,
God send him a long journey never to return
Thru the green wood and below.

Samuel Harmon also told this story and sang of "clear applesom."[10]

"The Enchanted Lady" might also be called a cante-fable. Jack sings the bowl full:

Your youngest daughter she come down,
  Oh fer to buy my drill;
She hugged me and she kissed me well,
  Fill, bowl, fill.

In both "Little Dicky Wigbun" and "Lazy Jack and His Calf Skin" "old passenger" or "Mr. Passenger" plays a part. Jane said she did not know what the old passenger was. "They uz men use to travel about and they called 'em the old passenger." Maud also used this name for the man who came calling on the wife while the husband was away.

Jane Gentry's descriptions are rich in imagery, and her dialogue is vivid. Jack calls his calf hide "you blobber mouthed thing," the king "put out an oration," and the old witch "popped her back against that hackle and popped like a rubber ball and danced all over the floor." There are wonderful phrases that invite the listener to join in. "Stiff Dick killed seven at a lick." The "municorn" smells him, and "here it come, Whippity cut, whippity cut, whippity cut." The old woman "tuk out down the road a-hollerin, Gally Mander, Gally Mander, all my gold and silver's gone and my great long leather purse." Old Bluebeard was "comin' up the holler with his beard as blue as indigo, his teeth as long as pipe stems and his thumbs tucked behind him." Mrs. Gentry always spoke this last refrain rapidly just as she did riddles. Maud's descriptions are also colorful, but she did not use the rhythmic refrains as her mother did. She described "Old Fire Dragaman" as "just a monster of a thing with a big old long forefoot, a pipe in his mouth, and a big long blue beard that reached from his chin and was draggin' the ground and his hands stuck behind him."[11]

Some of the tales are not about Jack, and they have been called "Grandfather tales," for they have been told by grandfathers to their grandchildren. They are fantastic tales and have been told by the same people who told Jack tales. Of the fifteen tales collected from Mrs. Gentry, four did not have Jack as the principal character—"Whiteberry Whittington," "Old Catkins" ("Catskins," a Cinderella-type character), "Little Dicky Wigbun," and "Old Gally Mander." It is important to remind ourselves that these stories have derived through oral tradition, although, of course, we do see them in print. They were composed orally and perpetuated orally. Indeed, Maud Long found it very difficult to write them down. "For me writing down of these tales has often been a difficult and tedious process. And I just couldn't do it. It all went stale on me."[12]

In transcribing Maud Long's stories from the Library of Congress tapes, I was inclined to stop typing and just listen. Hearing the tales from such a marvelous storyteller is a splendid experience even though it be from a recording. Writing them down is tedious work.

The descendants of Old Counce have always known that the tales were meant to be told. Reading is an entirely different process from telling. The teller leaves no trace except in the mind of the listener and seldom tells the story the same way twice. He embellishes, he forgets, he is reminded, he reacts to his audience. Although some storytellers do say that they tell the story the same every time, it is more usual to hear that they do not. Marshall Ward said that he adapted his stories to his audiences, and Ray Hicks admits to a creative process in which he adds to his stories to make them better. Monroe Ward said, "I allers try to tell 'em the old way, but I hardly ever use jest exactly the same words."[13] When Jane was telling about "Old Foster" who liked "stout" women, she remarked, "He'd a'been right atter me un your mother." Her audience at this time was another woman. It is doubtful she would have said this to a man.[14]

In telling "Old Catkins" Mrs. Gentry adapted the story to include material that would be understood in Hot Springs but perhaps not on Beech Mountain or Meadow Fork. "Catskin" goes around to the back door of the king's house looking for work. She knocks on the door. The door is answered by a "colored" girl who goes to get the queen. The queen asks if she wants to work with "darkies," and "Catskin" answers, "Yes, I don't mind. I'd jest as soon work with the colored girls as anybody." Long before the Gentrys moved to Hot Springs, African Americans had been working at the hotel. Farther along in the story she tells of going to a dance at the "club house."[15]

No two members of the same community or even the same family would be apt to tell a tale exactly the same. It is interesting to compare Maud's stories with those of her mother. "Old Bluebeard" becomes "Old Fire Dragaman," the title used by Chase in *The Jack Tales*, which had been published several years before Maud recorded for the Library of Congress. Ray Hicks calls it "Old Fire Dragon." Maud told Jack tales her mother did not tell Carter, and her mother told stories Maud did not record for the Library of Congress. Mrs. Gentry did not tell Carter all of the stories she knew just as she did not sing all the songs she knew for Cecil Sharp. Maud clearly said that she learned the tales from her mother, but since Maud did her recording about twenty years after her mother's death, it would be amazing if their repertoires and deliveries were identical.

The differences in Jane's and Maud's telling of the stories are generally in the descriptive words and phrases and in minor incidents. Jane sends Jack off with a "haversack full of rations" while Maud sends him off with a cake and a bottle of wine. There are, however, a few discrepancies that affect the outcome of the story. Mrs. Gentry has Jack speak of Old Bluebeard as being a friend of his and, although he does not give Jack anything to eat, he does not try to kill him. Maud's Old Fire Dragaman tries to kill Jack with fire and Jack "whacks" off his head, more like the telling of Ray Hicks and Chase's version in *The Jack Tales*. In Jane's "Hardy Hardback" Tom and Will die as a result of their encounter with the hackle, as they do in Ray Hicks's story. Maud sends the boys home crippled for life with broken backs. Maud explained that a hackle was "a great big old spiked thing that you used to get all of the old wood pulp out of the flax with." In the same story Maud has Eatwell eat a mountain of bread. Jane had Eatwell eat "a horse, a cow or two, a couple of sheep and some pigs," more like the Chase version. Maud was influenced by the Chase collection, but not in every tale, and in some instances the Chase version is more like Jane's.

In 1914 Jane told Irving Bacheller the story "Sop, Doll, Sop," and in 1923 she told the same story to Carter. It is essentially the same story, but the details differ. The tabby cat is a big black cat in the later version and Sarah has become Nancy. In Carter's version the witch puts "pizen" in the "sop" and Jack wraps the severed hand in tissue paper, drops it in his pocket, and goes about the business of getting his supper. In the 1914 telling Jack drops the hand into his pocket, where it begins to jump around, and he runs to tell the miller. As Maud said, it is difficult to tell a tale the same way twice. In recording for the Library of Congress Maud sometimes told parts of stories a second time. The two renditions were never exactly the same. She must have told the stories hundreds of times, but each telling was fresh, and Maud's creative disposition was always at work, as was her mother's.

Though both Jane and Maud had ample repertoires of stories, one might assume that they would have favorites and that they would tell their favorites to collectors. Maud said that she liked all of the tales, but her favorites were "Jack and the Varmints," "The Heifer Hide," and "Jack and the Giants' New Ground." The tales Maud recorded were, in fact, all tales in which Jack was the protagonist.

Council Harmon's legacy continues through the storytelling skills of his descendants, spanning four generations. His grandchildren, Jane Gentry, Monroe and Miles Ward, Roby and Ben Hicks, and Samuel Harmon, all learned from Old Counce and his children, except for Samuel, who said he learned from his maternal grandfather, Samuel Hicks, with whom he lived as a child. His great-grandchildren, Maud Long, Marshall Ward, Hattie Presnell, Stanley Hicks, and Nathan Hicks, learned from their parents. His great-great-grandson Ray Hicks is still telling tales and influencing untold numbers of would-be storytellers.

# Chapter 8

# Balladry

The effect of good music is not caused by novelty. On the contrary, it
strikes us more the more we are familiar with it.

—Goethe

In 1916 Cecil Sharp, an English musician and collector, came to Madison
County. He was interested in songs and ballads of British origin. The "Laurel Country" along the North Carolina—Tennessee border proved to be fertile ground. Sharp
visited singers in five Appalachian states, but here he found the most primitive
conditions and the most songs. Sharp brought with him an assistant, Maud Karpeles,
and for the first time both texts and tunes were written down. From Jane Gentry
he collected seventy songs and ballads, more than from any other singer he encountered in the Southern Appalachians. Forty of these are included in Sharp's
*English Folk Songs from the Southern Appalachians,* a collection unparalleled in
America. We know about Jane Gentry and her songs because of an incredible set of
circumstances linking John and Olive Campbell, the Russell Sage Foundation,
Frances Goodrich, the Presbyterians, Dorland Institute, and Cecil Sharp.

Sharp came to the southern mountains at the request of Olive Dame
Campbell, wife of John C. Campbell, director of the Southern Highland Division
of the Russell Sage Foundation. Beginning in 1907, John Campbell traveled throughout the southern mountains for more than ten years doing a social survey, and his
wife often traveled with him.[1] It was in December 1907, on one of their first field
trips, that they visited Hindman Settlement School in Kentucky. Olive Campbell,
a New Englander, had sung "Barbara Allen" as a child, but during this visit she
heard it sung by Ada Smith, one of the students.

> 'Twas in the merry month of May,
> The green buds were swelling,
> Poor William Green on his death bed lay
> For the love of Barb'ra Ellen.

Campbell was overwhelmed by this experience:

Shall I ever forget it! The blazing fire, the young girl on her low stool before it, the soft strange strumming of the banjo—different from anything I had heard before—and then the song! I had been used to sing "Barbara Allen" as a child, but how far from that gentle tune was this—so strange, so remote, so thrilling. I was lost almost from the first note, and the pleasant room faded from sight; the singer only a voice. I saw again the long road over which we had come, the dark hills, the rocky streams bordered by tall hemlocks and hollies, the lonely cabins distinguishable at night only by the firelight flaring from their chimneys. Then these, too, faded, and I seemed to be borne along into a still more dim and distant past, of which I myself was a part.[2]

Campbell began right away to try to learn the ballad. She found it a difficult undertaking for she found the intervals "subtle" and the modal sound strange to her ear. This fascination for the songs, particularly the melodies, began a search that continued for years. She called it "one of the most illuminating and rewarding experiences of my life, leading . . . into realms of pure and lasting beauty and opening the way into many related . . . .fields—folk hymns, folk games, folk dances, folk tales, folk arts, folk material in general."[3]

Frances Louisa Goodrich came to Allanstand in the Laurel section of Madison County in 1897 and stayed there for thirty-five years. Goodrich, who had attended Yale School of Fine Arts, came to the southern mountains to be of service in the Presbyterian mission work in the Asheville area. She established schools and Sunday schools, a craft program, and Allanstand Cottage Industries in the Laurel Country. She was called the "Godmother to the Guild" (the Southern Highland Handicraft Guild). These missions established by Frances Goodrich attracted outsiders looking for a base in the mountains. By 1909 Olive Campbell had carried out an appraisal of Allanstand Industries as a part of John Campbell's survey of mountain life.[4]

In October 1913 the Campbells attended the Country Life Conference in Big Laurel, one of Frances Goodrich's missions in Madison County, at the invitation of Warren Wilson, who was superintendent of the Country Life Department of the Presbyterian Church. There Olive Campbell heard some ballad singing and had an opportunity to explain the significance of the ballads. By 1914 she had visited singers in the Laurel Country, Rosie Hensley and Mrs. Sotherland, and in 1915 she took down a song from Mandy Shelton. At John Campbell's recommendation, Dr. George Packard, a medical doctor, and his wife had begun work in April 1914 in the Laurel Country. So long before Olive Campbell met Cecil Sharp she had become familiar with Frances Goodrich and the Laurel area, and she knew there were ballads to be found there.[5]

William Chauncy Langdon, who was working with the Russell Sage Foundation, recognized the importance of the ballad study and put Mrs. Campbell in touch with the Fuller sisters, English folksingers. Through Langdon and the Fullers, arrangements were made for an introduction to Cecil Sharp, who was in the United States because war conditions prevented his going home.[6] Olive Campbell was ready to meet Sharp. This collection had indeed been a labor of love. She had to learn each song and then find a piano and set down the tune as best she could. In 1911 she had gotten some help from a musician with the melodies and had sent some manuscripts off to Professor Leo Lewis at Tufts University, her alma mater, and to ballad scholar George Lyman Kittredge at Harvard University. Both men were very enthusiastic about her collection.[7]

By the time Cecil Sharp came to America, Olive Campbell had collected about 225 ballads. In 1916 she took a portion of her valuable collection and went to see Sharp at the home of Mrs. James Storrow in Lincoln, Massachusetts. She found Sharp incapacitated with gout, but he seemed to improve when he saw her manuscripts. It became clear to him that ballads were being sung in the southern mountains. Campbell convinced him of that. He considered her manuscripts "really original and valuable material."[8]

The result of this collaboration was the collection described as "the most important and permanent contribution made to ballad-lore since the time of Child."[9] David Whisnant, although critical of Sharp's favoring certain types of material over others and the limitations brought about by financial and time constraints, considers the Sharp-Campbell work a "landmark in the history of an enterprise that witnessed more than its share of greed, pettiness, and misrepresentation." Of Sharp, he said: "He was by all odds the best-trained, most humane and open-minded collector working in the area at the time. He was a conscientious and productive worker, and it may indeed be that his Appalachian collection is—as Bertrand Bronson [outstanding scholar of the ballad tunes] has asserted—the best regional collection we are likely to get."[10] Folklorist Archie Green simply said: "For the record, Sharp's collection is unparalleled; it cannot be whittled down in magnitude or power."[11]

The Campbells lived in Asheville, and Sharp and his assistant, Maud Karpeles, arrived there in the summer of 1916. From there he hoped to make treks into the mountains seeking out ballad singers. He could not have chosen a more inopportune time. On Sunday, July 16, a tremendous storm hit the Asheville area resulting in what was to be known as the Great Flood of 1916. Hundreds were homeless, six people died, dams were swept away, telegraph lines were down, railroad tracks twisted. In Marshall, the county seat of Madison County, fifty-eight buildings were washed away and two lives lost. In Hot Springs guests at the Mountain Park Hotel were taken out by boat, and the bridge over the French Broad River was washed away. Madison County was to be Sharp's first destination.

The only train that could get close to Asheville was the Murphy train, which could make it to the Murphy junction two miles west of Asheville.[12] So Sharp and Karpeles came by way of Knoxville, Blue Ridge, and Murphy to Asheville, arriving ten hours late on July 25.[13] After a day's rest, Cecil Sharp and Maud Karpeles, accompanied by John Campbell, were driven to Weaverville, where their mode of transportation became a four-wheeled dogcart, locally called a "surry." The trip to Marshall and on to White Rock was a harrowing one with hairpin curves and steep inclines on one side or the other. The forty-mile trip took eleven hours.[14] John Campbell wrote to Frances Goodrich, "I have just returned from a trip introducing Mr. Sharp and his secretary, Miss Karpeles, to the 'Laurel Country.'"[15]

By July 28 Sharp was already writing down the tunes and Maud Karpeles the words of "some wonderful stuff." They made their headquarters with Presbyterian missionaries and mission schools.[16] Sharp and Karpeles began their stay with Dr. and Mrs. Packard. In a letter to Jennie Moore, who taught the day school at Flag Pond, Tennessee, Campbell gave credit to Olive Campbell, Goodrich, and

Edith Fish, one of the teachers in the Laurel section who had collected ballads, for having opened the way for Sharp. He explained that although the people wanted to entertain the Englishman, Sharp insisted that he was to be treated as a paying guest and all travel expenses were to come from his fund.[17] Sharp found the songs to be of high quality, the tunes for the most part modal, and the singers much like English peasant folk.[18] By August 13 he had exhausted his supply of tune books and was writing tunes on loose paper.

Sharp spent time in Allegheny, Carmen, Big Laurel, and Spillcorn. It was Lucy Shafer, principal of Dorland Institute, who sent word for Sharp to come to Hot Springs to see a Mrs. Gentry.[19] On Wednesday, August 23, Cecil Sharp and John Campbell caught the 1:55 train for Hot Springs. They were met there by Shafer, who accompanied them to Dorland Institute. Campbell returned to Asheville by the evening train and Sharp went to bed with a bad asthma attack.[20] On Thursday, August 24, Sharp's diary entry read: "Asthma rather better, but weather still terribly hot and stifling. Had breakfast at 7 and at 8:30 sallied forth with Maud, crossed the river in a punt with the aid of wire manipulated by the ferryman, a peculiar_____[The bridge having been washed away in the flood in July] and called on Mrs. Gentry. She sang till 11:30 some excellent songs. Returned to lunch at 12 and called on her again at 2:30 till 4:45. I got more songs—20 in all—and then after a short stroll by the river returned to supper at 6. Spent evening writing tunes in my book. Very tired and rather late getting to bed."[20]

Jane told the Asheville Normal School students about Cecil Sharp's first visit. He must have taken her to be very shy for he suggested that if it would embarrass her to sing for him he might sit in one room while she sat in the other. This was not her first experience with such a person as Sharp. Irving Bacheller had preceded him. She replied, "If you can stand to look at me, I can surely stand to look at you."[21]

It would be interesting to know whether Jane Gentry felt tired after singing twenty songs. The next day Sharp returned for more songs. Nola Jane was twelve years old when Sharp first came and she remembers well his coming to see her mother many times. That Sharp crossed the river to get to the Gentry home indicates that they did not live in Sunnybank at that time but in the house on the banks of the French Broad River.

On Friday, August 25, 1916, Sharp wrote in his diary:

Packed and said good bye after a 7 o'clock breakfast and talked with Miss Schafer [Shafer] about Emma Hensley. She said she would accept her for thirty five dollars, but that she must enter her name and pay 3 dollars down at once if she wanted to secure a place. [Emma, a beautiful girl of thirteen, was the daughter of Reuben and Rosie Hensley of the Carmen community from whom Sharp had collected thirty songs. Emma had sung "Barbara Allen" for him. She and her parents seemed anxious for her to go to Dorland Institute. Sharp was not sure that school was the best thing for Emma, but he paid for clothes and helped with the fees.] Then went to Mrs. Gentry and got several more ballads—making 30 in all—some splendid ones. Then wandered in the wood for a while, bought some bread and cheese for lunch and caught the 12:40 back to

Asheville. Mrs. Campbell delighted to hear of our good luck. Wrote my tunes out in the evening before dinner and went to bed fairly early— evening nice and cool.

In a letter to John Glenn of the Russell Sage Foundation, dated August 26, Campbell related, "He [Sharp] has just returned from Hot Springs, North Carolina, where we got him in touch with an old ballad singer and he has returned highly elated, having secured thirty from her—all of them very valuable, and some of them very rare."[22] He surely meant Mrs. Gentry for he did not collect as many ballads from any other singer in Hot Springs. This "old ballad singer" was fifty-three years old at the time. Sharp, who was fifty-seven years old, had never before had such an experience. He had collected no more than 300 songs and ballads in a year in England, but in less than a month in a very limited area he had collected more than 160 songs and ballads.

His visit with Jane Gentry on August 24, 1916, gleaned "The Cherry Tree Carol," "Fair Annie," "Lord Thomas and Fair Eleanor," "The Wife of Usher's Well," "Little Musgrave," "Johnny Dials," "The Sheffield Apprentice," "Pretty Peggy O," "William and Polly," "Jack Went A-Sailing," "John Riley," "The Grey Cock," and a humorous song, "My Mother Bid Me." All of these were published in *English Folk Songs from the Southern Appalachians*. On that day she also sang "Jesus Born in Bethany," "The Little Maumie," "Young Beichan," "The Bloody Warning," "Once I Did Court," and a song she called "Anything." On August 25 she sang again for him. The ballads included "Young Hunting," "Johnny Scott," "Edwin in the Lowlands Low," "Shooting of His Dear," "The Brisk Young Lover," "The Rejected Lover," and "The Broken Token," all of which appear in *English Folk Songs*. She also sang "Barbara Allen" on that day, but the text is missing. Her daughter Maud Long sang a very good version of this ballad which she said she learned from her mother.

In September Sharp came back to see Mrs. Gentry. He was feeling very low in spirit for the war news was bad. It was at about this time that he received word that three English country dancers had been killed and a fourth was missing in action. His diary entry for September 11 read:

Feeling so feeble and about decided to give up Georgia idea and go for a few days to Hot Springs having ascertained that the hotel was now open. I feel that I cannot rough it anymore for a while. So Maud and I went there by the afternoon train and secured quite decent rooms. Immediately after arriving we called on Mrs. Gentry who at once fired off "The Two Sisters" and . . . said she knew the "Golden Vanity" and sang the first verse in a modal tune. Promised to give it me tomorrow. Told her not to die in the night or catch cold or anything that would endanger my getting the song on the morrow.

On Tuesday, September 12, 1916, he wrote:

In the morning crossed the river . . . after breakfast and walked to the Garrets [a prominent family who lived across the river] where we had a nice and pleasant chat, called on Mrs. Weir [Sally Royce Weir, author of

*Hot Springs Past and Present*] on way back, did a little shopping. Lunched at 1:30 and again crossed the river to see Mrs. Gentry. She gave me fifteen more songs, a . . . lot including "Lamkin"—a new Child ballad! Quite tired me out taking down so many and very glad to get home to some tea. After dinner began to write all her songs . . . but couldn't finish before bedtime."

He wrote a letter to John Campbell from Hot Springs on September 12:

We did a lot of prospecting this morning, . . . and this afternoon had a nearly three hour seance with Mrs. Gentry. Tell Mrs. Campbell the tune to the "Gold Vanity" is a beautiful one, Dorian. Then we got from Mrs. Gentry a version of "Long Lamkin" (No. 93) and a second variant of "The False Knight." So, with the "Two Sisters" which she gave us last night, we have now three new "Children" to go on our list. Others that we got from her were "The Green Bed," "The Tree in the Wood," two other cumulative ones, a good variant of "The House Carpenter," and several nursery ones and one or two scraps of good songs with nice tunes—altogether about 14 from her. That makes well over 40 that we have taken from her, and I dare say I shall get a few more."[23]

September 13 was a disappointing day for Sharp. He went to see a singer who had promised to sing for him, but company came in and the singer reneged. He then walked "endless miles" to find another singer from whom he got nothing. But on September 14 he wrote in his diary:

At the ferry en route to Silver Mining [Mine] Creek the ferryman [Harry Roberts] told us his wife Mrs. Roberts sang, so we called on her. She promised to stand ready for us tomorrow morning. Then we met Mrs. Hester House where we got quite a lot of good songs including "Earl Brand," etc. Then to Mrs. Ellie Johnson. Directly after lunch we tackled Mrs. Gentry and came home richly laden. So we made up for a blank day yesterday. Sat up late writing. . . . Emma Hensley came to dinner with us at the hotel and behaved very nicely indeed. She is very homesick, poor girl, but we bucked her up a bit I think. [This was on the day Emma arrived to begin school and she came to dinner in her new gray school uniform.]

On Friday, September 15, 1916, he wrote: "At the ferry in the morning, between showers (It rained all night) who should we meet but Emma and another school girl, running away home. We tried to stop them but this was of no use. So we said tender farewells after she had invited us to go with them. Then to Mrs. Roberts, Mrs. House, Mrs. Ellie Johnson, and in the afternoon Mrs. Gentry once more. We got a splendid lot including 'The Two Brothers,' 'The Cruel Brother,' two new Child's. Quite a wonderful day!" This was the day Lizzie Roberts sang "Black Is the Color of My True Love's Hair" for Sharp. It is the only manuscript of this song in his collection.

Sharp recorded Mrs. Gentry's songs for five days, from September 11 to 16.

Many of the songs were those she sang for children, such as "Sing Said the Mother," "Froggie He Would A-Wooing Go," "The Farm Yard," and "There's Nothing To Be Gained by Roving" (a singing game), and there were more ballads, among them "Old Wichet" (also known as "Our Goodman" and "Three Nights Drunk"), "The Gipsy Laddie," "The Drummer and His Wife" ("Father Grumble"), and "The Wagoner's Lad." Sharp's diary entry for September 16 read: "Packed early then off again to Mrs. House, Mrs. Johnson, and Mrs. Gentry. Took several photographs. Got several more songs making this the richest week I have yet had. 70 songs including 5 new children!"

Sharp wrote to Professor Alphonso Smith at the University of Virginia in Charlottesville on September 17 telling him of his very successful week. He was especially pleased with "The Cruel Brother," "The Two Brothers," "Lamkin," and "The Golden Trinity," which he had not previously collected in America.[24] Sharp wrote of his experiences in the southern mountains, "I discovered that I could get what I wanted from pretty nearly everyone I met, young and old. In fact I found myself for the first time in my life in a community in which singing was as common and almost as universal as speaking."[25]

Sharp has been criticized because his collection is heavily weighted toward ballads and folk songs in British tradition at the expense of sentimental songs, religious songs, and native American materials. In other words, he did not record all the songs the singers knew. There are few collectors who have been able to do this. Most collectors have a bias, and Sharp's resulted from his goal, which was to collect English folk songs. To write down all of the songs Jane Gentry knew would have been a gigantic task. He was not interested in collecting most of the hymns he heard, but Jane could have kept him busy for quite a while recording hymns.

He made at least eight visits to listen to Mrs. Gentry, the last one on July 27, 1917, perhaps in response to the following letter dated June 16, 1917:

Dear Mr. Sharp,
As I have been looking for you several days and you haven't come thought I would write you. I have a few more songs I can give you if you don't already have them. I can give you the crow song for one if you haven't gotten it already. Now Mr. Sharp if you are in the mountains anywhere when you get this letter and it doesn't cost you too much to get here I sure want you to come and see me. For you don't know how much pleasure it would be for me to get to see you and the lady that is with you once again. May God bless and keep you both.
Sincerely,
Mrs. J.N. Gentry
P.S. I forgot to say our Mountain Park Hotel is filled with Germans but you can find board at the Lance Hotel.[26]

The Lance sisters ran a boardinghouse. Miss Sue did the cooking; Miss Georgie rang the bell; and everybody in town could set their clocks at 7:00, 12:00, and 6:00. No one really knew what Miss Fanny did.[27] It seems safe to say that Mrs. Gentry had no rooms available. It had been announced in May that the Mountain Park Hotel would be leased by the government for an internment camp. Sharp told of an occasion when rumors were flying that he and Maud were German spies. This might well have been in Hot Springs during that first summer before the Germans and the residents came to terms.

The letter from Jane to Cecil Sharp takes on some importance because no other documents, letters or manuscripts, written by her have been found. One writer has attributed a large trunk tray filled with broadsides and "song ballets" to Mrs. Gentry, as well as a repertoire of songs that she sang to instrumental accompaniment. Jane Douglas, who stored the household goods after Maud, the last Gentry to live in Sunnybank, moved out, says there were no manuscripts. Sharp did not visit any singers who had printed song sheets. A few had handwritten copies, some done by their children, which they called "ballets." Mrs. Gentry was not among those with "ballets." Nola Jane says that she never knew her mother to write down the words to songs. "They were just in her memory." Jane could write, but Maud Long did most of the letter writing for the family. Mrs. Gentry was good at delegating chores and this one fell to Maud. This letter to Sharp was a typed copy and so we have no way of speculating by the handwriting who actually wrote it.

As for instruments, Jane's brother Doc made banjos, and he and his sons played both banjo and guitar, but no one in the family has ever heard of Jane playing instruments. Maud's instruments were piano and organ, and Nola Jane played ukulele and piano. Lalla played piano and organ. Jane "played" crochet and knitting needles while she sang.

It does seem clear that Mrs. Gentry freely gave the songs to Sharp and, indeed, enjoyed his company and that of Maud Karpeles. Berzilla Wallin of Sodom Laurel (Revere) remembered Sharp coming to her community. She said that after they found out that he did not want to buy land and that all he wanted was ballads, they got along fine.[28] He did like his informants, and his admiration of them was as genuine as his admiration of their songs. "I like the people very much indeed," he said, "and find them readier to sing to me even than the English singers."[29] He attributed to them an "easy, unaffected bearing and the unselfconscious manner of the well-bred."[30]

The willingness of the singers may have had something to do with the method of collecting. Sharp learned the songs, and although he was not an outstanding singer, he could sing some of them. This was in contrast to his experience collecting with Professor Alphonso Smith. Although Sharp found Smith a strong ally and liked him, he thought that he treated the singers as he did his students and that his questions left the people bewildered. He was not what Sharp called a "natural collector."[31] They were in agreement on the importance of the tunes, however, and Smith was glad to see a collector who could write down tunes. Smith wrote: "The truth is that the ballad heritage of the English-speaking race has been studied as poetry but not as song. Yet it is as song that the ballad was born and it is as song that it survives."[32]

Jane Gentry's reputation as a singer extended far beyond Madison County and Hot Springs. Her picture appeared in the *Asheville Citizen* on Sunday, September 23, 1923, with the caption: "Mrs. Jane Gentry of Hot Springs, N.C. who is credited by Dr. C. Alphonso Smith, the noted English authority, as knowing more folk songs and old English ballads than any other person in the United States and probably in the world. She can sing 67 ballads which have been handed down to her from generation to generation by word of mouth."

Smith had met Mrs. Gentry on July 17, 1920, when the North Carolina

Ballad Society was formed in Asheville. He was at that time head of the English Department at the United States Naval Academy. Before that he had founded the Virginia Folk-Lore Society and served as Edgar Allan Poe Professor of English and head of the English Department at the University of Virginia. The *Asheville Citizen* for July 17, 1920, contained the following article:

> Dr. Smith spoke of the wonderful privilege he was enjoying by meeting a lady so rich in memory of so rare a type of literature, and the great joy it gave him to have the honor of hearing them sung. Mrs. Gentry knows by memory sixty five ballads and can sing them with qualities of voice rare in an untrained voice and a woman of her age. Her simplicity, charm of manner, and wonderful smile won for her the audience in the crowded hall, even before she spoke.
>
> After Dr. Smith introduced Mrs. Gentry, she expressed her amazement at being invited to sing, but said she was glad to be of service and glad to accommodate Dr. Calfee [head of Asheville Normal School which two of her daughters attended]. Dr. Smith told the story of each ballad before Mrs. Gentry sang. Her voice, although untrained, is sweet and clear. Very remarkable for an elderly woman. Her wholesome smile alone would win any audience and the cheers that came from her audience were responses from the heart. Mrs. Gentry sang the following ballads: "Lord Thomas and Fair Elinor," "Over London Bridge" or "Poor Charlie," "Golden Vanity," "Two Sisters," "The Drummer and his Wife," and "Frog Went A-Courtin'." She also sang a quaint song called "The Tree in the Wood," which is not a Scotch and English ballad. Dr. Smith wanted the students to see the difference between the true ballad and a more modern song.
>
> Dr. Calfee closed the program by expressing the pleasure and honor she had bestowed upon the summer school by responding to the invitation. The audience gave a rising vote of thanks to Mrs. Gentry.

Some of the people mentioned at this meeting suggest that it was held at Asheville Normal School. It does not seem to have been a function of the North Carolina Folklore Society, which has been active from 1912 to the present. Professor Alphonso Smith taught the summer session at Asheville Normal School. He was said to be the most popular instructor ever to speak at the school.[33]

Cecil Sharp was wary of recording machines. He thought they might make the singers self-conscious. Only the cylinder machines were available to him and they were heavy and unwieldy for one getting around by foot, horseback, and wagon. So we have no recordings of Jane's voice, but Elizabeth Dotterer, who heard her often in her own home, said that she was fascinated by Mrs. Gentry's singing. "I have never heard as good a ballad singer as she was. She was a generation back, more genuine than anyone else I have ever heard. Maud Long was a good singer, but there was something pure about Mrs. Gentry's singing. She was absolutely natural . . . . The sweetest most cheerful, pleasant person always.[34] Bill Moore said it well when he called Jane "a singer among singers . . . a wonderful person . . . and the most beautiful singer you ever heard."[35]

# Chapter 9

# The Songs She Sang

A bird does not sing because it has an answer. It sings because it has a song.

—Chinese proverb

When a genealogical study was compiled to gather information on the current musicians and the musicians from whom Sharp collected in Madison County, it was found that most of them belonged to one extended family and were descended from one early settler.

Through a review of county vital statistics, census records, and interviews with older residents of the county, Frances Dunham has found that almost all of the Sharp contributors were descendants of one man, Roderick Shelton. Of the thirty-nine contributors to Sharp from Madison County, twenty-eight have been identified as Shelton descendants, three as spouses of his descendants, and five with family members who married his descendants. Three appear to be unrelated to the Sheltons. The notable exception to the dominance of the Shelton family in Madison County is Jane Gentry, whose parents moved to Madison from Watauga County. The only connection between her family and the Sheltons is that a niece married into the Shelton family. The others who have not been identified as Shelton descendants contributed a total of six tunes.[1]

The Sheltons, like the Hicks family, came from England to Virginia and then to North Carolina. According to the Shelton family history, Roderick Shelton was the "first settler in this part of the state," at least in the part of Madison County known as Shelton Laurel.[2]

Of Mrs. Gentry's seventy songs, only about seventeen were known to Madison County singers from White Rock, Alleghany, Carmen, Allanstand, Big Laurel, Spillcorn, and Hot Springs. Of these Mary Sands sang five—"Lord Thomas," "Lord Bateman," "The House Carpenter," "The Broken Token," and "The Sheffield Apprentice." William Riley Shelton sang three—"George (John) Riley," "House Carpenter," and "Lord Thomas." Mrs. Tom Rice sang three—"Frog He Went A-Courting," "Lord Thomas," and "The Cherry Tree." Hester House of Hot Springs sang three of the same songs that Jane sang—"Lord Thomas," "Gypsy Laddie," and "Early, Early in the Spring." There were fourteen other singers who sang one or two of her repertoire, three of whom sang "The Wife of Usher's Well."

Ellie Johnson of Hot Springs sang "Barbara Allen." At least half of the singers did not sing any of Jane's repertoire. The lack of a significant number of mutually known songs suggests that Mrs. Gentry did not have contact with other singers in the county and that they did not have a common source. All of the singers, including Jane Gentry, were of English descent. All of them had lived their lives in the mountains where they were not exposed to other music. One would expect them to know some of the same songs.

Of course, none of the singers sang all of the songs they knew for Sharp. There might well have been more overlapping if we could know the complete repertoire of each singer. It is also possible that the singers in Hot Springs knew each other and deliberately avoided songs they thought of as another person's song. The singers who lived in Hot Springs had lived in a village for some years while the Laurel singers were still in a remote rural setting. The only other source of music in Hot Springs would have been the Mountain Park Hotel, and these singers were not exposed to the music there. Radio and recordings were not yet factors. The boys had not come back from World War I with songs from other places.

In comparing the ballads sung by Watauga County singers in Tom Burton's *Some Ballad Folks* with Mrs. Gentry's ballads, out of eighteen ballads, twelve of them were known to Jane Gentry. The singers were Rena Hicks, Buna Hicks, Hattie Presnell, Bertha Baird, and Lena Harmon. All of the singers lived in Beech Mountain, North Carolina, when they were recorded between 1969 and 1971. All of them except Bertha Baird, who was from Alexander County, are a part of the Hicks-Harmon family. The common ballads were "The Two Sisters," "Edward," "Young Beichan," "Lord Thomas," "Little Musgrave," "Barbara Allen," "Lamkin," "The Gypsy Laddie," "The House Carpenter," "The Grey Cock," "Our Goodman," and "The Golden Vanity." Jane Gentry's repertoire seems more closely related to those of Beech Mountain singers than to those of Madison County singers.[3]

Both Maud and Nola Jane spoke of their mother learning songs from other people. While she was in college, Nola Jane told a writer that her mother had learned all of her songs "by rote" from her mother and from other folk singers in her community. "She added others to the ones she had always known by learning others from various sections of the mountains near our home." [4] We are not told who these other singers were, but we can assume that this practice of learning songs from other people continued after Jane moved to Hot Springs. Jane was a warm, open person who obviously loved the songs and enjoyed singing, so we should not wonder that she would learn songs from other people. But she did not have a reputation as a collector.

Singers of traditional songs sing what they want to sing. They may not be inclined to explain why they sing a song. They may sing a ballad, a hymn, a playparty song, in no particular order. Jane would not analyze the song or try to put it into a category. The song would simply be called an "old love song." Yet Jane Gentry might explain words in the songs or the content of the song if she thought the listener did not understand. For collectors, singers often sing what they think the collector wants to hear. For Sharp she sang twenty Child ballads, nine broadsides, and the rest were songs of various kinds. There was a generous helping of children's songs and even some religious songs, and Sharp collected very few of these. It would seem that Jane kept some control over what she would sing. It is obvious that she knew he wanted the old ballads, and no one was better at singing them.

On August 24, the day of Sharp's first visit, Jane Gentry sang twenty songs. First she sang sixteen verses of "Little Musgrave" ("Little Matthy Groves"). Was she flustered by the presence of this proper English gentleman? This was the first time she saw her songs written down on paper. Seeing Sharp writing notes and Karpeles writing words would be enough to confuse anyone. But it must have been exciting that someone thought her songs important enough to put down the notes and the words. They had always been important to her. They were as much a part of her as her busy hands. We know that she turned down Sharp's offer to go into the next room while she sang. At any rate, she kept her composure and went on to sing "Pretty Peggy O," an American version of an English broadside, "Pretty Peggy of Derby." "Lord Thomas and Fair Eleanor" was the next ballad. Sharp has left us only the tune and one verse. In all probability Mrs. Gentry sang the complete ballad. The tune is close to Maud's tune, and Maud sang nineteen verses which she had learned from her mother. Cecil Sharp was careful with the tunes, but for whatever reason, he did not record more than the first verse of some ballads, usually ballads of which he had multiple variants. Other ballads of Mrs. Gentry's with only one verse are "The Wife of Usher's Well," "Lord Bateman," "The Sheffield Apprentice," "Barbara Allen," and "In Seaport Town," ballads he had collected in the weeks before in the Laurel section. "Fair Annie," a ballad rarely collected in this country, was followed by a humorous song, "My Mother She Bid Me." Her next song was a ditty called "Anything."

> Now, gentlemen, you must not think me wrong,
> I'm sure you asked me to sing a song,
> I asked you all what I should sing,
> And you said you'd like just anything.

This could very well have been in response to a conversation with Sharp about what she should sing, as well as to give her a rest from the big ballads. Maud Kilbourne, a singer from Kentucky who sang for Sharp, once remarked that you need to sing some little songs in between the big ones. Jane then proceeded to sing for him some of her best ballads, among them "The Cherry Tree Carol," a ballad based on Pseudo-Matthew's gospel. Jane's version sings of "the fifth day of January," whereas many versions speak of "the sixth day." The fifth was the date of Christmas between the years 1752 and 1799. She sang some broadside ballads and even managed to include "Jesus Born in Bethany," a folk hymn. A concert artist could not have sung a better program. And Sharp could not have been happier with her selection.

Sharp was pleased with the ballads he was finding in America. A ballad tells a story, but seldom the whole story. It is more like a short story, leaving much to the imagination of the listener. How much of a story a traditional ballad tells is the result of its treatment at the hands of singers who forget, who do not always hear well, who exercise creativity. But ballads have a lyrical quality. They were made to be sung. Ballad tunes are there to carry the story, some more beautiful than others. Sharp thought that "The False Knight in the Road" was a "splendid example of the genuine ballad at its highest pitch." The tune is nothing more than a vehicle and of little value alone. The ballad tells the story of a child on his way to school when he encounters a demon or a devil. If he answers all of the questions correctly he belongs to God, if not, he belongs to the devil. Of course, the clever child outwits the devil and sends him on his way by letting the devil know that he knows who he is: "And you that deep in hell, / Said the child as he stood." "Old Wichet," also known as "Our Goodman" and "Three Nights Drunk," has a tune that effectively supports the tale but no more. Mrs. Gentry's ballad begins with an unusual verse:

> She beats me, she bangs me,
> It is her heart's delight
> To beat me with a poking stick
> When I come home at night.

This ballad in America usually begins with the husband asking about the horses in the stable, as Jane said, "where my mules ought to be." As she sang it, the husband is a fool. Rena Hicks and Hattie Presnell both sang:

> The first night I came home
> Drunk as I could be;
> Saw a horse standing in the stable
> Where my horse ought to be.

We do not know whether this ballad was one Jane learned from her mother or her grandfather, but since hers was recorded fifty years before those on Beech Mountain, we would certainly expect significant changes in the song. Older variants describe the husband as a fool, later ones say he is drunk and include verses with zippers and J.B. Stetson chamberpots, rather than a churn with heels and a nightcap trimmed with fur. Maud sang the ballad as her mother did with additional verses. Both of them concluded with "a baby your mammy sent to me," not a cabbage head as it is sung on Beech Mountain.

Not all ballad tunes are mere vehicles. Some of Jane's more beautiful tunes are "Young Hunting," "Geordie," and "The Golden Vanity." Some of the song tunes Sharp found very different from English tunes and very beautiful, such as her "The Rejected Lover," with essentially the same tune as "Young Hunting" and similar to the tune for "The Wife of Usher's Well." It is not unusual for singers to use the same tune for more than one song. Bascom Lamar Lunsford once said that was why the mountains had so much music; they just kept using it over and over. "Come All Ye Fair and Tender Ladies" was another of Jane's melodies which Sharp considered especially beautiful.[5]

Cecil Sharp pointed out that the songs collected in the Appalachians were generally cast on "gapped" scales, scales containing five or six notes, rather than the seven we expect today.[6] Pentatonic scales have been noted among early music cultures in China, Africa, and Polynesia, as well as among American Indians and in Celtic and Gaelic folk music. "Gapped" does not imply that the tune is not complete. The beauty of the melodies establishes that they were not limited by the five-note scale. They were indeed complete and often very beautiful. The ballad tune is repeated over and over, and yet a good singer like Jane Gentry can hold the attention of listeners through long ballads, the tune supporting the story.

Twenty of Mrs. Gentry's songs were the A variant or the first version of the song given in *English Folks Songs*, which suggests that Sharp thought well of them. The A variants are usually fairly complete with good tunes. Eight were B variants, and there were seven songs and ballads which were the only variant given, among them two fine ballads, "The Grey Cock" and "Fair Annie." Jane's "Fair Annie" is a lovely ballad, the story dating back before 1200. After Annie has borne seven sons for Lord Thomas he goes away and returns with a bride who has ships loaded with riches. The two women discover that they are sisters and take proper action: "And we'll have Lord Thomas burned."

At a North Carolina Folklore Society meeting several years ago, Holgar Nygard of Duke University suggested a Scottish connection for Jane Gentry's repertoire. It is true that several of her ballads are firmly rooted in Scottish tradition—"The False Knight in the Road," "Edward," "Fair Annie," "Young Hunting," "The Wife of Usher's Well," "Little Musgrave," "Lamkin," "Johnny Scot," "Geordie," and "The Grey Cock." "Billy McGee McGore" is the Scottish counterpart of "The Three Ravens." Some of her other ballads have been sung in Scotland as well as in England—"The Two Sisters," "Lord Thomas," "Barbara Allen," and "Old Wichet." This covers almost her entire repertoire of Child ballads. Among her broadside ballads with Scottish connections were "The Green Bed," "Jack Went A-Sailing," "John Reilly," "Johnny Dials" "The Broken Token," and "The Brisk Young Lover." Many of these ballads can be found in William Christie's *Traditional Ballad Airs* and Gavin Grieg's *Folk-Songs of the North-East*. Both of these collections were done in Scotland. The Hicks family came from England, and in time perhaps we will discover which part of England. It is possible that they came from the north of England, where the tradition is much the same on both sides of the border.

"My Boy Billy," which Bertrand Bronson calls a parody of "Lord Randall," as sung by Jane Gentry may show evidence of her creative bent. Maud Clay Gibbs, a granddaughter, said that she was good at making up songs but that she never knew which part was made up. The last verse shows his sweetheart rolling (rowing?) a boat and making a door.

> Can she roll a boat ashore, Billy boy, Billy boy,
> Can she roll a boat ashore, charming Billy?
> She can roll a boat ashore,
> And make her own door,
> She's a young girl and cannot leave her mammy.

Jane Gentry spent a good portion of her life singing to children. Her repertoire reflects this. For Sharp she sang "The Farm Yard," "Cock Robin," "The Tree in the Wood" (a cumulative song well collected in English nursery and folk song tradition), "Three Little Mice," "Baby's Ball," "The Frog He Would A-Wooing Go" (a popular song for over four hundred years), and "I Whipped My Horse." She did not limit her children's repertoire to obvious materials. She also sang such songs as "The Drummer and His Wife" and "The Bird Song," as well as other ballads she considered appropriate. Maud recorded "Jenny Jenkins" and "Soldier, Soldier, Won't You Marry Me," which she learned from her mother. Mary Kestler Clyde's account of Jane's concert at Asheville Normal School confirms that Jane sang "Soldier, Soldier." She may have learned some of the above songs from other singers in the community. She may have learned songs from people who stayed in her boardinghouse. Some of them do seem to be of more recent vintage. "Sing Said the Mother" was included in the first edition of the Sharp-Campbell collection but omitted from the last because Sharp apparently came across information that made him doubt that it was a genuine folk song. The singers in the Laurel section sang no more than half a dozen songs that might be called children's songs and no singer more than two or three. Perhaps they did not realize that Sharp would welcome these songs. In 1921 he published *Nursery Songs from the Appalachian Mountains*.

Most ballad singers sing the ballads in a straightforward manner without theatrics. Sharp said that he did not see them closing their eyes or assuming a rigid posture, but that they were just natural. Nola Jane said that her mother did react to the mood of the song and that sometimes she would close her eyes when she was singing sad songs. This did not seem to be a habit but just a reaction to the song. She also reacted to humorous and happy songs. It seems clear that she sang in a way that seemed natural to her. Miss Peggy confirmed this: "What she did just seemed natural." Jane instinctively knew that the story was the important thing and that it must unfold, not be "produced" by the singer. If allowed to, the ballad will tell itself. With songs, however—love songs, hymns, humorous songs— the singer expresses whatever emotion is appropriate for the song. The song is of utmost importance. No audience is necessary, and so the singing is not an artistic production. Sharp said it well: "The wonderful charm, fascinating and well-nigh magical, which the folk-singer produces upon those who are fortunate enough to hear him is to be attributed very largely to his method of singing . . . quite as traditional as the song itself."[7]

Mother and daughter, Jane and Maud, both fine singers, afford an opportunity to take a look at songs transmitted orally within a family. It is important to keep in mind that Jane's songs were recorded by hand. Bertrand Bronson said of Cecil Sharp: "There has never been a collector with such quickness and tact in seizing and accurately reporting melodic characteristics from individual singing."[8] Although we mourn the fact that we cannot hear Jane Gentry sing, we are fortunate that her tunes were written down so well. No two singers sing a song exactly alike. A singer singing the song twice on the same day would not sing identical renditions. Indeed, both Sharp and John Forbes, who notated Maud's songs from the Library of Congress tapes, found that often no two verses in a song were exactly the same. Maud's songs were recorded by machine more than twenty years after her mother's death. Now, almost fifty years later, they have been taken down by hand from those recordings. Of course, there were variations. It would be much more amazing if there were none. The songs are alive when they are being sung. They are always in process, always changing.

It is virtually impossible to notate every nuance in a song, and it would be confusing to see each verse notated in an attempt to get exactly what the singer was singing. Sharp, in a letter to Philips Barry, said that the publishing firm "had no proper reader and they had a nasty habit of altering my M.S. without drawing my attention to it."[9] We can assume that Sharp made every effort to correct the errors, but having spotted an error in the second measure of "The Cherry Tree

Carol" and because there were about thirty manuscripts attributed to Jane Gentry not included in *English Folk-Songs from the Southern Appalachians*, I made the decision to work from Sharp's original manuscripts rather than from the Oxford University Press edition. That edition is now out of print and in the public domain. In notating Maud Long's tunes, John Forbes and I sent manuscripts back and forth until we were both satisfied that the tunes were as accurately transcribed as possible. When Forbes heard Maud's voice, his reaction was: "I like your singer, Maud Long. She has straight pitch and good rhythmic accuracy. And her voice is wonderful to listen to."[10] Maud's clear enunciation made taking down the texts much simpler than capturing the tunes.

Most of the tunes shared by Jane and Maud were recognizable as the same. There were some variations in tune and text in all of the songs. There were verses sung by one and omitted by the other, as with "Little Matthy Groves," "The False Knight," "Old Wichet," "Sing Said the Mother," and "Johnny Scot." Jane began "Little Musgrave":

> The first come down was a raven white,
> The next come down was a polly,
> The next come down was Lord Thomas's wife,
> And she was the fairest of them all,
> And she was the fairest of them all.

When Maud recorded this ballad for the Library of Congress, she began with a verse often heard at the beginning of "Little Musgrave":

> It fell upon a gay holiday,
> As many there be in a year,
> When young men and maids together did go,
> Their mathen [matins] and mass for to hear,
> Their mathen and mass for to hear.

Maud sang thirty verses, and she sang of "Lord Barnard." Jane sang of "Lord Thomas." She also sang of Lord Thomas in "Fair Annie" and we assume in "Lord Thomas and Fair Eleanor." Maud's ballad is so different from her mother's that one wonders if she had learned another version in the ensuing years. It is possible that Maud learned verses from sources other than her mother, but her purpose was to record Jane's songs, so she must have believed she was doing that.

The variations in the tunes for the most part can be attributed to memory lapses and the passage of time. Tunes are not static, and changes may be made unconsciously. In "The Grey Cock," not an easy song to sing, there were marked differences. A mental lapse may have occurred in Maud's "Bruton Town (In Seaport Town)." She sang the same tune that she sang to "The Broken Token," not at all like her mother's beautiful mixolydian tune. This was one of the songs of which we have only the tune and one verse. In "The Cherry Tree" Maud repeated the last two lines of each verse as a refrain. Jane did not; at least Sharp's manuscript does not indicate that she did.

Maud Karpeles quoted the daughter of a singer who described her mother's singing thus: "Her tongue wrapped so lovingly round the words."[11] Could this have been Maud or Nola Jane speaking? Jane, as is typical of good singers, sang as she spoke. So did Maud. This has created interesting differences in the texts of the songs. Maud spent the twenty years after her mother's death as a teacher and as a leader in the church and the community. She may have started out singing the ballads as she heard them from her mother, but in time, without this constant model, "afeard" became "afraid," the tears no longer "run down," they "ran down," and "Joseph flew in anger," no longer "in angry." Maud spoke proper English and constantly met the public, so it is not surprising in "The False Knight" to hear Maud sing, "I wish you were in the sea," rather than "I wish'd you was in the sea," as Jane sang it, or "kisses gave her" rather than "kisses give her" in "The Broken Token." Jane called this ballad "The Soldier's Return" and sang of "a ring that she had given him," while Maud sang of "a ring that was broken between them." In "The Green Bed" Jane said "drawed handfuls of gold" while Maud said "drew handfuls of gold." "My green beds they are empty and has been all this week" became "have been" when Maud sang it. It is probable that Maud never consciously made such changes. After twenty years they rolled off her tongue as though she had always sung them that way. Other expressions that were the idiom of her people gave her no pause and she sang "a-drinking" in "Barbara Allen"; the farmer's wife was "a-sitting" and the sister was "a-floatin" in "The Two Sisters." It is interesting that Jane did not say "a-sitting" but "sitting." The daughter's dear was still a "princy boy" in "In Seaport Town." In "The Rejected Lover" both singers sang "I'd a-died when I was young, or never had a-been born." In "The Golden Vanity" Maud sang of the "low-de-lands" just as her mother did. In "Jackie's Gone A-Sailing" Maud rhymed "bleeding wound" with town. One might assume that her mother sang it that way, although Jane did not always insist that her verses rhyme. In "The Cherry Tree Carol" she sang:

> On the fifth day of January
> My birthday shall be,
> When the stars and the elements
> Shall tremble with fear.

Joan Baez sang a melody for this ballad which she said was derived from the singing of Maud Long on the Library of Congress recording,[12] but the guitar accompaniment makes use of harmonies it is doubtful either Jane or Maud "heard" when they sang this song.

Forgetfulness is a plight faced by singers who have large repertoires, especially those who know a number of songs with similarities in tune or text. Mrs. Gentry was singing "Lamkin" when she could not remember the rest of the ballad. Of course, she had not forgotten the story and she told Sharp that the maid was sent to warn the lady's husband of the murder, and she does so by saying that Dunkins has killed a doe and a swan.[13] Maud sang "The Tree in the Wood" without the first two lines of the first verse. Three times she recorded it, in 1944 with Artus Moser and the seventh grade of Hot Springs High School, in 1947 at the Library of Congress, and again in 1950 when Maud Karpeles returned with Sidney Robertson Cowell to record three of her songs. The song had become etched in her memory without the introductory lines. When Maud was recording for Artus Moser she forgot a verse. Her response was, "I don't know what went wrong, but just something, and I failed to think of the next verse."[14] Then she sang the song again.

Jane's "Gypsy Laddie" has an unusual refrain: "All a lipto tally boney, hair, hair, / All a lipto laddy." In her final verse the lady says:

> The night before last I lay on a feather bed,
> Lord Thomas he lay with me.
> Last night I lay on a cold straw bed
> With the calves a-bawling all around me.

Maud's last line is "with the gypsies a-dancing all around me." Bertrand Bronson refers to a version of "Gypsy Laddie" in James Watt Raine's *The Land of Saddle-Bags* as Mrs. Gentry's, collected the same year Sharp collected it from her. Sharp's text, beginning with the second verse, is printed beside it, and Bronson remarks that the text is quite different after the first stanza. Raine does not give the source, and when one takes a closer look, his version appears to be Jane's first verse and refrain. The remainder of the text is from the singing of Hester House, another singer from Hot Springs. The refrain becomes "All a lipto tally doney" with the explanation that "doney is a mountain word for sweetheart." It also contains the line, "With the gypsies a-dancing all around me."[15]

In 1923, the year before *The Land of Saddle-Bags* was published, Raine published a song book, *Mountain Ballads for Social Singing.* He called it, not a collection but a selection of mountain ballads for use with Berea College students at Vesper Hour gatherings and other social occasions. The music for the book was collected by Cecil J. Sharp. Among Raine's papers was the music for "Gypsy Laddie," a Sharp manuscript on which Jane Gentry's name had been marked through. There were changes in House's text which would make the song easier for group singing.

> It's he caught up his old grey horse,
> His blanket being so speedy O.
> He rode all night and he rode all day,
> And he overtaken of his lady O. [Hester House]

> It's he caught up his old grey horse,
> And he caught up his pony;
> He rode all night and he rode all day
> Till he overtook his doney. [James Raine]

The songbook version was published in Raine's *The Land of Saddle-Bags,* and Bronson apparently assumed it was collected by Raine. There is no evidence that Raine ever called on Jane Gentry, but he clearly gave Sharp credit for the ballads.[16]

The words were usually meaningful to the singers. Ballad language becomes second nature to singers such as Jane and Maud. They sing "ruby lips," "make a mourn" (or "moan," as Maud said), "lily white breast," and "bloody warning," and they and the listener understand that it often means more than what the actual words are saying. There are a few instances in which Jane had carried the song with words or phrases that we question, and we wonder if she ever did. In "John Riley" we hear the phrase "We'll sail the ocean high o'er promo-

tion." I... ...cording to Child, this is in all
probabili... ...ohnny's head "like a swallow"
and is ru... ...rded this song it sounded like
"tavern."

Son... ...t of misunderstanding on the
part of the p... ...ped My Horse" the refrain as
Maud Karpel... ...kill ko, / Coy ma lin dow, kill
ko me." Maud ...ngo, kil-ko, kil-ko, / Coy ma
lingo, kil-ko ne... ...gotten, and it is possible that
Jane also sang i... ...g" Jane sang of a "deathlike
blow," according ...ow," which somehow sounds
more like a ballad

Irregulariti... ...blems for those committing
them to print. Not ... ...ng unaccompanied. She certainly felt a steady be... ...tune and the words without
worrying about note v... ...th the tune because she had
no accompanying instru... ...creating harmonies she might not hear or rhythms she might not feel. She could linger on a note if it felt right and still effortlessly fit the words to the tune. At times it was obvious that Maud had forgotten her mother's exact tune or text, but she had not forgotten the shape of the tune or the meaning of the text, and she brought the tune and the words together in her own way. It would not have occurred to Maud to imitate her mother, just as Jane did not imitate her mother. They sang the same songs, but each sang in her own way, in her own natural voice.

Jane Gentry's contribution to Cecil Sharp's collection did not exhaust her repertoire; far from it. Maud recorded quite a few songs that were not among the Sharp manuscripts. Maud said, "Not all of the songs that my mother and father sang were the ballads or some little ditty to amuse us children. They loved to sing the old hymns." Then she sang two of those hymns, "Alas and Did My Savior," which Maud said was sung to an old Welsh tune, and "Calling Now for Me."

Chapter 10

# Riddles and Rhymes

Had I but words to say how these tunes are bound with the life of the
singer, knit with his earliest sense-impressions, and therefore dearer
than any other music could ever be—impossible to forget as the sound
of his mother's voice.

—Emma Bell Miles, *The Spirit of the Mountains*

There was great respect and love among Jane and Newt Gentry and their
children. Although they worked hard and much was expected of them, the children felt fortunate to have them for parents and said as much. There was laughter
and fun in the Gentry home. At a family reunion in 1980, Lalla said to those
gathered: "I tell you that was one of the happiest homes and there's nothing in the
world that makes a happier home than a bunch of kids."

When Maud recorded for the Library of Congress she went into some detail about life in the Gentry home:

Mother sang practically all the time as she went about her work. There
were nine of us children and that saved her having to answer the call of
each one, because as she sang we knew where she was. And then in the
evening as we would sit around the fire, each child busy with pulling
the burrs from the wool or raveling up a piece of worn woolen goods
that she might re-card the wool, then she would sing these songs to us
and tell us the Jack tales.[1]

There were so many children in the family we didn't have to hunt
playmates. And on cold winter evenings and in the afternoon, the oldest one of the children who was free from work would often gather the
smaller ones of us together to play. And one of the games that we especially liked was called "Travel." The older one would sit down and the
rest of us would bring our little chairs or kneel around her knee, and if
there were a number of us playing we only got to put down one finger.
But if there were just two or three of us playing we could each put on
two fingers—on her knee—and then she would go 'round the circle of
fingers, counting:

Intery mintery cutery corn,
Apple seed and apple thorn,
Wire briar limber lock,
Three geese in the flock.
One flew east, one flew west,
One flew over the cuckoo's nest.
The clock fell down,
And the mouse ran out,
You old dirty dishrag, you.

And whoever's finger she ended on with "you," that was the person who was "It." And they got to travel.

So they went and stood in a corner and then all the rest of us gathered 'round this older sister and whispered the things we'd like to be. Oh, we could be a horse, or a cow, or a pig, or a sheep, or the skillet, or the coal shovel, or we could be a wagon, or a cloud, or a rainbow—just anything in the world that you wanted to be. But you had to remember what you were and tell her so she could remember it. Then we named the one in the corner, too. Then after everybody was named, the older sister would say:

Now would you like to come home on a cow, or a sheep, or a rainbow, or a wheelbarrow, or a pig?
(We'd say there were five of us playing.)

And then the person who had traveled would guess the thing that she'd like to come home on. Well, if it was one of us, we would have to go get her, put her on our back or pick her up in our arms, and carry her back to the big sister. And she would say:

What've you got there?
And we would say:
A bag of mitts.
She'd say:
Shake her till she spits.

And so we'd give her a good shake, and everybody would have a good laugh, and we'd sit down and begin all over again. But if the one who had traveled guessed their own thing that we had secretly named her, then we all would yell out:

Come home on your own tiptoes.
And that wasn't half as much fun as being carried in. But it was a game that we all dearly loved to play.[2]

Jane Gentry was the hub around which everything revolved. Much of what the children learned from her was not taught but was, indeed, "caught." She sang

"Ten Little Indians" to teach the children to count, and Newt Gentry told the children that the Indians counted like this:

> Onery, twoery, zickory zon,
> Holly bone, cracker bone,
> Whale-a-bar dollery dockason, and ten.[3]

At least, it sounded like this to Maud. There is an English nursery counting rhyme that goes thus:

> One-ery, two-ery,
> Ziccary zan,
> Hollow bone, crack a bone,
> Ninery ten.

Roby Hicks, son of Samuel and Becky Harmon Hicks, told collectors Anne and Frank Warner that his parents were raised "in this country" but that their parents "come from Cherokee." Though not far away, by Roby's reckoning Cherokee was another country. He said that they counted Cherokee fashion in his youth—one to ten: "saki, tally, choway, nikki, whiskey, su-tally, sook-nail, sink-nail, squay." Dorothy Hartley suggests that medieval farm people, without formal education, used finger counts and tallies in place of arithmetic and that many of these rural counts came to America and were picked up by the Indians. In the nineteenth century they were called "Indian counts."[4]

The Jack tales and the songs and ballads were for the most part learned by the children as their mother worked in the kitchen or at the loom or at the fireside at night. Many ballad singers do not remember learning the songs. Often they were "absorbed" before they were old enough to start to school. Some were sung as lullabies. Maud Long was observed picking up the baby before she began to sing, saying that she always felt more like it when she was holding a young'un.[5] She learned only one song deliberately. The song was "Jenny Jenkins" with the refrain "So buy me a double whirly gurley whirly silk satin blue beamole." When Maud was asked how she could twist her tongue around to say that, she answered: "It isn't so very hard, but I did have a hard time learning that one. It really is the only one that I consciously made an effort to learn. And after I'd begged my mother all one evening to teach that song to me, she said, 'Never mind, tomorrow you are going to help me put a piece in the loom and while we thread the loom, then I'll sing this song for you until you learn it.' And so the next day I really learned every word of this. And the 'blue beamole' was always a marvel to me. I wondered what kind of a dress that could have been."[6] The song the children loved best when they were young was "Fiddle-I-Fee" or "The Farm Yard" with all the animal sounds. They would beg Jane to sing it over and over until she would tell them her "tongue was slick" and she could not sing it any more.[7] "Three Little Mice" is a song with fingerplay that she taught her children. "Over in the Meadows" was another nursery song the children never tired of. One the boys especially liked was called "The Old Gray Horse" by the Gentrys. Sharp used the title "I Whipped My Horse."

After the move to Hot Springs they learned another way of counting out to determine who would be "It."

Eeny, meeny, miney mo,
Catch a Negro by the toe,
If he hollers let him go,
Eeny, meeny, miney mo.
O-U-T spells out goes she.

Until they moved to Hot Springs the Gentry children had probably only known the children of family members and neighbors who knew the same songs and games they knew. In town they had a more eclectic group of playmates. There were at least fifteen African American families living in Hot Springs. Most of them worked at the hotel. Colonel Rumbough's son Henry Thomas gave land to these families to build their own church, which they used for a school on weekdays. Whites were invited to attend church, and some did go on Sunday afternoons. The only slaves in the area were said to have been owned by Thomas Garrett, whose home was a stage stop called Garrett Inn.[8] The following story suggests that there may have been families of former slaves still living in the area.

H.B. Parks, who was in charge of the agricultural work at Dorland Institute in 1912, was riding through the meadows on Big Rich Mountain where the school kept cattle when he came upon this scene: "I heard the following stanza sung by a little Negro boy who was picking up dry sticks of wood near a Negro cabin:

Foller the drinkin' gou'd.
Foller the drinkin' gou'd;
No one know, the wise man say,
Foller the drinkin' gou'd."

He said that he might not have been attracted had not the old grandfather gotten up and, with his cane, given the boy a sound lick across his back. He asked the old man why he did not want the boy to sing the song, but his only answer was that it was "bad luck." After further inquiry, he found that the song had to do with the underground railroad movement.[9]

Nola Jane, who was born in Hot Springs, remembered games such as "Drop the Handkerchief" and "Who Has Got the Thimble." She liked games in which one side acted out things and the other side did the guessing. Of course, the boys liked games like mumbly peg. They played a game similar to hopscotch, and during World War I marching games became popular. When the German prisoners at the Mountain Park Hotel gave afternoon concerts the children marched to the music.[10] Although she did like some of the sad ballads, Nola Jane also liked for "Mama to sing snappy songs like 'Soldier, Soldier, Won't You Marry Me?'"

One of Nola Jane's favorite activities was "preaching," which was patterned after a street preacher she heard on Bridge Street. On one occasion she was "preaching" from the back of a wagon in the middle of a field of sagebrush. She had her "congregation" all around her when Roy set the field on fire and broke up the meeting. Splashing in the swirl hole in Spring Creek was a favorite summer pastime for the children.[11] Mischievous children would trap unsuspecting prisoners on the swinging bridge over Spring Creek and try to shake them off. Even goats were sometimes the victims of this game.

"My mother knew a great many riddles, and she could say them so fast that it would just make your head swim," said Maud. In the summer of 1923 Isabel Carter collected riddles along with the Jack tales, and these "Mountain White Riddles" were published in 1934 in the *Journal of American Folklore.* Jane Gentry contributed many of the riddles in this collection. She told Carter that in her "mother's day they used to tell riddles all night long and the best riddle got a prize, but in my day they sang all night long and the best song got a prize." By 1923 riddles did not hold much fascination for most people. Although they were heard occasionally, Jane said she "hadn't heard a good 'un in many years."[12]

As one might expect, Jane Gentry did not forget the riddles, and sometimes they came in handy. One of those occasions was her encounter with the rash young stenographer in New York. Here is the answer to the riddle.

> As I went around my willy-go-whackum,
> [As I went around my cornfield,]
> There I spied old Bow Backum.
> [There I spied a pig.]
> I went home after Tom Tackum,
> [I went home after my dog,]
> To run Bow Backum out of my willy-go-whackum.
> [To run that pig out of my cornfield.]

Compare Maud Long's version recorded in 1944. Carter may have misunderstood and Jane may have been saying "whirly," as Maud did:

> As I went around my whirly-go-whackum [wheat field],
> There I spied old Bo Backum,
> And I called Tom Tackum,
> To run Bo Backum out of my whirly-go-whackum.[13]

The following riddles were recited by both Mrs. Gentry and Mrs. Long:

> Love I sit and Love I stand,
> Love I hold in my right hand,
> I love love and love loves me,
> Guess this riddle and you may hang me.

> Answer: A young man was going to be hung if he could not make a riddle that the king's courtiers could not guess. So he had a beautiful collie dog that he loved very much and the dog's name was "Love." He took some of the hair from Love and sewed it into his glove, put some in his shoes, sewed some in the seat of his pants, and then he made his riddle. They didn't guess it and the man got to live.

The above was Maud Long's explanation. In Carter's notes the person was a woman who gained her freedom by killing a little dog named Love and putting patches of skin in her shoes and so on.

> As I went up a heeple steeple,
> There I met a heap of people.
> Some was licker, some was lacker,
> Some was the color of a chaw of tobaccer. Answer: Ants

> Hickey-more, hackey-more,
> Hanging over the kitchen door,
> Nothing so long and nothing so strong,
> Hickey-more, hackey-more,
> Hanging over the kitchen door. Answer: The Sun

> Threw a rock, threw a reel,
> Threw an old spinning wheel. [This line is omitted in Carter's collection]
> Threw a sheep shank bone,
> Such a riddle never known. Answer: Lightning[14]

Jane Gentry was a natural teacher. A grandchild, Maud Clay Gibbs, often stayed with her grandmother. Jane called her "Dixie Dan" because that was Maud's favorite song. As Mrs. Gentry went about her work they played a game.

> I do recall there being this game we played. She repeated a song, poem, or short ditty, and I had to respond with one that I knew. The fun part being many times she would have to leave the kitchen where this would usually take place and go into the dining room, pantry, or even the back porch to do or get something as she cooked the meals for the boarders and her family. She would just continue as she came back into the room, or it would give me time to think up "mine," as we called it. Only after I was married and had three children did I find out why I stayed with her so much . . . and I realized why she took so much time with me. . . . I asked this question of Aunt Maud and she said: "Dearie, didn't you know . . . that your folks thought you were "simple" [retarded]. . . . But Grandma was making me use my brain and most of it worked.[15]

As a child Maud Gibbs had a speech impediment that was mistaken for a mental problem.

Jane Gentry could have collaborated with Jean Piaget, who began defining his developmental theory in the 1920s when heredity was considered to be the only factor determining intellectual level. She was doing what seemed reasonable, sensible, and just plain fun. Her methods agreed with Piaget's theory that the quality of experience has a profound impact on intellectual growth—that one experience builds on another, resulting in more and more complex learning and problem-solving skills.[16]

Jane's expressive use of language prepared her children well for formal education. Language is a highly efficient way to store and recover information and to solve problems. It is a good tool for organizing and structuring data. The Gentry family's days were filled with conversation, stories, riddles, and songs. The children were kept busy with tasks, but there was also time for creative play and activities that enriched their young lives.

The three Gentry daughters who became teachers, Emily, Maud, and Nola Jane, told the Jack tales to their students. "I never left out any story that was in the Jack tales. The school children seemed to enjoy all of them. Although the Jack tales were published and the book sent to us, we nearly always preferred her [Jane's] version—even if they were not in the Jack tale book." (She referred to Richard Chase's *Jack Tales*.[17])

Jane could come up with a Jack tale any time and tell it beautifully as if it were in the back of her mind—"no, the front of her mind," Miss Peggy would say. Haladine Gentry Sink, Alfred's daughter, remembers how she looked forward to her grandmother Jane coming to the school and how quiet the children were. "I loved for her to come and tell Jack tales," she said. It was the same with Maud. On rainy days at school the children would be brought to the lunchroom and she would tell Jack tales. You could hear a pin drop, and that was remarkable because the children were not generally that attentive. But they did love to hear Maud tell Jack tales. Maud also turned out good singers in the schools where she taught. They especially enjoyed singing "The False Knight in the Road" because they got to sing the word "hell."[18]

One of the stories Mrs. Gentry told her children was about "Stiff Dick." There are two published versions of this story, one collected by Carter in 1923, and this version, written down by Irving Bacheller about 1914 and published in 1938.

> Onct there was a boy an' I never did see no one so outdacious brave. He were one o' the bravest humans that ever did live. He were a-shamickin' erlong the road one day an' were passin' through a town. A king pops out an' says:
>
> What be your name?
>
> Stiff Dick.
>
> Be you a right brave man?
>
> Yes, bedads, I be.
>
> Well, now, we have got a wild municorn over in this yere country an' we want to git him killed. I will give anybody a thousand dollars that will kill him.
>
> Well, bedads, pay me five hundred down an' I will kill him for you.
>
> The king slaps down the money.
>
> Stiff Dick, he says to himself: I've got five hundred dollars now an' I'm ergoin' to leave hur.
>
> So he started over through the woods an' mount'ins an' the municorn smelled him an' tuk right a'ter him. So Dick started to run an' he run an' run an' run. Late in the evenin' he were gettin' mighty nigh tard to death an' he didn't see no chanct 'cept to clomb a big oak. He made for the tree. He didn't have time to clomb hit so he run eround hit. The municorn giv a jump at him. He were tryin' fer to nail him to the tree with one long horn that stuck out o' his forehead. Dick dodged

an' the municorn he jus' stove his horn plumb into the wood an' couldn't pull hit out.

The boy come eround an' he seed the municorn were ketched tight. Dick went on back to town.

King come out an' says: Did you git the municorn?

Lord o' mercy! Never seed no municorn! A little bull calf with one horn come at me back in the mount'ins. I picked him up by the tail, stove his head agin a tree an' stuck him thar by his horn. If you want him killed you cain go up thar an' kill him yourself. I reckon 'twould pleasure you to kill him.

So the king got him an army o' men an' went up an' killed the municorn. Come back. Paid Stiff Dick his other five hundred dollars.

Well, now, bedads, I'm gettin' rich, says Dick. I'm ergoin' to git out o' this part o' the country while I've got a thousand dollars.

The king says: Now, we've got one more thing that we want you to kill.

Well, what be hit?

Well, hit's a lion, a wild lion.

King paid him five hundred dollars more an' he started to git out o' the country. Went up the mount'ins on his way home, an' the lion smelled him an' tuk a'ter him. He run an' run all day long an' were jist tard to death. The lion stopped to kill a dog that were out thar a-huntin'. That give Dick his chanct. He seed a long, slim pine an' he clomb hit an' the lion come a'ter Dick an' started to gnaw the tree down, an' he gnawed an' gnawed an' while he were ergnawin' Dick jumped right erstraddle o' the lion's back. Hit skeered the lion an' he started to run an' Stiff Dick he held right tight into the lion's ha'r. The lion were so skeered he didn't know which erway to git to, so he done made a straight line right to the town. Skeered the men an' they run out with their guns an' shot the lion down.

Stiff Dick he got off an' 'gun to cut a terrible rusty. He swore straight up an' down that he were breakin' that lion to make the king a ridy horse, an' he cut up so that the king made the men pay him another thousand dollars an' when he left thar he had riches an' riches.[19]

# Chapter 11

# Time Passes

Thyme, thyme it is a precious thing;
It's a root that the sun shines on;
And Time it will bring everything unto an end,
And so our time goes on.

—Folk Song

The children grew up and, one by one, married and moved away from home. Nola Jane would go through the house saying, "Mama, they're taking too much." Each one who left took some things from home, but her mother smiled and made little of it. They took memories that were more important than the objects they took. They took memories of a busy, singing mother who could figure out how to do almost anything. They took memories of a gentle father who taught them how to grow vegetables and who told scary stories about hunting and trapping game to put meat on the table. They took memories of games and songs shared with brothers and sisters. They took memories of growing up in a hardworking, loving family.

Nora, the oldest, left first. She married Thomas Keener on October 6, 1895. Her grandfather Ransom was the preacher who performed the ceremony. This was before the family left Meadow Fork, the year Roy was born. She married at about the age her mother did, just before she was sixteen. Nora and Thomas, who were later divorced, had two sons, Virgil and Billy. She had a daughter, Mae, by her second husband, Dave Lyda. Later she moved to Texas, and after her husband's death she owned and operated a small diner for many years.

Emily was teaching in a little mountain school in Madison County when in 1905 she was recommended for a job that would change the direction of her life. An army officer, a Colonel Taylor, and his wife and son were staying at the Mountain Park Hotel. The colonel was being transferred to the West Coast and went to Dorland Institute in search of a young woman to care for his son, McNay. Emily accompanied the family by train to Fort Lawton near Seattle, Washington. From there the colonel was transferred to Fort Liscom in Valdez, Alaska. Emily, who had been brought up to raise the vegetables she ate, found that she could not have a garden at the foot of a glacier. She was not happy living in Alaska. Then she met Enoch Virgil Byford, who was employed as a civilian carpenter at the military post. He strongly resembled her father, whom she loved and missed. They were married in May 1907 and moved to the White River Valley south of Seattle. About 1912 they moved to Whidbey Island, north of Seattle, to farm. This life was more to Emily's liking. It was isolated, not by mountains but by water. They cleared the land, and it was like pioneering all over again; they raised most of what they ate. Emily and Virgil had two children, Jeannette and Virgil, and she reared her children as she had been brought up, singing ballads and old hymns and telling her children about the adventures of Jack, Will, and Tom. She sang most often "Sweet Hour of Prayer" and "I Am a Pilgrim and a Stranger."

> I am a pilgrim and a stranger,
> Traveling through this wearisome land,
> I got a home in yonder city,
> Lord, it's not made, not made by hand.

Perhaps she thought of herself as a pilgrim and a stranger. North Carolina, "back home," was so far away that she never got home again. Her remains were brought back to Madison County after her death in 1958. Emily Gentry Byford was a very private person but, like her mother before her, was never discouraged, was devoted to her family, and was a good neighbor.[1]

The third daughter, Mary Magdalene ("Maggie"), married a hometown boy, Bud Sanders, in 1908. They lived on the banks of the French Broad River near her parents. Bud Sanders died, and Maggie joined Nora in Texas. There she was married to Will Moses, and they had a son, Roy.

The next to marry was Alfred, on August 26, 1910. He and his wife, Mae Lamkins, settled in Hot Springs. Alfred became a Western Union operator, was town clerk, and was elected mayor for two terms. Like his father, he was always a dedicated farmer. Alfred and Mae had five children—Patrick, Haladine, Lalla Maud, James, and Bill. Alfred and his son James opened Gentry Hardware after James came back from service in World War II. James and his wife, Dorothy, still operate the hardware store on Bridge Street next to the Spring Creek bridge.

Another Gentry child also married in 1910. Mae attended business school and worked as a secretary in Knoxville. On November 19, 1910, she was married to Luther Clay. They lived in Shull's Mills, Montezuma, and Boone, North Carolina, the part of the mountains the Hicks family had come from when her mother was a child. Mae died in April 1928 while their five daughters, Maud, Lalla Mae, R.L. (Bobbie), Betty, and Margaret, were still young. Nola Jane spent the summer helping the children get adjusted.

In 1913 Mrs. Woodrow Wilson had the Blue Mountain Room in the White House decorated with handwoven bedspreads, draperies, and rugs, all woven by women who lived in the Appalachian Mountains. This came about because Frances Goodrich had engaged the women of Laurel in weaving as an industry. Crooked-seam coverlets had become straight-seam coverlets because they were more marketable. The saying was, "A crooked seam throws the devil off your track." Most women had looms that made it very difficult to weave two perfectly matched panels. When the coverlets were washed, they were taken apart and sewn back together with the seams on the opposite side and end to end to decrease wear. Some of Mrs. Gentry's coverlets have straight seams and some have crooked seams.

Frances Goodrich was pleased with twenty ends per inch for coverlets. Jane Gentry's have thirty-two ends per inch. We know that Elmeda Walker wove the fabric for the furniture covering and Josephine Mast wove the overshot rug, but no record of the other weavers has been found.[2] Jeannette Armstrong, Emily's daughter, was told that her grandmother had a part in weaving the draperies, but this has not been verified.[3] Mrs. Gentry did use some of the same patterns that were sold in the Allanstand shop—Whig Rose, Chariot Wheel, and Zion Rose.

During these busy years Irving Bacheller came and wrote down Jane's stories, and in the summer of 1914 she went to New York. Maud, who was teaching in Raleigh, came home to run the boardinghouse. Jane's trip did not make the newspapers. It was an exciting interval in her life, but she was glad to get back to her children and her boarders.

Lalla, the next to youngest daughter, was described as beautiful, happy, and carefree, interested in everything and everybody. One summer Lalla came home and brought with her a white parasol trimmed with lace. The students at the school next door thought she looked pretty and envied the white parasol. But when she walked down the street, the teachers commented that she would not be "showing off" if Maud were at home.[4] Lalla was named by a Campbellite preacher who was at the Gentry home when she was born. He later baptized her and performed the wedding ceremony when she was married on October 3, 1914, to Charles Hemphill, a Presbyterian minister's son.[5] Charles's father was an instructor at the Presbyterian Seminary in Louisville, Kentucky, and Charles worked for the YMCA. They were later divorced, and Lalla married L. Frazier Bailey, who had done missionary work in South America. Lalla's children were all given Gentry as a middle name—Frazier, Victor, Tinha, Vona, and Guinevere. She lived her later years with her daughter Tinah Anderson in Atlanta.

On November 26, 1916, Roy, the youngest son, married Josephine Braswell, and for a few years they lived in Hot Springs, where he worked as a policeman. Later they moved to West Virginia, where he worked in the mines and became night superintendent of a mine. Their last move with their eight children was to East Canton, Ohio. Roy was the prankster of the family, but his children spoke of him as one of the "kindest, finest Christian men who walked the face of the earth." While he was working in Hot Springs he was threatened by a local man. Uncle Doc, who had moved to Marion, heard about it and came back to help take care of the situation. According to Nola Jane, they all shook hands and settled on friendly terms.

World War I, "the war to end all wars," broke out. There were wheatless days and meatless days. The women knitted socks and sweaters for servicemen. During the war years, the Germans came to Hot Springs. Cecil Sharp came and wrote down Jane's songs, and life went on with the same philosophy the Gentrys had always lived by—"While you're resting go chop some wood." In 1918 Jane lost her first child, when Maggie died in Texas. She was only thirty-two years old. Isabel Gordon Carter came and wrote down the Jack tales and the riddles. This collection that was to be highly interesting to many people later on went almost unnoticed. And Jane went right on cooking meals for the boarders. Nola Jane, the youngest, the "spunky" one, graduated from Dorland-Bell in 1918, the year Dorland Institute merged with Bell Institute at Walnut. She went on to graduate from Asheville Normal School and then worked her way through Duke University waiting tables. She earned two degrees, both A.B. and B.S. "Monk," as she was called, was known in her college days for her store of songs and ballads, some of which she sang to the accompaniment of a ukulele. "Individuality" was the word used to describe her. She graduated in 1927 and taught school for sixteen years in North Carolina. In 1930 Nola Jane and Lawton J. (Jack) Blackwell were married. They lived in a cabin on Snowbird Mountain and taught at Robbinsville, where he was principal. She swapped with the Cherokee children—meal and flour for berries. Then the Blackwells went to Alaska to teach in remote Athabaskan Indian villages in the Yukon. Jack was an avid fisherman, and he would often fish for an hour before school in the mornings and leave the catch with a needy family. In 1957 Jack was stricken with a heart attack and died. Both Nola Jane and Jack were much loved by the native people. Twenty years later, when a new school was built it was named the Lawton J. Blackwell Elementary and High School. Nola Jane came back to Hot Springs for a short time, but she was too well entrenched in Alaska. She returned and married W.H. (Bill) Yrjana. In June 1969 Nola Jane retired from teaching and enrolled at the University of Alaska, Fairbanks, in business administration so that she could help Bill with the bookkeeping in his coal business. Her last days were spent in the Pioneer Home in Fairbanks, where some of the Indians she had taught periodically made the trip up the frozen Yukon to check on her.

Maud was the daughter who stayed home the longest. She graduated from Asheville Normal School and did graduate work at the University of North Carolina, Chapel Hill. Maud was an outstanding teacher at Dorland-Bell School and public schools in Hot Springs and Greeneville, Tennessee, as well as a piano teacher for many Madison County youngsters. She was ordained to the office of ruling elder in the Dorland Memorial Presbyterian Church in 1931, one of the first women to hold this office. She married Grover Cleveland Long, a railroad employee, on June 10, 1922. They had one daughter, Jane Douglas, who teaches music in Athens, Georgia.

During all of the comings and goings of this large family, Jane Gentry and Maud continued to run the boardinghouse. They shared mountain food, songs, and tales with hundreds of students, boarders, and travelers who passed through Hot Springs. Among the boarders were Dorland-Bell teachers. In Mrs. Gentry's day, Sunnybank's dining room featured an extremely long table where food was served family style. Jane and Maud were known far and wide for their excellent cooking, and the table was filled to overflowing with fresh vegetables and fruits, home-cured meats, fresh baked bread, pies and cakes, and homemade preserves and jellies. The following recipe comes from Jane's cookbook, courtesy of Jane Douglas.

*Scalloped Apples and Cheese*

| | |
|---|---|
| 6 to 8 day-old biscuits | 4 to 5 apples, pared and sliced |
| 2 cups grated American cheese | Salt |
| Milk | 2 to 3 tablespoons butter |

Line a greased baking dish with biscuit halves. Place a layer of thinly sliced apples on the biscuits. Cover with cheese and sprinkle with salt. Repeat layers until all apples and cheese are used. Cover with milk. Put remaining biscuits with butter on top. Bake in moderate oven for 30 minutes (or until apples are soft). Serve hot as a main supper or lunch dish.

Jane's grandson James Gentry, though he was very young, remembers the wonderful aroma of her bread baking. He could smell it before he got in the house. She grew her own hops. Sunnybank had an unusual water supply system for the time. A windmill pumped water from a spring into a tank in the attic.

After the evening meal Jane and Maud often sang ballads and told tales. These evening sessions were rare experiences for the guests, warm and delightful, for there was great love and respect between these two marvelous singers and storytellers. Long after Jane's death, Maud continued to take in guests. She kept registers from the 1940s until she left Sunnybank in 1972. The comments clearly indicated that Sunnybank was no ordinary boardinghouse.

I have had a most enjoyable stay in your home. The night you sang folk songs I shall long remember.

You all don't know southern cooking until you have stopped here. The best food in our 700 miles.

We came hungry and disgusted with southern cooking. We stayed to eat and left reluctantly. Southern cooking is swell.

Thanks so much for a lovely breakfast and your beautiful garden was worth the hard mountain driving.

In five thousand miles and fifteen states this is the best meal I have eaten.

Guests came from every part of the United States and some from other countries. They were always met with easy hospitality.[6] Jane and Maud shared a love for flowers. Newt grew good vegetable gardens, but there always had to be flowers blooming in the summertime—dahlias, sunflowers, lilies.

Correspondence kept together the family members who had scattered as far as the West Coast. It was Maud who did the letter writing. On Whidbey Island Emily took time to walk Jeannette to school. Jeannette looked fragile, and a neighbor had assured Emily she would "never raise that child." This fear seemed to haunt her until Jeannette was grown. Emily had another ESP experience. Again it came in the form of a dream. She was walking Jeannette to school when she saw beside the road a tired, exhausted blue bird. She picked it up, and fastened beneath a wing was a note that read, "Father's dead." For nearly a month Emily mentioned the dream from time to time. She thought perhaps she should write and tell her parents to be extra careful. One day Jeannette came home from school with a headache and was put to bed. She awoke several hours later to the sound of Emily sobbing. She had received a letter. It bore a blue special delivery stamp, the same blue as the blue bird that had brought the message in her dream. It was a letter from Maud telling her that her father had suffered a stroke on March 18, 1922. About a week later, another letter came, and she held it for a long time before opening it. Her father had died on March 24. He was buried in the Oddfellows Cemetery just south of town. Emily had always felt very close to Newt. As the second child, she had "tagged along" behind him everywhere, planting and cultivating.[7]

When Newt died, Eugenia Elliott was in Maud Long's sixth grade class. She never forgot that Ellie Pollock, a teacher at Dorland, sent all of the sixth grade girls out to pick violets for a funeral arrangement. Nola Jane was in her last year in Asheville Normal School. It was hard after her father died. "We were lonely," she said. It happened so suddenly. He had a stroke while he was working in the barn. Typically, Jane said that everybody would have to help. Nola Jane asked what she could do, and typically, Jane said that she could bring in some stovewood. They did pull together, and that summer Maud and Grover were married in a simple ceremony at Sunnybank. With Grover's railway pass the newlyweds took a trip to the West Coast to visit Emily, stopping along the way to visit Nora. They returned to Greeneville, Tennessee, Grover's home, and Maud taught school. What Nola Jane called "Maud's most distinguished work" was with a group of neglected, troublesome boys in Greeneville in a program funded by the Rotary Club. She found their strong points and brought them out. Like Jane, she did what seemed the practical thing to do and it worked.

Jane Gentry's life with her great talent for living, and her rich store of oral literature came to an end the hot summer of 1925, the summer it did not rain at all. They tried putting reservoirs in different places around Hot Springs. People went up to Silvermine to wash clothes. Gardens dried up. Creeks dried up. You could walk across the French Broad River almost anywhere. Maud had been staying with her mother, but she had to go to Greeneville overnight to take care of some business. Maud Clay, her "Dixie Dan," was there. Lily, a young girl from up in the mountains, was helping with the housework. Lily and Maud had spent two or three days cleaning up the old servants' quarters off the back porch. They tried to sleep there and were "eaten up" by bedbugs. Mrs. Gentry had them take out the junk, clean the room, and "kerosene" the bed. "Grandma told us we could move into the room and we were sleeping in there for the first time. I had been in Aunt Maud's old room next to Grandma, but that night she came across the kitchen on to the back porch up a couple of steps into the room where we were. She woke us and said for one of us to run next door to Rufty's and get help. She was sick."[8]

Mrs. Gentry had had a heart condition for several years. Dr. Edward Peck was her doctor, "Dear old Dr. Peck," who never seemed to look where he was going, striding up the road with his coattails blowing in the breeze, Dr. Peck, who once rode an ox to get to a sick child, who would sit with his patients all night. He took care of the Dorland Bell students and prescribed hot mustard foot soaks to ward off pneumonia. He never seemed to take his doctor's bag off his arm.[9] But there was nothing he could do for Jane. The death certificate called it "rheumatism of the heart." She was sixty-two years old—sixty-two years of living life as though every day were her last.

Dorland-Bell students sang at her funeral. Nola Jane said they sang her favorite hymn, "How Beautiful Heaven Must Be." Eugenia Elliott sang in the choir and remembered singing, at Mrs. Gentry's request, "Will There Be Any Stars in My Crown?" The casket was placed on a wagon, and the mourners walked behind it to the Oddfellows Cemetery south of town. It was a hot, exhausting walk. Jane was buried beside Newt.

How beautiful Heaven must be,
How beautiful Heaven must be,
Fair haven of rest for the weary,
How beautiful Heaven must be.

After Jane's death the Board of National Missions of the Presbyterian Church published a brochure in her honor. It contained the Irving Bacheller article "The Happiest Person I Ever Knew," preceded by this tribute:

A number of years ago the principal of Dorland-Bell School, Hot Springs, North Carolina, visited the Gentry home, at that time twenty miles up Spring Creek, "away back in the sticks," as Mrs. Gentry expressed it. As a result of that visit the eldest daughter became a pupil in the school and one by one the other eight children followed, the Gentrys moving to Hot Springs in order that their boys and girls might have the advantages the school offered. Mrs. Gentry's buoyant faith and happy personality, as pictured by Mr. Bacheller, have always been an inspiration to the Board's missionaries.[10]

Jane Gentry died on May 29, 1925. On June 7 her picture appeared in the *Asheville Citizen*, a photograph that had been taken in a Fletcher, North Carolina, church when she had told mountain stories at the Western North Carolina Mountain Service. No mention was made of her death. The picture was labeled "Happiest Person."

Years later one of Mae's daughters, Bobbie Shuping, with her husband, Roy, and two-year-old son, Clay, came to visit Aunt Maud. Aunt Maud prepared a good meal, and after supper they set up a portable crib in an upstairs bedroom and everybody retired for the night. Bobbie Shuping recalled what happened that night:

Sometime that night, I can't tell you what hour, someone came into the room from the room next to us, walked by the baby's crib . . . checked the baby. The person, silhouetted in the light, walked back by the baby's crib and walked out.

At that time there was nobody in the house but us and Aunt Maud, and Aunt Nola, and they were downstairs. We thought maybe someone had come in for a room in the night and lost their way.

In the morning I told Aunt Maud about it. I said, "Someone came in our room during the night." And she said, "Oh, yes, dear, I understand. That was Grandma Gentry. She always comes and checks the babies who stay in this house."[11]

Wherever Jane is, we can be sure she is looking after the babies, telling them stories, singing them to sleep. Her life epitomized the words Thomas Jefferson wrote to Mrs. A.S. Marks in 1788: "It is neither wealth nor splendor, but tranquility and occupation, which give happiness."

# Chapter 12

# Epilogue

The times they are a-changing.

—Bob Dylan

During Jane Gentry's lifetime there was a great deal of activity in the fields of folklore and collecting. Folklore societies had been formed in Missouri, Virginia, West Virginia, and North Carolina. In the 1920s regional collecting and publishing were going on in New England (Phillips Barry), Kentucky (Josiah Combs, Hubert Shearin, Josephine McGill, Loraine Wyman, Howard Brockway), South Carolina (Reed Smith), Virginia (C. Alphonso Smith, Arthur Kyle Davis), West Virginia (John Harrington Cox), Missouri (H.M. Belden), North Carolina (Bascom Lamar Lunsford, Frank C. Brown), and in other states as far-flung as Nebraska (Louise Pound) and Texas (John Lomax, J. Frank Dobie). In 1928 the Library of Congress Archive of Folk Song was established.

In October 1925, about six months after Jane Gentry died, Robert Winslow Gordon arrived in Asheville to begin his fieldwork in the southern mountains. Bascom Lamar Lunsford was collecting and recording, and within three years of Mrs. Gentry's death the Asheville Dance and Folk Festival drew attention to the ballad singers, fiddlers, and string bands in the mountains. Many of these musicians were from Madison County. Frank C. Brown of Duke University and others were collecting throughout the state of North Carolina. This work resulted in the finest state collection of folklore to date—*The Frank C. Brown Collection of North Carolina Folklore*, seven volumes of ballads, songs, riddles, and remedies. It seems a glaring omission that neither Jane Gentry nor any of the other singers from Madison County, with one exception, are represented in the Brown collection. The explanation may be that the Sharp-Campbell collection had already been published, and with such a wealth of contributors from all parts of the state, there was no wish to duplicate materials. The real question remains, however. Did North Carolina collectors miss Mary Sands, Mrs. Tom Rice, the Hensleys, Jane Gentry, and Maud Long?

Bertrand Bronson in his collection *The Traditional Tunes of the Child Ballads*, published in 1959, included twenty-two of Jane Gentry's ballads and four of Maud Long's. Jane's "Old Gally Mander" was published in *A Harvest of World Folk Tales* (Viking Press, 1949) with credit given only to Isabel Gordon Carter.

MacEdward Leach included Jane's "Fair Annie" in *The Ballad Book*, credited only to Sharp.

The music was not only being put into collections, it was on its way into mainstream music. Traditional ballads and songs such as Jane Gentry sang were performed and recorded and became a part of the first country music heard on radio and recordings. In 1922 WSB, the first powerful radio station in the South, went on the air and featured folk performers. Ralph Peer came south to find and record folk musicians for Okeh Records.[1]

Would Jane Gentry have left her home to travel around singing before audiences and recording her music if she had had an opportunity to do so, as the Carter family did? A.P., Sara, and Maybelle Carter, too, came from a remote mountain area. They were auditioning for Brunswick Records the year Jane died. Times were changing. A.P. Carter wanted to get into the music business. The Carters were pioneers of a sort, opening the way for other country musicians. Jane did not join with other musicians to entertain groups of people. She did sing for the guests in her home, for the Ballad Society, and for the schoolchildren, but she was sharing music that was dear to her. Jane and Maud sang songs and told stories for the guests at Sunnybank, but we do not know of them joining with other musicians. The Carters played instruments very well. Jane did not play instruments. The Carters, Jimmy Rogers, Uncle Dave Macon, and Bradley Kincaid all were "going public" with their music. The world of commercial music was growing and expanding to include traditional music, but it never reached her.

When Mrs. Gentry died, Nola Jane was a student at Duke University. This was the year that Trinity College changed its name to Duke University after James B. Duke, the tobacco magnate, gave the school $40 million. Nola Jane gained a reputation as a folksinger who was carrying on the traditions of her family. She was the subject of a newspaper article headlined "Miss Gentry Collecting Folk Songs of Mountains Just Like Her Mother." She gave private concerts for her friends and small recitals in which she talked about the songs and about her mother's song tradition. In some of her programs Nola Jane was joined by Mary Kestler (Clyde), who was her roommate at Asheville Normal School and at Duke, and by Bessie Copeland (McCastlain). Nola Jane and Mary sang and Bessie strummed chords on guitar. Their most memorable performance was one given at the Washington Duke Hotel in Durham.[2] After graduation, however, Nola Jane did not continue as a performer but put all her energy into teaching—making use of the songs and stories in her classroom.

It was Maud who became known as a performer of both songs and Jack tales. She recorded some materials for Annabel Morris Buchanan and Richard Chase in 1936. Buchanan was associated with the White Top Festival in Virginia. Maud told Chase some of her mother's tales, which he included in his collection *The Jack Tales*. In 1944 she recorded some of her mother's songs for Artus Moser, ballad singer, folklorist, and principal of Hot Springs School. He did the recording in Hot Springs on equipment made available to him by the Library of Congress. The recordings were done on aluminum disks coated with acetate and the disks were actually cut.[3] This was the equipment used in radio recording at that time.

A larger recording project of tales, riddles, songs, and ballads was done in Washington for the Library of Congress. In 1947 Maud received a letter from Caroline Pond, a former Dorland-Bell teacher, who had retired to Washington,

D.C., with her sister. The two elderly ladies had no living relatives, and Maud realized that Pond was losing her eyesight and that she and her sister had become incapable of taking care of themselves. Maud was teaching in the public school at the time, and her daughter Jane was in college. Her husband had died the year before. Like her mother, Maud had a history of helping her friends and neighbors. Her nephew Pat Gentry and his wife, Queen, came to live in Sunnybank, and Maud left for Washington. She lived with the Pond sisters and took care of them until they died. One day a week a maid came in and the two sisters said, "Maudie, you go see Washington." She spent many of those days recording at the Library of Congress.[4]

Although she played piano and organ well and taught other people to play, Maud sang the songs unaccompanied as she had heard her mother sing them. Her fee for one and one-half twelve-inch sides was $22.50 and a copy of the records. The songs used were "The Cherry Tree Carol" and "Fiddle-I-Fee." For $35.00 she gave the Library of Congress permission to make and sell recordings of "The False Knight in the Road," "My Sweet William," "Jackie's Gone A-Sailing," "My Grandmother Green," and "The Broken Token." This was in 1947. By 1955 the library had received a grant to issue long-playing records, and she was paid $300.00 for permission to make and sell two albums of Jack tales. The recording of the Jack tales was Maud's idea. She had suggested this to Artus Moser, and it was also her idea to include the "Introduction to the Jack Tales," which explained when and where the tales were told. It was clear that she knew the value of these oral materials and was able to articulate this better than anyone else could have. It must have pleased her to be told that this project would be a scholarly presentation for use in schools, colleges, and libraries.[5] For all of this recording and use of the songs and tales she received less than $400.00. She had been told in the beginning that it was not the practice of the library to pay singers for songs considered to be in the public domain. This was before the songs and tales were used on commercial albums.

Duncan Emrich was chief of the Folklore Section when Maud began recording for the library. At the end of 1955 Emrich left to become cultural affairs officer in Greece, and Rae Korson, who had been the reference librarian, took his place as head of the Archive of Folk Song. In typical Gentry fashion, Maud became friends with Rae Korson, comparing notes on grandchildren in their letters. In 1957 Korson planned a long-playing record for children. It was to be called "A North Carolina Childhood: Songs, Games, and Riddles" recorded by Maud Long. Maud was delighted with this project, and in June 1957 she was paid $75.00 for the duplication of recordings of "Tree in the Wood," "Froggie Went A-Courtin,'" "Paper of Pins," "Soldier, Soldier, Won't You Marry Me?," "The Old Gray Horse," "Jenny Jenkins," "Over in the Meadow," "One Little Indian," "Indian Count," and "Travel Game," as well as the riddles she had recorded.[6] Apparently this recording was never done.

Maud Long is listed in *Folksingers and Folksongs in America*, compiled by Ray Lawless. B.A. Botkin included Maud's "Jack and the Calf Hide" as told to Artus Moser in 1941 in *The Treasury of Southern Folklore*. "Jack and the Giant's New Ground" as told by Maud Long is contained in *Folklore on the American Land* by Duncan Emrich. Emrich also used Long's "False Knight Upon the Road" from the Library of Congress recording in *American Folk Poetry* (Little, Brown,

1974). W.K. McNeil included Maud's "False Knight Upon the Road" as collected by Buchanan and Chase in *Southern Folk Ballads*, volume 2 (Little Rock: August House, 1988).

For the most part, Maud treated the ballads and songs and tales much as her mother had. She traveled more and sang in places her mother never did, but she was always aware of her heritage. She knew the importance of the songs and tales. She was a mainstay of the community and of the church. She served as a ruling elder in the Presbyterian Church, taught Sunday school and held almost every office in the church and many in the presbytery. In March 1963 she was named "Woman of the Week" by the *Asheville Citizen* and recognized for the years she had spent teaching piano to mountain children and for her determination to see that as many children as possible had music in their lives.[7]

Maud carried the legacy to the very end. She lived in Sunnybank until 1972, when she left to be near her daughter in Athens, Georgia. She took her old-timey organ with her, and her second-floor neighbors at Lanier Gardens would gather to hear her play and sing hymns, often joining in. She never forgot the tunes or the words. She died in October 1983.

In September 1990 I flew to Fairbanks, Alaska. Nola Jane had moved to a nursing home maintained by the state of Alaska for its "pioneers." I checked into a motel and walked over to visit her every day for about a week. I had heard that she was like her mother, and after corresponding with her for several years I felt compelled to meet her. She was bright and cheerful, but she seemed tired and had not completely adjusted to this enormous change in her lifestyle. I was asked to give a program for the residents of the home, and Nola Jane and I talked about what I should do. She said she was not sure the people would like "those old songs." The librarian from the public library gave me a ride that night. She was excited to hear that Nola Jane was the great- granddaughter of Council Harmon. She was a storyteller who knew about the Hickses and the Harmons. I did sing the old songs and I talked about Jane and told some stories. Nola Jane said the residents came into her room at all hours telling her they hadn't heard those songs in sixty years or so. She was pleased. Her niece Jane Douglas and the staff thought that the deep conversations about her family and the recognition from those around her gave her the strength she needed to cope with her new surroundings.

On August 21, 1993, Nola Jane died peacefully in her sleep at the Pioneer Home. She would have been ninety years old in October. She looked frail and "elfin," but she was spunky and a fighter, gentle and fun-loving to the last. She had sung the songs and told the tales to several generations of schoolchildren. The youngest of the nine Gentry children, she was the last to go. But this will not be the end of the songs or the stories.

Daron Douglas, Maud's granddaughter, a classically trained musician, has turned to the music she heard her grandmother sing. She sings the old ballads, plays mountain dulcimer as well as fiddle, and weaves on her grandmother's loom. There are other grandchildren and great-grandchildren who tell the family stories and the Jack tales. Betty and Lalla Rolfe, Mae's daughters, have been interested in keeping the tales alive. Before Betty's death in 1995, Lalla was taping Betty telling the Jack tales. Phyllis Davies, Jeannette's daughter and Emily's granddaughter, lost her teenage son, Derek, in a plane crash. Her book *Grief: Climb toward Understanding* (Secaucus, N.J.: P.D. Lyle Stuart, 1988) was written to help others deal with grief. In her own way she is reaching out to help her neighbors as did her great-grandmother Jane. Eugene Hicks, Uncle Doc's grandson, bought the hotel and springs property and retired to Hot Springs. He reopened the springs and developed a campground. He has never forgotten where his people came from, and his venture has added a spark of life to the town of Hot Springs.

We will never know who may be singing a song or telling a story or lending a hand because Jane Gentry went around singing and telling stories and "takin' the blues off" wherever she happened to be.

Part II

# Jane Hicks Gentry's Jack Tales

# The Jack Tales

The tales published here were collected in the summer of 1923 by Isabel Gordon Carter and published in her "Mountain White Folk-Lore: Tales from the Southern Blue Ridge" (*Journal of American Folklore* 35 [July-September 1925]). In her notes on the tales, Carter refers to Johannes Bolte and Georg Polivka's *Anmerkungen zu den kinder- und Hausmarchen der bruder Grimm*, 5 vols. (Berlin, 1913-32), a commentary on the classic Grimm tales. Carter's references are noted at the end of each tale.

Folk tales have been classified into recurring types, which transcend political and ethnic boundaries. The types indicated in the notes here are from Stith Thompson, *The Folktale* (New York: Holt, Rinehart, and Winston, 1946). Thompson, a professor of folklore and English at Indiana University, enlarged on Antti Aarne's earlier tale-type index, so this is referred to as the Aarne-Thompson Type-Index; it is an important key to the study of tales.

Gentry called these stories "old Jack, Will, and Tom tales." Other members of this extended family have told these tales as well; when known, that information is noted. Jane's daughter Maud Long recorded some of her mother's stories for Duncan Emrich of the Archive of American Folk Song at the Library of Congress in 1947. All of the eleven tales she chose to tell were about Jack, Will, and Tom. Some of Long's tales are available on Library of Congress recordings. Mother and daughter did not always give the same name to a story. The following are stories told by both Gentry and Long:

| Jane Gentry | Maud Long |
|---|---|
| "Jack and Old Bluebeard" | "Jack and the Fire Dragaman" |
| "Lazy Jack and His Calf Skin" | "Jack and the Heifer Hide" |
| "Hardy Hardback" | "Hardy Hard Back, or Sail, Ship, Sail" |
| "The Enchanted Lady" | "Jack and the Drill" |
| "Jack the Giant Killer" | "Jack and the Giant's New Ground" |
| "Sop, Doll, Sop" | "Jack and the Sop Dog [Doll?]" |
| "Old Stiff Dick" | "Jack and the Varmints" |
| "Jack and the Northwest Wind" | "Jack and the Northwest Wind" |

Jane Gentry told the following stories which Long did not tell: "Jack and the Fox"; "Whiteberry Whittington"; "Old Foster"; "Old Catkins"; "Jack and the Beanstalk"; "Little Dicky Wigbun"; and "Old Gally Mander."

Maud Long seems to have been partial to tales about Jack. Her stories are generally lengthy and detailed. Long told the following stories that Gentry did not tell: "Jack and the Doctor's Daughter"; "Jack and His Hunting Trip"; and "Jack and the Bull." It is probable that Jane knew these stories, because Maud stated that she was recording her mother's stories. Perhaps each was telling her favorites.

## Old Stiff Dick

They uz a little old boy long time ago, didn't have no mammy or poppy, jest growed up in the hog weeds, and he didn't even know his name, but everybody called him Jack. And he jest stayed here and yonder, wherever he could drop in at night. So one day he was a walkin' the road and he had him a belt around his waist and he had him a little old knife and he was a whitlin' and makin' him a paddle. So he come along past a mud hole and there was a lot of little old blue butterflies over hit. So he struck down with his paddle and he killed seven of the butterflies. So he goes on a little piece further and he comes to a blacksmith shop, and he gets the blacksmith to cut letters in his belt, "Stiff Dick killed seven at a lick." So he goes on a piece further and he passes the king's house. King runs out and says, "I see you're a very brave man; I see where you've killed seven at a lick."—"Yes, bedads, I'm a mighty brave man." So the king says, "Stranger, I want to hire a brave man to kill some animals we have here in the woods. We have a wild municorn here killin' so many people, soon we'll all be kilt. If you'll kill that municorn, we'll pay you one thousand dollars, five hundred down, and five hundred when you bring the municorn in." So Dick says, "All right." So the king paid him five hundred dollars. Stiff Dick stuck that in his pocket and said to hisself, "Bedads, if they ever see me around here again." And he tuk out. When he got way up in the mountains the municorn smelled him and here it come,

> Whippity cut,
> Whippity cut,
> Whippity, cut.

Stiff Dick tuk to runnin' and the municorn after him. The municorn was jest clippin' Stiff Dick. They run up the mountains and down the ridges. So long late in the evening they started down a long ridge, the municorn jest a runnin' after Stiff Dick. And away down at the end of the ridge Stiff Dick saw a big oak and he made a beeline to see if he cud clumb hit. So the municorn was jest a gettin' so close that agin they got there the municorn was jest behin' him. Jack jest slipped around the oak right quick and the municorn stove his horn into hit and he just rared and plunged. As soon as Stiff Dick saw he was fastened for all time to come, he went on to the king's house. King says, "Did you get the municorn?" Dick says, "Municorn? Laws a massy, never was nothin' but a little old bull calf come tearin' out there after me. I jest picked it up by one ear and tail and stove it agin a tree and if you all wanst hit, you'll have to go up thar and git hit." So the king got him a great army and went up and killed the municorn, come back and paid Jack five hundred dollars more, King says, "Now, Stiff Dick, there's one more wild animal living up here, a wild boar. I'll give five hundred dollars now and five hundred more when you ketch hit." Jack tuk the five hundred dollars and says to hisself, "You'll never see me anymore." But after he'd gone a little ways here come the wild boar after him,

Whippity cut,
Whippity, cut,
Whippity cut.

All day long around the mountains, across the mountains and down the ridges, all the day just a runnin'. So along late in the evenin' away down in the holler he saw an old house and when he got down there the door was open. So he run right in the door and up the wall and the wild boar run right after him and laid down under him. Boar was tired and soon fell asleep. So Dick eased up the wall and over and down the outside and shut the wild boar up in there. So he went down to the king's house. King says, "Did ye git the wild boar?" Stiff Dick says, "Wild boar? Laws a massy, I never saw nothing but a little old boar pig come bristlin' up after me. I jest picked hit up by the tail and throwed hit in an old waste house. And if you all wanst hit, you'll have to go up thar and git hit." So king got up an army of men and went up and killed the wild boar and went back down and paid Stiff Dick his other five hundred dollars. King says, "Now, Stiff Dick, there's one more wild animal we want to git killed. That's a big brown bear." So he give Dick another five hundred dollars. Stiff Dick says to hisself, "If I can jest get out of here no brown bear ul never see me." So he got way up on the mountain; old brown bear smelled him and here he come,

Whippity cut,
Whippity cut,
Whippity cut.

Across the hills, up the ridges, every way to dodge the bear. The bear uz right after him. So late in the evenin,' way down at the end of a ridge he saw an old pine tree that had been all burned over and was right black. Jack made a beeline fur that tree. The bear was jest a little ways behind when Jack run up the tree. Bear was down at the root of the tree and he was so mad he tried to gnaw the tree down. Hit gnawed and gnawed. Jack keep a easin' down on another old snag and another old snag and directly he got on a snag jest above that old bear and the old snag broke and Jack fell just a straddle the old bear and they jest burnt the wind. Stiff Dick was so tickled and so scared, too, that he was jest a hollerin' and screamin' and directly he run the bear right thru the town and the soldier boys heared him a screamin' and they run out and shot hit. Stiff Dick got off it when it fell, and he was jest a swearin' and a rarin'. He was swearin' he was breakin' hit for the king a riddy [ridey?] horse and he got mad and made the soldier boys pay Dick five hundred dollars. And when I left there Stiff Dick was rich.

*"Jack and the Varmints" as told by Maud Long; "The Lion and the Unicorn" as told by R.M. Ward. Type 1640, The Brave Tailor. Bolte & Polivka XX (1:148-65).*

# Hardy Hardback

A man, an old king, he got so rich that he put out an oration that anyone that could do more than his old witch or could find anyone who could do more might have his youngest daughter and half his kingdom. So they was an old poor man and he had three sons, Jack, Will and Tom. And they decided that they'd try for a fortune. So Will he told his mother he was going over to the king's house to see if he could break the enchantment of the lady. He had to walk way long ways. His mother cooked him up a haversack full of rations. So Will started out but if he couldn't do as much as the old king's witch could, the king would kill him, cut his head off and set it up on a pole. So when he got over to the king's house he hollered, "Hello," and the king come out and said, "What'll you have?" He said, "I come over to see if I could break the enchantment of the lady." King says, "Now if ye can't do as much as my witch, I'll kill ye and cut your head off and set hit up on a pole." "I know hit," says Will. King says, "Do you think ye can hit the iron hackle as hard as my witch can?"—"Yes, bedads, I think I can." King says, "Come, old witch," and she popped her back against that hackle and popped like a rubber ball and danced all over the floor. Will he come in and pounced agin that hackle and stove hit through his body and hit killed him and the king cut his head off and set hit up on a pole.

So then Tom decided he wanted to go. His mother said, "Oh, Tom, don't go. Will was killed." "Well, bedads I'm going anyway," says Tom. So Tom, he starts out and meets the same little old dried up man that Will met, so he said, "Good morning, Tom." Tom says, "Good morning." He said, "Where ye started?" Tom says, "None of yer business." So Tom had his haversack of rations and he tramped a long ways over to the king's house and he says, "Hello," and the king come out and says, "What'll ye have?" Tom says, "I come over to see if I could break the enchantment of the lady." "Well, if ye don't, I'll kill ye," says the king. "Ye know that, don't ye?" "Yes I know hit," says Tom. "Come in," says the king. "Can ye hit that iron hackle with your back as hard as my old witch can, or can ye find anyone who can?"—"Yes, bedads, I think I can." so the old witch come in, hit agin the iron hackle, bounced off like a rubber ball and danced all over the floor. Tom he come in, stove his back against the hackle and hit stove into his back and killed him. King cut his head off, put hit up on the pole. By that time he was a gettin' a pretty long pole full of heads.

So Jack decided he wanted to go and he got to beggin' his mother to cook up a haversack full of rations. Mother said, "Jack, you're all we've got." Jack said he was a goin' anyway. But his mother wouldn't cook up a haversack full of rations so he jest tuk some old dried bread un started out. When Jack got out he met the same little dried up man. He says, "Good morning, Jack." Jack says, "Good morning, father—good morning, uncle, ain't ye goin' to have some breakfast with me?"—"Where ye started, Jack?"—"Well, uncle, I've started to try to make a ship sail on dry land."—"Well, you take my stick, Jack, un go back around the way I've come to a spring. And you stir my stick in that there spring until hit turns to wine and you'll see a new tin bucket and tin cup. Gin ye get back here I'll have yer ship made." So Jack went and stirred in the spring until hit turned to wine and there sat the tin bucket and he filled hit and come back and the little old man had the ship made, and they sat down and eat their bread and drank their wine. He said,

"Now, Jack, you git in this ship and say, 'Sail, ship, sail' and hit'll sail. Now, Jack you take in every man that you see between here and the king's house. Now when you see a man you say, 'Hey! what's your name?' and when he tells you say, 'Come here and git in this ship and say, 'Sail, ship, sail,' and it ul sail right along." So Jack was sailing along and he looked up on the mountains and he saw a man hitting his back against the trees and knockin' 'em every which way. Jack says, "Hey! What's your name?" "Hardy Hardback."—"Hardy Hardback? Hardy hard back I think you are, come un get in here." So they sailed on a little ways and he saw a man out in the pasture jest a eatin' up the sheep and hogs. "Hey! What's your name?" says Jack. "Eat Well."—"Eat Well? Eat well I think you are, come and get in here." Went on a little ways and he saw a man up the holler jest drinking up the little springs and branches. Says, "What's your name?"—"Drink Well."—"Drink Well? Drink well I think you are, get in here." So Drink Well got in and Jack said, "Sail, ship, sail," and it sailed right on. So went a little ways and saw a man running. He'd run a ways on one leg, then take hit up and run a while on tother. Jack says, "Hey! What's your name?"—"Run Well." "Run Well? Run well I think your are. Come git in here." So Run Well got in and they sailed right out. Went a little further saw a man standing with a gun like he was a shootin' a hare in the skies. "Hey! What's your name?" says Jack. "Shoot Well."—"Shoot Well? Shoot well I think you are," says Jack. "Come on git in here." So he got in and Jack said, "Sail, ship, sail," and they sailed right out. Little further saw a man a listenin'. He'd put one hand over one ear, and one over the tother. "Hey! What's your name?" says Jack. "Hark Well." "Hark Well? Hark well I think you are. Come on git in here." So Hark Well got in and Jack says, "Sail, ship, sail," and it sailed right out. So they sailed on a little ways 'til they got to the king's house. Jack hollered, "Hello," and the king come out and says, "What ul ye have?" Jack says, "I come over to see if I could break the enchantment of the lady."- "Well, if you don't, I'll kill ye." "Yes, I know hit," says Jack. Said, "Do you think you can hit the iron hackle as hard as my old witch can or can ye find anyone who can?"—"Yes, bedads, I think I can." So the king called his old witch and she stabbed her back agin the iron hackle and bounced off like a rubber ball and danced all over the room. "Hardy Hardback, come in here," says Jack. Hardy Hardback come in and struck that iron hackle and stove hit through the wall, jumped off on the floor and danced all over. King says, "Well, now do you think you can eat as much as my old witch can, or can ye find anyone who can?"—"Yes, I think I can. Come in here, Eat Well." So Eat Well come in and they assigned each a horse apiece. Eat Well jumped out and eat up his horse, and a cow or two, and a couple of sheep, and some pigs, and the old witch didn't have one horse eat up. So they called 'em in. Said, "Well, now do you think you can drink as much as my old witch can, or can ye find anyone who can?" "Yes, I think I can," says Jack. "Drink Well, come in here." So they assigned them a creek apiece and Drink Well jumped in and drank his up, and a spring or two, and was drinking the river up when they called 'em in. "Well, now," says the king, "can you find a man that can run as fast as my old witch can?" "Yes, I think I can. Run Well, come in here." So they give 'em an egg shell apiece and started 'em to the ocean after an egg shell full of water. So Run Well run on to the ocean, got his water and come on back and met the old witch half way. She said, "I'm tired." He said, "I'm tired, too." She says, "Let's sit down and rest and not run ourselves to death for other people."

So they went up above the road a few steps to a nice grassy place and sat down and rested. She says, "Lay yer head over here and rest." She had an old jaw bone in her pocket and if she could git anybody to sleep and put that under their head they wouldn't wake up until that was knocked out. So Run Well being tired, she waited 'til he uz asleep and put that jaw bone under his head. She poured his egg shell out and started on to the ocean. Jack began to get uneasy and said, "Hark Well, hark well and see where Run Well's at."- "Jack, he's layin' asleep half way between here and the ocean with a jaw bone under his head, and he'll never wake 'til that's knocked out." "Shoot Well, shoot well and shoot hit out," says Jack. So Shoot Well shot and knocked hit out. Run Well jumped up and picked up his egg shell and started to the ocean. When he was comin' back he ketched up to the old witch and knocked the old witch, and come on back to the king's house. And they was married 'fore the old witch got there and when I left they was rich.

*Mrs. Gentry omitted Will's encounter with the old man as well as the fact that the lady's enchantment must be broken until Will mentions it. When the person has told the story hundreds of times and the plot is so vivid in the mind of the teller, it is understandable that she might have thought she had already told that part of the story. It is interesting, however, that in spite of these omissions the listener is able to understand the story.*

*Known as "Hardy Hardback" or "Sail, Ship, Sail" by Maud Long. Known as "Hardy Hardhead" by R.M. Ward and Ray Hicks.*

*Type 513 B, The Land and Water Ship. Motif F601ff, "Extraordinary companions who are each endowed with some remarkable power." Bolte & Polivka, LXXI.*

## Old Bluebeard

One time they was an old man and woman had three sons, Jack, Will and Tom. Will was the oldest one, Tom he was next and Jack was the least one. The old woman and the old man died and left Jack, Will and Tom to look after the place. They was workin' away over in the field and each tuk his time goin' to git dinner. Tom [Will] he was the oldest, was first and he tried to see what a good dinner he could git up. He hung the meat up afore the fire to boil and he fixed some turnips and some potatoes and fixed everything nice for his brothers and when hit was ready he went out to blow the horn—they didn't have no dinner bell in them days—and when he blowed the horn down the holler he saw an old man comin' with his beard as blue as indigo, his teeth as long as pipe stems and his thumbs tucked behind. And the man says, "Have ye anything to eat?" Will says, "No," cuz he didn't want the old man to come in and eat up the nice dinner he'd fixed up for his brothers. Old Bluebeard says, "Well, I'll see about hit!" And he went in and eat up everything Will had cooked up. And Will had to fly around and fix up something for his brothers. He fixed up what he could, but he couldn't fix much cuz he didn't have time. Then he went out and blowed down the holler and when his brothers come in they says, "What in the world tuk you so long to fix up such a shabby dinner?" And Will says, "Well, I fixed ye up a good dinner, but when I went out to blow for ye to come in an old man come up the holler with his beard as blue as indigo, his teeth as long as pipe stems and his thumbs tucked behind him and he walked in and ate up everything I'd fixed. So I had to fly around and fix you something else."

Tom says, "Well, I knowed he wouldn't eat it all up if I'd been here." Will says, "All right tomorrow is your day and we'll see what he does to you." So next morning Tom put him on some meat to boil in front of the fire and when he come in from the new ground he got him some turnips and potatoes and pumpkin and baked him some bread and fixed him up a good dinner. And when he went out to blow the horn he saw an old man comin' up the holler with his beard as blue as indigo, his teeth as long as pipe stems and his thumbs tucked behind him and he said, "Have ye anything to eat?" And Tom says, "No," Old Bluebeard says, "Well, we'll see about that." And he went in and eat up everything Tom had fixed except jest a little bit of pumpkin. And Tom had to fly around and git up something for his brothers and when they come in Jack says, "Why didn't you keep him from eatin' hit up?" Tom says, "Tomorrow is your time to git dinner and see if you can keep from hit." And Jack says, "Bedad, I will."

So next day Jack put him some meat to boil in the fireplace and got some turnips and potatoes and fixed 'em and when he went out to blow the horn for his brothers to come in, old Bluebeard was a comin' up the holler with his beard as blue as indigo, his teeth as long as pipe stems and his thumbs tucked behind him. Jack says, "Now, uncle, you jest come in and have something to eat." Old Bluebeard says, "No, I don't want anything." Jack says, "Yes, but you must come in and have dinner with us. "Old Bluebeard says, "No, I don't want to," and he tuk around the house and tuk out down the holler. Jack tuk out down the holler after him and saw him git down a den—a hole in the ground—and when the brothers come home and Jack was gone they thought old Bluebeard had eat Jack up 'stead of his dinner but after a while Jack come in and they says, "Jack, where you bin?" Jack says, "I bin watchin' old Bluebeard, watchin' where he went to and I watched him go down a hole in the ground and I'm goin' to foller him." So Jack tuk a big old bushel basket out and put a strop on hit and him and his brothers went to old Bluebeard's hole. Will says he was agoin' down. Jack says, "We'll take turns. Will, go first." So Will he climbed in the basket and they let him down in the hole and when he shuck the rope they pulled him up and asked him what he found. Will says, "Well, I went until I saw a house and then I shuck the rope." "Oh shaw, Will, what ud you shake the rope then fer? Why didn't you find out what was in the house? Will says, "Well, you go in and find out." Tom says, "All right I will." So he clumb in the basket and went down 'til he was on top the house and then he shuck the rope and they pulled him up. When he told 'em he shuck the rope when he was on top of the house, Jack says, "You're nary one no account but me." So he went down and looked in the room and there sat the prettiest woman he ever saw in his life. And Jack says, "Oh! you're the prettiest woman I ever saw in my life and you're goin' to be my wife." "No," she said, "Old Bluebeard ul git you. You better git out of here." "Oh, no, he won't," says Jack. "He's a good friend of mine and I'm goin' to take you up and marry you." "No," she said, "you wait 'til you get down to the next house. You won't think nothin' of me when you see her." So Jack put her in the basket and shuck the rope. And when she come out, Will says, "Oh!

you're the prettiest woman I ever saw in my life!" and Tom said, "Oh! you're the prettiest woman I ever saw in my life."

Jack went on down to the next house and looked in and there was the prettiest woman he ever did see, the other wan't nothing along side this one. Jack says, "You're the prettiest woman I ever saw and you're goin' to be my wife. My brothers can have the other one but I'm goin' to have you." She says, "Oh, no, Jack, when you go down to the other house you won't think nothin' of me." "Yes, I will, too," says Jack. "You jest come git in this basket." So he put her in the basket and shuck the rope. Then he went down to the next house and there was the prettiest woman. Jack says, "Oh! you're jest the prettiest woman I ever did see and you're goin' to be my wife. My brothers kin have the other two but you're goin' to be my wife. Come git in the basket." But afore she was pulled up she give him a red ribbon and told him to plait it in her hair so he'd know her when she come out and she give him a wishin' ring. Jack put her in the basket and shuck the rope. When the brothers saw her they stopped talkin' to the other two and fell in love with her right away. Tom says, "You're going to be my wife." Will says, "No, she's goin' to be mine." And they started fightin'. She says, "I won't have nary one. I'm goin' to marry Jack." They said, "No, you won't fer we'll leave Jack down there." So they pulled up the basket and they commencet to fight and left Jack down there.

Jack jest sit ther and Old Bluebeard come in and walked around but he didn't give Jack nothin' to eat. Jack jest sit there and after a while he turned the ring on his finger seein' how he'd fell away and said, "I wish I was in my old corner beside the fire smokin' my old chunky pipe." And there he was and there was the woman with red ribbon plaited in her hair and she said, "Oh, Jack!" And they was married and they uz rich when I left there.

*Known as "Old Fire Dragaman" by Maud Long and R.M Ward. Type 301 A, The Three Stolen Princesses. Bolte & Polivka, CLXVI.*

## Whiteberry Whittington

Whiteberry Whittington was a hired boy and he lived with the king, and he loved the hired girl. So he was out helpin' to kill beef one day and he got some blood on his shirt. The king's daughter she was kinda in love with him. So when he got back he says to the hired girl and the king's girl, "Whichever one washes this stain out my shirt, that's the one I'm goin' to marry." So the hired girl she washed hit out, he knowed she would, and he married her and lived with her until they had three children.

One day King's daughter says, "I washed that shirt and you said whichever one washed that stain out your shirt, that's the one you was goin' to marry." "Yes, I did," says Whiteberry Whittington, so he left with the king's daughter. And the hired girl she was home jest a mournin,' and at last old woman come by and says, "Why are you always a grievin' and a cryin'?" The hired girl told her how her

*Left*: Newt and Jane Gentry, ca. 1917, in a photograph by Herbert Pelton, a well known Asheville photographer. *Below*: The Gentry family at Sunnybank, Christmas Day ca. 1919. *First row, left to right:* Maud Clay, Margaret Clay, Mae Lyda, and Emma Reese (Margaret's daughter). *Second row:* Lalla, Maud, Mae with Lalla Mae, Newt, and Jane. *Back row:* Nora with Lavetta Jane, Margaret Reese, Nola Jane, and William Ransom Hicks ("Uncle Doc"). Courtesy of Haladine Sink and Jeannette Armstrong.

*Left*: Ransom and Emily Harmon Hicks, Jane's parents. Courtesy of Nathan Hicks and Pat Gentry. *Below*: Harriett Reese Hicks and William Ransom ("Uncle Doc") Hicks.

*Left*: Jane with her ever-present handiwork and J.W., the poodle they credited with saving their lives when the house caught fire in the night. Courtesy of Jeannette Armstrong. *Below*: The house that Newt built on Meadow Fork. Photo by Bill Smith.

*Above*: Sunnybank, ca. 1919. Courtesy of Elmer Nall. *Below*: Cecil Sharp and Maud Karpeles note a song (singer unknown). From A.H. Fox Strangeways, *Cecil Sharp* (London: Oxford University Press, 1933), plate xviii. Courtesy of North Carolina Division of Archives and History.

*Left*: Elizabeth ("Miss Peggy") Dotterer. As a young girl she rode her horse throughout the mountains around Hot Springs. Her observant nature made her a natural historian for the town. Courtesy of Mars Hill College Appalachian Center. *Below*: The Mountain Park Hotel, Hot Springs. Courtesy of Hazel Moore.

*Left*: Emily with her husband, Virgil Byford, and children Virgil and Jeannette. Courtesy of Jeannette Armstrong.

*Below, left*: Maud Gentry Long, ca. 1954. Courtesy of Jane Long Douglas and Elmer Hall. *Below, right*: Nola Jane, from the Duke University *Chanticleer,* 1927. Courtesy of Duke University Archives.

*Above*: Jeannette Armstrong and Phyllis Davies, daughter and granddaughter of Emily. Photo by Bill Smith. *Below*: Dorothy and James Gentry in Gentry Hardware, Hot Springs. Photo by Betty Smith.

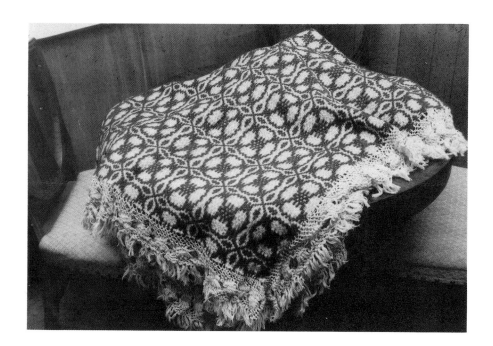

*Above*: One of Jane's woven coverlets, blue and white, in "Gertrude's Fancy," with crocheted trim. *Right*: Family and friends gather for the dedication of the "Balladry" historical marker. *Back row, left to right:* Lalla Rolfe, Jane Douglas, Betty Rolfe, Daron Douglas, and Elizabeth Dotterer. *Front row:* Collins Moore (son of Daron) and Cora Elkins.

husband had left her and gone away with the king's daughter. Old woman says, "If you'll give me one of these children, I'll tell you where your husband is. But," she says, "you'll have to climb the glassy hills and wade the bloody seas to git to him."—"I don't mind that but I hate to give up one of my little children." She wasn't a aimin' to give hit up to her at all. Old woman says, "Well, when you find your husband you kin come back and git the child." So she wouldn't give it to her and the old woman says, "Well, listen, if you give me this child, I'll give you this beautiful fan and help you git your husband." So she give her a child and started on her way with the two children and she travelled and travelled until she met another old woman who looked like the first one.

"Oh! these two pretty children," she says. "You've jest got to give me one of them." So the hired girl says, "No, I've already had to give one to the old witch and I can't give way nary nother one." Old woman says, "Give me one of them children and I'll give you this pretty comb and it'll help your husband to love you and I'll help you find him." So she give the old woman one of the children and she tuk the comb and started on. So she clumb the glassy hills and waded the bloody seas and went on. Travelled on for about two more days and met another old woman who says, "Oh, this pretty baby, I'm bound to have this pretty baby."—"No, I jest can't give you this baby. I've had to give the other two children to the old witches and I have to hunt my husband and I jest don't believe I could live if I had to give up this one." The old woman says, "If you'll give me this one, I'll give you this pretty string of beads, and if you don't, you'll never find your husband and you'll never live nuther." So she tuk the string of beads and give the old witch the child and went on to the place her husband and the king's daughter was, and it want but a few more days 'fore she saw the king's daughter. King's daughter says, "Oh, that pretty fan, I've got to have that pretty fan." "No," hired girl says, "You got my man and that's enought for you."—"No, I've got to have that fan. I'll send my husband over to spend the night with you."—He wasn't her husband of course because he'd married the hired girl. The king's daughter jest said that. She was anxious to git him to come over so she could tell him how the king's daughter had lied her and lied him. So she give the king's daughter the fan.

So the king's daughter went home and told him he was to go over. So he went over, he jest minded the king's daughter like he was a little brown puppy, and the king's daughter says, "You got to take this dost of laudnum because I don't want her a talkin' to you." So when he got over there, she wanted him to have some supper with her. But he said no, he was sleepy and wanted to go to bed. So she fixed the bed and he went to bed. She crawled in behind him. So she says,

I've clumb the glassy hills and waded the bloody seas,
My three little babes I've give for thee,
Turn over to me, my fair Whittington.

But he was jest so sound asleep he couldn't wake. So in two or three days the king's daughter happened to notice the comb. "Oh, what'll you take for that comb, I just must have that comb."—"No, you have my man and that's enought for you."—"Say, if you'll give me that comb, I'll send him back to stay all night with you." So she give her the comb. So the king's daughter give him another dost of laudnum and he wouldn't eat supper and during the night she'd talk to him, but couldn't git him to wake enought to speak to. She'd say,

> I've clumb the glassy hills and waded the bloody seas,
> My three little babes I've give for thee,
> Turn over to me, Whiteberry Whittington.

He'd never move. So in two or three days the king's daughter saw her beads. "Oh, I'm jest bound to have them beads."—"No, you got my man, you got my fan, you got my comb. I'm jest not goin' to let you have these beads."—"I'll let my man come and stay all night with you if you'll jest let me have them beads." So she let her have the beads. So that night when she give the laudnum to Whiteberry Whittington, he jest spite [spit?] hit down in his boot and went on over. So she told him what a hard time she'd had to git to him, how she had had to give up her children. She told him that the king's daughter had lied to him and that she was the one that washed the blood out. So he went back to the king's daughter and says, "You jest lied me and I'm goin' back with my wife, kill the old witches and git my children." So he tuk his wife and they went on back and stopped at every house and killed the old witch and tuk the children and when I left there, they was rich and livin' happy.

*"Whitebear Whittington" as told by R.M. Ward, Nancy Ward, and Mrs. Kel Harmon.*

*Type 425 C, The Girl as the Bear's Wife. The Search for the Lost Husband. Bolte & Polivka XC, XCIII, CXXVII.*

## Old Foster

They used to be an old man, he lived way over in the forest by hisself, and all he lived on was he caught women and boiled 'em in front of the fire and eat 'em. Now the way my mother told me, he'd go into the villages and tell 'em this and that and get 'em to come out and catch 'em and boil they breasts. That's what she told me, and then I've heard hit that he jest eat 'em. Well, they was a beautiful stout woman, he liked 'em the best (he'd a been right atter me un your mother) so every day he'd come over to this woman's house and he'd tell her to please come over to see his house. "Why, Mr. Foster, I can't find the way."—"Yes, you can. I'll take a spool of red silk thread out of my pocket and I'll start windin' hit on the bushes and it'll carry ye straight to my house." So she promised him one day she'd come. So she got her dinner over one day and she started. So she follered the red silk thread and went on over to his house. When she got there, there was a poor little old boy sittin' over the fire a boilin' meat. And he says, 'Laws, Aunt,"—she uz his aunt,—"what er you doin' here? Foster kills every woman uz comes here. You leave here jest as quick as you can."

She started to jump out the door and she saw Foster a comin' with two young women, one under each arm. So she run back and says, "Jack, honey, what'll I do, I see him a comin'?" "Jump in that old closet under the stair and I'll lock you in," says Jack.

So she jumped in and Jack locked her in. So Foster come in and he was jest talkin' and a laughin' with those two girls and tellin' the most tales, and he was goin' to taken 'em over to a corn shuckin next day. Foster says, "Come on in and have supper with me." So Jack put up some boiled meat and water. That's all they had. As soon as the girls stepped in and seed the circumstance and seed their time had come their countance fell. Foster says, "You better come in and eat, may be the last chanct you'll ever have." Girls both jumped up and started to run. Foster jumps up and ketched 'em, and gets his tomihawk and starts up stairs with 'em. Stairs was shackly and rattly, and as they went up one of the girls wretched her hand back and caught hold of a step and Foster jest tuck his tomihawk and hacked her hand off. It drapped into whar she was. She laid on in there until next day atter Foster went out. Then Jack let her out.

She jest bird worked [walked?] over to where the corn shuckin' was. When she got there Foster was there. She didn't know how to git Foster destroyed. The people thought these people got out in the forest and the wild animals ud ketch 'em. So she says, "I dreamt an awful dream last night. I dreamed I lived close to Foster's house and he was always a wantin' me to come to his house."

Foster says, "Well, that ain't so, and it shan't be so, and God forbid it ever should be so."

She went right on, "And I dreamt he put out a red thread and I follered hit to his house and there uz Jack broilin' women's breasts in front the fire."

Foster says, "Well, that ain't so, and it shan't be so, and God forbid it ever should be so." She went right on, "And he says, 'What'er you doin' here? Foster kills every woman uz comes here.'"

Foster says, "Well, that ain't so, and it shan't be so, and God forbid it ever should be so."

She went right on, "And I seed Foster acomin' with two girls. And when they git thar the girls their hearts failed 'em and Foster ketched 'em and gets his tomihawk and starts upstairs with 'em."

Foster says, "Well, that ain't so, and it shan't be so, and God forbid it ever should be so."

She went right on. "The stairs was shackly and rattly and as they went up, one of the girls wretched her hand back and caught hold of a step and Foster jest tuk his tomihawk and hacked her hand off."

Foster says, "Well, that ain't so, and it shan't be so, and God forbid it ever should be so."

She says, "Hit is so, and it shall be so and here I've got the hand to show."

And they knowed the two girls was missin' and they knowed it was so, so they lynched Foster and then they went and got Jack and bound him out.

*Bolte & Polivka XI.*

# Old Catkins

There was an old man and an old woman and they had three girls and the mother died. One of the girls was awfully lazy when she was a growin' up, and the other two girls jest fairly hated her. So she'd always say when they was a fussin' at her, "That's all right; Catskins ul come out the big end of the horn someday." So when the mother died the father tuk her wedding dress and put it away and said whenever he found another woman who looked as nice in that dress he'd marry again. So the girls, they fussed so much at Catskins they really made her father think she was no good and he didn't get her no pretty things or nothin'. So one day the two oldest girls were off visitin' so Catskin, she jest tried herself to see what a nice dinner she could git for her father. So they was eatin' dinner that day and her father said, "Catskin, I believe you're the smartest girl I've got." That tickled Catskins pretty near to death. So after she washed and cleaned up, she thought she'd try on her mother's wedding dress. She'd never been dressed up before in her life.

So her father was up on the hill a ploughin' and he looked down in the yard and he saw someone with his wife's wedding dress on. So he loosed the horse from the plough jest as quick as he could and went down and said, "Who was that with my wife's wedding dress on?" She said she didn't know. He said, "Yes, you do know and you've got to tell me too."—"Well, I'll tell you what I'll do. If you'll get me a dress the color of every cloud that ever floated in the ereal I'll tell ye." So he went and got the dress just as quick as he could. Then she said she had to have one the color of every bird that ever flew in the air and then she'd tell him. So he went and got a dress the color of every bird that ever flew in the air. And then she said she had to have a dress the color of every fish that ever floated in the sea. So he went and he got that. And then she said, "Twas me." And that made him mad and he said he was goin' to beat her up and she had to leave home. So she tuk her dresses and started out to git work. And on the way she left her dresses at the dressmaker's and told her she'd come and redeem 'em. So she went on to the king's house and she went round to the back door, and so she knocked and a colored girl went to the door and she said, "Could I see the queen, please?" And the colored girl hunted the queen and brought her to the door and the girl says, "Do you want to hire some more help?" Queen says, "Do you want to work with the darkies?" She says, "Yes, I don't mind. I'd jest as soon work with the colored girls as anybody." So Catskins just went in and pushed up her sleeves and went to work, and she soon had the rest of the girls jest ashamed of theyselves. She had the kitchen jest a shinin'. So the queen come and says, "My goodness, you'll have the other girls ashamed of theyselves." Says, "There's goin' to be a big dance down at the club house Saturday night and I'll dress you up in some of my clothes and let you go and have a good time."

So Saturday night rolled around and the queen come and dressed Catskin up and started her down to the ball to have a good time. Catskins went down where her dresses was and drug out the one the color of every cloud that ever floated in the ereal and she put hit on and went down to the ball. So she sure enough did have a good time. The king's son was there and he danced with her, and he got to liken her and thought she was the prettiest thing he ever saw. So they give out they'd be another ball the next Saturday night and wanted 'em all to be there. So she promised 'em she'd be there. So she went back and tuk the queen's dress to her and told her what a good time she'd had and the queen said, "You jest keep a workin' like you been and you can go to all the balls they is and I'll dress you in a heap fine dress next time." So she jest made things shine that week. And the queen just fell in love with her and so the next Saturday night she brought her a fine dress. But Catskins went and got her dress the color of every bird that ever flew in the sky and she fixed herself up and went on to the ball. So the king's son was there and jest fell in love with her. So he told her he loved her and he told her he'd bring the ring next week. So that week Catskin jest spread herself to see how much she could do. So next Saturday night the queen brought out the finest dress and sent her to the ball to have a good time. But Catskins went out and got her dress the color of every fish that ever floated in the sea. So the king's son was there and he brought her the ring and when the ball was over, he wanted to take her home. She said, "No, you're not goin' to take me home. If you take me home, I'll not get to come back no more." He was bound to take her home, but she said, "You're not goin' nary step." So she went on home alone. Well, there was nary nother dance give out and there they was. The king's son didn't have no way to know whar she was and he couldn't find her nowhere. So he got sick; got bad sick. So his mother was jest gettin' all kinds of doctors. He said, "Now, mother, don't get nary doctor fer me 'cause my heart's broke." So he went to bed and wouldn't eat nary a bite. The queen, she was all the time a cookin' tryin' to get him to eat a bite. One day Catskins says, "Let me cook him a cake." She said, "Oh Catskin, he won't eat what you cook him." She said, "Well, he did eat my cookin' every day. Let me try hit. I jest believe he would." So his mother said, "Well, honey, go ahead and bake. I'd jest give anything in this world if I could see him eat jest one bite." So Catskins went to work and she baked a little cake and she put the ring in hit and carried it to his mother and she begged his mother to let her carry hit upstairs. So his mother consented to let her carry hit upstairs. Catskins says, "I'll jest take it to the door and hand it in to you." So Catskins carried hit up to the door and handed hit in to the queen and Catskins jest peeked in and smiled. And the king's son said, "Oh, mother, let Catskins come in, she smiles jest like the girl at the ball." So his mother says, "Eat a little cake." Catskin fixed hit so he could find that ring. So then he bit the cake and found the ring he said, "Oh, Catskins, you're the girl I saw at the ball, come help me up." So she holped 'em up and they uz married and when I left there they uz rich.

*When asked why the girl was Catskins, she said, "She was raggy and she didn't have no new clothes, her sisters jest wouldn't give hit to her, so they patched her dress with the old cat's hide." When asked to repeat where the dance was to be held, she changed from "a big dance at the club house," to "a big dance Saturday night." Carter titled this story "Old Catkins" in spite of the fact that Mrs. Gentry consistently called the protagonist Catskins or Catskin. R.M. Ward also told this tale and called it "Catskins."*

*Type 510 A, Cinderella. Bolte & Polivka LXV.*

# Jack and the Beanstalk

Once there was a little boy and he didn't have no mother or no father and his grandmother was a raisin' him and she uz awfully mean to him. So she whipped him one morning and she whipped awfully hard and he was cryin'. So she was sweepin' the house and she swept up a bean and she says, "Here, take this bean and go out and plant it and make you a bean tree." He went out and planted it and he played around all day and was very good after that. So next morning he got up and ran out early to see about his bean tree and hit had growed to the top of the house. So he run and said, "Grandmother, my bean tree is as high as the house." So she slapped his face and said, "Go on out of here, you know it's not up yet." When she went out, sure enough it was as high as the house. So hit made her kind of sorry and she give him a piece of bread and butter. So next morning he jumped up and ran out and says, "Granny, my bean tree's as high as the sky." So she slapped him again and says, "Son, don't come in here telling such lies as that, you know hits not as high as the sky." So after a while when she got thru cleanin' up she went out and sure enough it did look like the bean tree had growed up thru the sky. So Jack played around all day and looked at his bean tree and next day he decided he'd climb hit. So he started and he told his grandmother, "I'll hack you off a mess of beans as I go up." So he clumb and clumb and throwed her down the beans. Atter a while he come to a big field. So he got out and got to wandering around in that field and he saw a house. So he went to this house and then he saw the old giant's wife was a sittin' thar and she says, "Law, little boy, what you doin' here? Don't you know the giant ul be in directly?" "Oh, hide me, do please hide me," says Jack. And atter a while she hid him under the bed. So directly the old giant come in and says, "Fi fo fiddledy fun, I smell the blood of an Englishman. Dead or alive I'll have his bones to eat with my bread and butter." His wife says, "Aw now, poppy, don't talk that way, that was just a little old boy that was here this evenin' and he's gone now." So the giant et his supper and Jack lay there under the bed and he looked out at the giant's boots and a gun. Fastened to the bed cords they was the prettiest china bells. So he wanted the china bells and he wanted the boots and he wanted the giant's gun. So he laid there 'til they was all asleepin' and he eased out and got the giant's gun and down the bean stalk he went. So he laid around all next day, he rested and next morning he started to climb the bean stalk again. So he clumb back up the field and went back to the giant's house. "Law, Jack, what you come back for? The giant thinks you stole his gun and he'll sure eat you up." "No, no, he wont, jest let me crawl under the bed one more night." So she let him crawl under the bed. So the old giant come in says, "Fi foo fiddledy fun, I smell the blood of an Englishman. Dead or alive I'll have his bones to eat with my bread and butter." "Aw, poppy, don't talk that way, it's jest that little ol poor boy comin' back here everyday." So Jack, he laid there and studied what he'd get next, so way in the night he got out and got the giant's boots and went down the bean tree. So atter he got down he laid around two or three days, but he wanted them bells so he decided he'd go again. So he clumb up the bean tree and went to the giant's house and when the giant's wife saw him she says, "Law, Jack, the giant's awfully mad at you, he thinks you stole his boots. You better go way before he ketches you." "Aw, he wont ketch me, jest let me come in one more time." So he crawled under the bed. So the giant come home and says,

"Fi foo fiddledy fun, I smell the blood of an Englishman. Dead or alive I'll have his bones to eat with my bread and butter." "Law now, Poppy," says his wife, "that little old boy's been here but he ain't comin' back again." So Jack laid there under the bed and he begun untying the bells and every now then one ud made a noise and the old giant ud say, "Fi foo fiddledy fun, I smell the blood of an Englishman. Dead or alive I'll have his bones to eat with my bread and butter." Then another bell ud go "dingle" and he'd say, "Fi foo fiddledy fun, I smell the blood of an Englishman. Dead or alive I'll have his bones to eat with my bread and butter." So finally at last Jack, he got 'em all untied from the bed cords and got 'em down. And he started out for the bean stalk and they begun to go "dingle." And the giant says, "Fi foo fiddledy fun, I smell the blood of an Englishman. Dead or alive I'll have his bones to eat with my bread and butter." And tuk out after Jack. And when they got to the bean stalk, Jack clumb down and then he looked up and here come the giant right atter him. And Jack hollers, "Give me a hand ax, granny, give me a hand ax." And he begun to hack and hack and down come the bean tree and down come the giant too.

*Type 328, The Boy Steals the Giant's Treasure. Bolte & Polivka, CLXV (2:511; 3:33-37).*

## Little Dicky Wigbun

He was a little bit of a man and his wife didn't like him nary a bit. She loved the old passenger. I don't know what the old passenger was. They uz men use to travel about and they called 'em the old passenger. So she was all the time playin' off like she was sick and sending little Dicky Wigbun to the Clear Apsul Springs to get clear Apsul Rum fer her. (I don't know what clear Apsul Rum were, it's just in the story; they didn't really have anything like hit.) She was hopin' the wild varmints ud get him and eat him up and she cud have the old passenger. So one day he uz going down to the spring and he met the peddler. Peddler says, "Dicky, where you started?" "I've started down to Clear Apsul Springs to git my wife some Clear Apsul Rum." Peddler says, "Dicky, I'm jest as sorry fer you uz I can be. Your wife don't care nothing fer you." "You think she don't?" "No, she's jest sendin' you off down here to see if you wont get killed by the wild animals. You jest get in this knapsack of mine and let me carry you back to your house and let you see what's going on." "Well, I believe I will," says Dicky. So Dicky got in the haversack.

Got to Dicky's house and the peddler says, "Kin I stay all night?" "Yes, I guess ye can, but my husband's not here." So he went in and says, "Mrs. Wigbun, kin I bring my haversack in? I dropped hit in a mud hole down the road a piece and I'm feared I'll get my rations wet." "Yes, I guess ye kin."

So the peddler went out and cut a couple of holes so's Jack [Dicky] cud see out and just picked him up and carried him into the house. So the peddler says, "Let's all sing some little ditties." "All right," the passenger says. "Well now, Mrs.

Wigbun," says the peddler, "you sing the first one, then Mr. Passenger, you sing the next one and then I'll sing one."

So Mrs. Wigbun sings:

> Oh Little Dicky Wigbun
> To London he's gone
> To buy me a bottle of Clear Apful Rum,
> God send him a long journey never to return
> Thru the green wood and below.

"Well now, Mrs. Wigbun, that's a pretty song, sing hit again."

> Oh, Little Dicky Wigbun
> To London he's gone
> To buy me a bottle of Clear Apful Rum,
> God send him a long journey never to return
> Thru the green wood and below.

"Well, now, Mr. Passenger, you sing yourn"

> Oh, Little Dicky Wigbun thinks
> Who eats of his sweets and drinks of his drinks,
> And if God spares my life I will sleep with his wife
> Through the green woods and below.

"That's pretty, sing hit again."

> Oh, Little Dicky Wigbun thinks
> Who eats of his sweets and drinks of his drinks,
> And if God spares my life
> I will sleep with his wife
> Thru the green wood and below.

"Now, Mr. Peddler, you sing yourn," says Mrs. Wigbun.

> Oh, Little Dicky Wigbun, he's not very fur,
> And out of my knapsack I'll have him to appear,
> And if friends he don't like, I stand to his back
> Thru the green fields and below.

> So they hung the old passenger all right away.
> And they burnt Dicky's wife the very next day
> Thru the green fields and below.

*Mrs. Gentry told Carter her grandfather, Council Harmon, used both "apsul" and "apful."*

# Old Gally Mander

Once they was an old woman and she was so stingy she wouldn't spend a penny and she lived on ash cakes and water. She had a big long leather sack hanging up in the chimney with her money in hit. She didn't have any money 'cept gold and silver. So her hired girls got so they pilfered around and tried to find her money. So she sent her son over the ocean to git a girl who wouldn't know anything about her money. So he went and got her a girl that evenin'. And the girl fixed 'em the supper. So after supper the old woman wanted to go out a visitin'. So the old woman says, "Don't you look up the chimney." So of course as soon as the old woman was out of the house, the girl went and looked up the chimney and got to gougin' 'round with her stick and directly the big long leather purse fell down and she looked in hit and seed the silver and gold and she just tuk hit and started out. Directly she passed old cow. Old cow says, "Oh, come pretty lady, milk my old sore bag." "I've got no time to fool with your old sore bag. I'm goin' over the ocean." Went on a little way and met an old horse. "Oh come, pretty lady, wash my old sore back." "I've got no time to wash your old sore back. I'm goin' over the ocean." Went on a little way, met a peach tree all loaded down to the ground with peaches. "Oh come, pretty lady, and pick off some of my peaches and rest my poor tired limbs." "I've got no time to pick your old peaches. I'm goin' over the ocean."

Old woman come home, seed the girl was gone, looked up the chimney and seed her purse was gone and just tuk out down the road a hollerin'. "Gally Mander, Gally Mander, all my gold and silver's gone and my great long leather purse." So she started off down the road at a loop-loopy-te-loop. Met the old cow. " Old cow, have you saw anything of a girl with a long leather purse?" "Yes, run, old woman, and you'll soon overtake her." "Gally Mander, Gally Mander, all my gold and silver's gone and my great long leather purse." Pretty soon met the old horse. "Old horse, have you saw a girl with a long leather purse?" "Yes, old woman, and you'll soon overtake her." "Gally Mander, Gally Mander, all my gold and silver's gone and my great long leather purse." Met the peach tree. "Peach tree, have you saw a girl with a long leather purse?" "Yes, old woman, she's right down there at the side of the ocean," "Gally Mander, Gally Mander, all my gold and silver's gone and my great long leather purse." And got to the ocean, caught her, flogged her up and pitched her into the ocean.

Old woman tuk her purse, went back home, lives long time by herself. Then sent her son out to hunt her another girl away out where nobody didn't know 'em. So the girl come and the old woman liked 'er very well. After while old woman says, "Now, I'm goin' out to visit, don't you look up the chimney while I'm gone." So when she got out of sight the girl wanted to look up the chimney for curiosity. Got her stick, got to gougin' into hit, and directly the leather purse fell down. Looked inside and it was full of gold and silver, and she tuk out down the road. Directly she met old cow. "Oh come, pretty lady, and milk my old sore bag." "I've got no time to milk your old sore bag, I'm goin' across the water." Went on, met the horse. "Oh come, pretty lady, and wash my old sore back." "I've got no time to wash your old sore back, I'm goin' across the water." Went on, met the peach tree. "Oh come, pretty lady, pick off some peaches and rest my poor tired limbs." "I've got no time to pick off your peaches, I'm goin' over the water." So old woman come in, looked up the chimney. "Gally Mander, Gally Mander, all my gold and silver's gone and my great long leather purse." So she tuk out down the road. Directly she come to old cow and said, "Have you saw a girl with a long leather purse?" "Yes, old woman, and you'll soon overtake her." "Gally Mander, Gally Mander, all my gold and silver's gone and my great long leather purse." Directly she met old horse. "Old horse, have you saw a girl with a long leather purse?" "Yes, run, old woman, and you'll soon overtake her." "Gally Mander, Gally Mander, all my gold and silver's gone and my great long leather purse." Come to peach tree. "Pretty peach tree, have you saw a girl with a long leather purse?" "She's right down by the side of the water." So the old woman shuck her and flogged on her and pitched her into the water. Then she tuk her long leather purse and went back home. "I'll stay by myself and eat ash cakes all the days of my life 'fore I'll bother with ary other girl."

But atter a while her son went way off where nobody didn't know 'em and brought her back another girl. Old woman, she jest stayed there and wouldn't go out un visit but atter a while she went to visit. Says, "Don't you look up that chimney." So the girl tuk her stick and went to the chimney un gouged, un gouged, un directly the purse fell down. She opened it and it was full of gold and silver, so she grabbed hit up and started. She passed old cow. "Pretty fair maid, come milk my old sore bag." She says, "Yes, I'll milk your old sore bag," and she milked it and bathed it and bathed it. She passed the old sore horse. "Pretty lady, won't you bathe my old sore back?" "Yes, I'll bathe your old sore back." So she bathed it and bathed it. So she come to the pretty peach tree. "Pretty fair lady, won't you come pick off some of my peaches and rest my poor tired limbs?" "Yes, I'll pick off some of your peaches." So she picked un picked un picked. Peach tree says, "You climb up here in my limbs. The old woman ul be here in a minute."

Old woman come home, looked up chimney seed her long leather purse was gone, "Gally Mander, Gally Mander, all my gold and silver's gone and my great long leather purse." She tuk out down the road. "Old cow, have you saw a girl with a long leather purse?" "Yes, she passed here long, long, long ago and forgot about hit." "Gally Mander, Gally Mander, all my gold and silver's gone and my great long leather purse." Met old horse. "Old horse, have you saw a girl with a long leather purse?" "Yes, she passed here long, long ago and forgot about hit." "Gally Mander, Gally Mander, all my gold and silver's gone and my great long leather purse." Come to peach tree. "Pretty peach tree, have you saw a girl with a long leather purse?" "Yes, but she's over the ocean long ago." Old woman, "What'll I do, what'll I do?" "Go home and eat ash cakes all the days of your life." And that's what she got fer bein' so stingy.

*Bolte & Polivka, XXIV.*


## Sop, Doll, Sop

They was a poor little old orphan boy growed up in the country and his name was Jack and he never could find anything he could do. So he found an advertisement of a man wanted a miller. So he tramped across the mountain and went a long ways 'til he come to the miller's house. Got there one Sunday afternoon. In them days they didn't never come up to the house and ring the door bell, they always hollered, "Hello." So Jack hollered, "Hello." Miller says, "What'll ye have?" "I've seen yer advertisement," says Jack, "and I've come to work fer ye."—"I'm in need of a miller."—"Well, bedad, I've come to tend your mill fer ye." "Well, I'll jest tell ye now I've hired lots of millers but they always died," says the miller. "Well, I'd jest as soon be dead as alive. I've got no home and no place to stay," says Jack.

"Well, you're the kind of man I'm looking fer," says the miller. "We'll, go down and I'll show ye around the mill. Now you'll have to cook here on this fire place; here's yer meal un yer meat and yer skillet. Jest make yourself at home and cook what ye need." "Well, bedads, I'll get along all right," says Jack. So Jack baked him some bread un made him some coffee un fried him some meat. So he didn't put his meat un bread up on the table, jest put 'em on the floor and sat down beside 'em. He had a little brass lamp and the light of the fire place and the moon was shining as bright as daylight. All at once the little old cabin got as dark as midnight. He got up and chared up his fire and when he looked around every crack in the house was full of cats—jest as thick as they cut stick—with their eyes jest shinin'. That sort of scared him and he jest sit down and commenced to eatin'. All of a sudden one big old black cat jumped out in the middle and hollered, "Sop, doll, sop." Then all the cats sat down on the floor. She walked up and popped her paw in his meat sop and licked hit and hollered, "Sop, doll, sop." He began to get scared and he said, "Stick your old paw in here again and I'll whack hit off." So she stick hit in and hollered, "Sop, doll, sop." "If you do hit again," says Jack, "I'll hack it off." She did hit again and he hacked it off. When he hacked hit off, it fell into the fryin' pan—hit was a woman's hand with a ring on the finger and she hollered, "Whar-a-a," and they all went out the cracks and the moon shined back in as bright as day. So he tuk the hand and he wrops hit up in some tissue paper and drops hit down in his coat pocket.

So next morning he wuz up bright and early and had his breakfast over and was grinding and whistling when the miller comes down. Said, "Why, hello, Jack, I see you're still alive." "Yes, bedads, I'm still alive," says Jack, "but I'll tell ye what I done last night." And he told all about the cats. "Show ye what I done too," and he pulled this hand out of his pocket. So he handed out this hand to the man. And he says, "That's my wife's hand." Jack says, "Oh surely not." He says, "Yes, hit is." Jack says, "Well, she was a big black cat when I hacked hit off."—"Well, hit is," says the miller, "fer this is a ring I put on her hand yestiday." So he tuk the hand and went up to the house. Says, "Nancy, let's see your right hand." She poked him out her left. Says, "Nancy, hit's yer right hand I want." She begin cryin' and said, "I haven't any." So he says, "Now tell me all about this, Nancy, and I won't have you burned."

"Well, I didn't want you to have a miller. I wanted you to keep the mill yourself. So I got all my friends and witched 'em into cats, and got 'em to witch 'emselves into cats and we put pizen in the miller's sop. And when I went, put pizen into this man's sop he hacked off my hand." So he gathered up all the other witches and had 'em burned and that made the other husbands mad, and they had his wife hung. He wouldn't let 'em burn her 'cause he had said she shouldn't be. So Jack made an end of a good many witches.

*Bolte & Polivka IV.*

## Jack and the Northwest Wind

Once they was a boy and he got awful trifling. He got so thinly clad he was about to freeze and he got hit into his head he cud stop the northwest wind. So he had an old uncle lived way out in the northwest so he thought he would go to that uncle. So he went out there and his uncle said, "Jack, where you started?" "Well, bedads, I've started to stop the northwest wind. I'm about to freeze to death." says Jack. "Oh, Jack, don't do that; if you'll go on back home and leave that northwest wind alone, I'll give you a rooster and you can jest pat him on the back and say, 'Lay a gold egg,' and he'll lay ye a cap full." So Jack tuk his rooster and stuck him under his arm and started. Uncle says. "Now don't you stay over at that house." So he told him how to go so as not to stay there. So boy tuk his rooster and went over to that house, and called to stay all night. So one of the boys come to take Jack's rooster to put it away and Jack says, "Now this rooster is all I've got to make my living so take good care of hit. You can jest pat him on the back and he'll lay gold eggs."

So the boy jest eased the rooster in his hen house and next morning he gave Jack his old rooster. They uz awful good to Jack; wouldn't charge him a penny. So he went on home. When he got there, he let the rooster down and patted him on the back and said, "Lay a gold egg," and he wouldn't lay none, so that made Jack mad and he killed him and eat him. So when he got his old chicken eat up, he uz cold and thought, "Bedads, I'm going to stop that northwest wind." So he went on out to his uncle's and when his uncle saw him, he says, "What you doin' back here?" "I've come to stop the northwest wind; I'm about to freeze to death," says Jack. "That old chicken was no account and I jest killed hit and et it."

"Now, Jack, you'll jest go on home and let that northwest wind alone. I'm goin' to give you a sword and hit ul cut forty inches through anything—cut trees down, cut heads—jest anything. If you'll jest go on home. Now don't stop over at that house, Jack, if you do, they'll steal hit. They've got swords jest exactly like hit and they'll put you in one of theirn." So Jack gets his sword and starts out an goes right over to that house and stays all night. So the boy says, "I'll take care your sword fer ye." "All right," says Jack. "But take good care because it'll cut forty inches through anything." So boy jest takes hit and puts hit in his box and puts one of his own swords in Jack's box. So next mornin' Jack gets up and takes his sword and goes on home with it. And when he gets there he takes the sword and puts it down in his wood yard and says, "Cut away, cut away, sword," and it wouldn't do nothin,' so he got awful mad and sold his sword for about a dollar and started back to stop the northwest wind. So he got back over there where his uncle lived. And his uncle says, "Jack, what you doin' here, and where's your sword?"—

"That sword want no good and I sold hit for a dollar and I'm goin' to stop the north wind." So his uncle says, "I'll tell ye what I'll do. If you'll go on home and let the northwest wind alone, I'll give ye a club and when you say, 'Play away club,' hit'll jest bust up anything."—"Well, bedads, I will." So he got his club and started and went right on over to that house and stopped to stay all night. And he told that boy all about his club. So way in the night Jack was layin' there awake and heard the boy say, "Play away club." And the club began to play away and just knocked the boy over and jest addled him. And Jack got his rooster and his sword and tuk his club and went on home and when I left there Jack was plumb rich.

*Type 563, The Table, the Ass, and the Stick. Bolte & Polivka XXXVI, LIV (1:349-61).*

## Jack and the Fox

One time they was an old man and three sons, Jack, Will and Tom. He called 'em up and divided his fortune. Give 'em all their portion and started 'em out to see who could marry the richest. Jack says to his father, "I don't want but one thing you've got, that's the old pet fox." Will and Tom got theyselves all dressed up fine and started out. They didn't want Jack to foller 'em, he looked like such a slab, so they made him go by hisself. So he tramped all day long. Finally along about dark he looked up the hill and saw a farm house and he thought he'd better go there and try to git lodgin' fer the night. Didn't have a penny, jest old pet fox. He went on up to the house and out in the yard he said, "Hello!" And here come the prettiest little cat walkin' to the door. "Who keeps house here?" says Jack. She says, "Cat and a mouse. I use to be a woman but the witches got mad at me and witched me into a cat, but," she says, "if you'll stay here three days and nights and not let a thing come into this house, not the least thing even down to a mouse, I'll be a pretty girl and I'll marry you." So he squeezed the old fox and it said, "Gold enough." "Yes, bedads, I will," says Jack.

So he put his old fox down and he cut him some clubs and fixed hisself at the door. Everything from a elephant to an ant tried to come in on him that night —all kinds of varmints. Next morning he went to the cat about hit and there's the prettiest baby he ever saw. So he got breakfast. The varmints weren't bad to try to come in of a day—always at night. And that night he got him some lamps and candles and he jest killed snakes and rats an other varmints all night long. Next mornin' he saw jest the prettiest little girl he ever did see. And he squeezed the fox and hit says, "Gold enough." So he fit all that night and she was a pretty woman and they uz married. So they hitched up the horses and carriage and started out fer his father's so as Jack cud show him his wife.

When they got near, they heard the banjo and fiddle and music and all, and Will and Tom and their wives was there. So Jack pulled out on a turnpike and left his wife and put on his old clothes and tuk his pet fox under his arm and went in. So Will he pushed his wife behind one door, Tom, he pushed his behind the beds so they wouldn't see Jack he was so shabby. So Jack come on in and he squeezed his fox and hit says, "Gold enough." And then Jack, he went and got his wife and carriage and all and drove up. And Tom tuk his wife out one door and Will tuk his out the other—'cause they weren't rich. So Jack he come out the right end of the horn. He married plumb rich.

*Known as "Cat 'n' Mouse" by Monroe Ward and Marshall Ward.*

*Type 401, The Princess Transformed into a Deer. Bolte & Polivka LXIII, XXXIII A.*

## The Enchanted Lady

One time they's an old king and he got so rich and he put out an oration that anyone who cud break the enchantment of his youngest daughter cud have her and half of his kingdom. And the way to break the enchantment was to stay in sight of a rabbit twenty-four hours. But if you couldn't keep the rabbit in sight twenty-four hours the king killed ye. But if ye cud, you killed the king. So they's jest lots and lots went over. Every time one ud start over they'd meet a little old dried up man. He's ask 'em where they was goin' and they jest sass 'em and go on. So this little old Jack, he started over. So he met the little old man. "Where you goin,' son?"—"Well, Uncle, I'm goin' over to the king's house to try to keep in sight of a rabbit twenty-four hours." "Take this drill down and the rabbit ul jest take right out around hit and go 'round and 'round until hit falls over dead." So Jack put hit in his pocket and went over to the king's house. Says, "Hello." King comes out and says, "What'll ye have?" "I've come over to try and break the enchantment of the lady," says Jack. "You know if ye don't I'll kill you, don't ye?" "Yes, I know hit," says Jack.

So the old king stove out and ketched a rabbit right down in the thicket and he give hit to Jack and while he was a ketchin' the rabbit Jack jest wretched down and stuck the drill in the ground and the rabbit tuk out around hit. So the old king begun to git kind of sick. He didn't know what was the matter but he seen Jack was a goin' to git him. So long in the evenin' he says to his daughter, "Jack's goin' to git to kill me. I wonder if you kin go down there and buy that drill." So she went down to where Jack was and tried to buy the drill off him. Jack says, "If you'll hug me and kiss me right good." So she did but he said, "No, I'm goin' to have you and half the old king has got." So she went on back and told the old king and he sent his oldest daughter. She offered Jack a pile of money. Jack says, "No, but if you'll hug me and kiss me right good, you kin have hit." So after a while he says, "Now you've hugged me and kissed me, but I'm goin' to kill him and have your sister." So the oldest sister went on back. "Well," says the king, (It was between sun down and dark.) "I guess Jack's goin' to kill me." So he went in where the queen sit a smokin' her pipe and says, "Mammy, you go down and see if you kin buy hit." She went down un told Jack all the disheartenin' tales she cud. Jack says, "If you'll hug and kiss me right good, I'll let ye have hit." So she hugged and kissed him right good, but when she got through, Jack says, "I'm goin' to kill the old king, and I'm goin' to have a half of his fortune and his youngest daughter. That's the oration and I'm goin' to stick to hit." So she went on back. Long in the evenin' old king says, "I'm goin' to die, I'm goin' to take this bowl and we'll have Jack sing hit full fer me 'fore I die."

So king went down and says, "Jack, will ye sing the bowl full for me?" Jack says, "All right."

> Your youngest daughter she come down,
>     Oh fer to buy my drill;
> She hugged me and she kissed me well,
>     Fill, bowl, fill.
> Your oldest daughter she come down,
>     Oh fer to buy my drill.
> She hugged . . . . . . . . . . . ..

"Stop! Jack, stop! Oh, oh, oh, don't sing that, Jack," says the old king, "jest kill me." So Jack killed him and married his daughter and when I left there Jack uz rich.

*Known as "Jack and the Drill" by Maud Long, "Fill, Bowl, Fill" by Monroe Ward. Type 570, The Rabbit Herd. Bolte Polivka III, 267-74.*

## Jack the Giant Kller

One time they was a fine wealthy man lived way out in the forest. But he couldn't have nothing, hogs and sheep and cows and sech like because the giants killed 'em. So he went out and put him up an ad-ver-tise-ment (Put up a board or hew out the side of a tree and write what he want to.) So he put up one for some one to clear land. Little old boy Jack saw hit and he tramped and tramped until he got away out in the forest and he called, "Hello." Old man hollered, "What'll ye have?" Jack says, "I've come to clear yer land." "All right," says the man. It was Sunday evenin' un they uz havin' supper. The old lady says, "What'll ye have for supper, Jack?" He said mush and milk. While they was makin' the supper a preacher come in an' they sit the mush away and they fried him a chicken and fixed some coffee and fixed a good supper. After supper Jack tol 'em he wanted a piece of leather so he made him a pouch, a sort of haversack thing to tie around his waist. Next morning they got up, asked Jack what he'd have for breakfast. Said, "Jest give me that cold mush and milk." He'd take a spoonful and then poke one in a hole in his pouch. So he got it full. Then he said he was ready to go to work. So man says, now he says, "Jack I don't want you to back out, but I'm no a wantin' any land cleared. I want to kill them giants over there and I'll give a thousand dollars a head for them—some of 'em has two heads and I'll give you five hundred dollars down, and five hundred dollars when you come back." Jack says, "Give me a tomihawk (that's a thing like a hatchet 'cept it has two heads to hit. They used hit in olden times. Indians use to use hit to scalp with.) and I may be in for dinner, and hit may be night when I git in." So they give him a tomihawk and he went over in the forest and climb a great long pine. Along about one o'clock he looked way down in the holler and saw a great old giant a comin' up with two heads. So he says to himself, "Land, I'm gone." So the old giant come, and he says, "What are you doin' up there?" Jack says, "I'm a clearin' timber." Giant says, "Come down from there, you ain't got sense enough to clear timber, you have to have an ax and chop down timber." So Jack come down a little way. "Have ye had yer dinner?" says the Giant. Jack says, "I've had my dinner." Giant says, "I'm sorry, I jest come to ask you to come down and take dinner with me. Come down, let's wrestle and play a while." Jack says, " All right, bedads, I'll be down." So Jack come down and down, till he got right on a limb a top the giant. He had no idea of comin' down when he started, jest tryin' to bluff the giant. Jack says to the giant, "I can do somethin' you can't do." Giant says, "What is hit?" Jack says, "I can squeeze milk out of a flint rock." Giant says, "Oh ye can't do hit?" Jack says, "Yes, I can, you hand me one and I'll show you." So Giant handed him up one and Jack gits hit right close to his little old pouch and squeezes milk out on the rock and drapped the milk on the giant. Giant says, "Hand me down that rock; if you can squeeze milk out of hit, I can." Jack handed it down to the giant. The giant was so stout that when he put his hands to hit, he just crushed it into powder. Jack says, "I told you you couldn't squeeze milk out of hit. I can do something else you can't do."—"What's that?"—"I kin take a knife and cut my belly open and sew hit up again." Giant says, "Oh you can't neither." "Yes, I can," says Jack. "I'll show you, hand me your knife." So the giant hands him up his knife and Jack cut that pouch open and sewed hit up again. "Now didn't I tell you I could?" Giant says, "Hand me down that knife," and he just rip his belly open and fell over dead. So Jack crawled back down and tuk his tomihawk and cut off his head. And that evening late he come waggin' him in a giant's head. That jest tickled the forest man and he paid Jack a heap of money and says, "Now Jack, if you kin jest get the rest of 'em; they's a whole family of 'em."

So next morning Jack took his tomihawk (or tommy hatchet) and went over and climb the big old pine agin. So long about noon he looked down the holler and saw two giants a comin' each with two heads on. So they begin to get closter and closter. Jack climb down and tuk out down the holler and as he went he filled his shirt tail with rocks. After a while he come to a big old holler log and he climb in hit with his shirt tail plumb full of rocks. So the giants went up and mourned over their brother. And they went down past Jack sayin', "Poor brother, if we jest knew who it was a murdered him, we'd shore fix him." Jack was a layin' in there with his heart jest a beatin'. They past the log and said, "Let's pick up this log and carry hit down to poor old mother for some kindlin'." So they each tuk an end and carried hit a little ways. Jack thought he'd try his rocks on 'em. So he crawled up pretty close to the end and throwed a rock and hit one of the giants. Giant says to the other one, "What you hit me for?" Giant says, "I didn't hit you."—"Yes, you did too." Jack crawled back and throwed a rock at the other giant. "What you hit me for? I never hit you."—"I didn't hit you."—"Yes you did too." So they fit and they fit and fit and directly they killed each other; one fell one side of the log dead and the other on the other side. So Jack crawled out and cut their heads off and went on back home. So he was gettin' him a pretty good load of money and was gettin' awfully tickled. The forest man were plumb tickled too and said, "Jack if you jest can get the rest. But watch out they don't get you." "Bedads they won't git me," says Jack. So next morning he says, "Give me my tomihawk," and he went on out. So along in the evenin' he looked down the holler and saw a little old giant comin' up about his size. "Well," says Jack, "I've about got 'em from the looks of this one." This little giant come up a talkin' to hisself. Looked up in the tree and saw Jack sittin' there. "Stranger, can you tell me who has killed my poor brothers?"—"Yes, I killed your brothers, and bedad, I'll come down and kill you if you fool with me."—"Oh please, Jack, please, Jack, I'm all the child my mother's got left, and you kill me there won't be nobody to git her wood this winter and she'll freeze to death. If you'll come down I'll take you home with me, and we'll have the best dinner." So Jack went on down. Giant went to his mother and says, "Jack come home with me, and he says he's the one who killed brothers but he's not much." So Giant's mother says, "Well, come on in, Jack, you'uns go out and play pitch crowbar awhile." Jack couldn't lift it. Little old giant pick hit up and throwed hit about one hundred yards. Jack went over and picked up one end and begin to holler, "Hey, uncle. Hey, uncle." Giant says, " "Hey, Jack, what you hollerin' about?"—"I've got an uncle in the Illinois who is a blacksmith and I thought I'd pitch hit to him."—"Oh don't do that, Jack, hit's all we have."—"Well if I can't pitch hit to Illinois, I won't pitch hit at all." Little giant slipped back to the house. "Mother, I don't believe Jack is much stout." "Well, we'll see," says the mother. "Here boys, take these pails down to the river." Little old giant tuk the buckets and when he got to the river he stove in his bucket and put hit up full and then he stove Jack's in and put hit up full. Jack begun to roll up his sleeves. Little old giant says, "What you goin' to do Jack?"—"Oh thought I'd carry up the river."—"Oh don't, Jack, mother might walk in her sleep and fall in."—"All right," says Jack, "but I wouldn't be ketched a carryin' that little old bucket." So they went on back. The mother had a big hot oven sittin' in front of the fire with a plank across hit. "Git on this plank Jack and I'll ride ye," says she. So Jack got up un she shuck him and shuck him trying to shake him into the oven but he fell off on the wrong side. "Let me show you," says old mother giant, and she got on and Jack give her a shake and popped her into the oven, and he had him a baked giant in a minute.

Little old giant came in, says, "Mother, mother, I smell Jack." Jack says, "No you don't, that's your mother ye smell." When little old giant sees Jack, he begin to holler, "Oh! Jack, I'll give ye anything if you won't kill me."—"All right, give me a suit of invisible clothes." So he give him invisible suit and Jack just went over the house and tuk what he wanted, all that was any account, because the giant couldn't see him. And Jack tuk a sword and walked up to the little old giant and stuck hit in him and went and got him some silver and when I left there, Jack was plumb rich.

*Type 1088, Eating Contest. 1640, Getting the Giants to Kill Each Other; The Brave Little Tailor. 1063, Throwing Contest with Club. 1060, Squeezing Water from a Stone. 1121, Ogre's Wife Burned in Her Own Oven.*

# Lazy Jack and His Calf Skin

They was an old man and old woman had three sons, Jack, Will, and Tom. Jack was awful lazy. So they didn't give Jack anything when they see they had to die, with the exception of one little old poor calf and Jack was too lazy to feed hit.

So the other boys was over in the new ground a clearin' away and Jack's little old calf were over there a buzzin' round eatin' lin bushes and sech, and they cut a tree down and killed it. So they come on over to the house and said, "Killed your little old calf over there, Jack. You can go over and skin it and eat it or just let it lay there." "Bedads, I'll go over and skin it," says Jack. So he went over and skinned it and come on back and brilled the meat. He sit there in a corner and brilled and brilled hit 'til he got the meat all eat up. Gin he got the meat all eat up the hide was good and dry. So he got the hide down and he sewed hit all up good and he left the tail on and filled it with old shucks and cobs so when he shuck hit he could make hit rattle good.

So he tuk hit by the tail and started off down the road one morning, a draggin' hit all day until late that evenin' he come to a house. He called, "Hello! Can I stop here this evenin'?" Woman come to the door, says, "Yes, I guess ye can. My husband's gone but Mr. Passenger's here and I guess ye can stop the night." So she met Jack at the door and jest sent him on up stairs. Didn't offer him no supper or nothin'. So instead of gettin' in bed, Jack lay down on the floor and peeked thru a knot hole to see what they all did there and he saw her fix the finest supper. They jest had everything that cud be thought of, baked pig and stuffed goose and roast chicken and pies and cakes. And her and Mr. Passenger sat down and started eatin'. So Jack was a lyin' up there jest starved to death. So they eat all they cud eat, then tuk and put hit all away and got out all kinds of drinks. Jack watched good where they put it. So they was sittin' a drinkin' and they heard her husband come a whistlin'. So the old man said, "Where'll I git. Where'll I git." She said, "Jump in that big chist and I'll lock you up." So he run jumped in the chist and she run got all the drinks put away and she run jumped in the bed. So the husband come in and said, "Old woman, got anything cooked to eat around here?"—"Yes, I guess you'll find some bread on the table," she says.

So Jack saw the old man a eatin' down there so he dragged the cowhide around and old man said, "What's that?" Woman says, "Little old crazy boy stopped here to stay the night. Guess that's him makin' that noise." Man said, "What's his name?"—"Says his name's Jack." So the man hollered, "Jack, come down here and have some supper with me." Jack says, "Don't care if I do." So Jack didn't eat two bites of bread 'fore he stuck his hand back and shuck that cowhide so hit made a noise. So he fired in on the old cowhide and went to beatin' on hit. "Shut your mouth, you blobber mouthed thing," he says. Old man says, "What's hit sayin, Jack? What's hit sayin'?" Jack says, "Oh I don't want to tell, the big mouthed thing. I'm afraid it will make the woman of the house mad." Man says, "Now, you go ahead and tell me. I don't care for the woman of the house. You tell me what hit said." Jack says, "Well, hit says over there in that buffet there's roast pig and stuffed goose and roast chicken and pies and cakes." Man says, "Is they, old woman?"—"Yes, little bit I was savin' fur my kinfolks." Man says, "Jack and I er your kinfolks, you bring 'em out here." So the old woman got up and set 'em out all the good eatings. They didn't eat long 'fore Jack reached out and shuck the little old calf agin'. Said, "You shut your mouth, you blobber mouthed thing." Old man says, "What's hit saying Jack? What's hit sayin'?" "Oh, I don't want to tell," says Jack, "I'm afraid it will make the woman of the house mad." "Now, you go ahead and tell me," says the man. "Well, hit says over in that cabinet is whiskey and brandy and gin and all manner of drinks."—"Is they, old woman?"—"Yes, little I was savin' for my kinfolks."—"Well, Jack and me er your kinfolks, you bring 'em out here." So she brung 'em out.

The man begin to git a little foxy. "What'll you sell that fer?"—"Oh, I couldn't sell hit."—"I'll give you five hundred guineas for hit." "Well," Jack says, "if you give me that chist over there and five hundred guineas you kin have hit." (My mammy always told that a five dollar bill was as much as a guinea.) So old woman says, "You can't sell that old chist. That's a chist my poor old father give me." Man says, "I bought that chist and I paid fer hit too, and I'm a goin' to sell hit." So the man and Jack traded and the man helped Jack git the old chist up on his shoulders. So Jack carried the old chist a little ways. He didn't want hit 'cept to tease the Old Passenger. He said, "Ill jest drap this in the well." Old Passenger says, "Oh, don't put me in the well. I'll poke you out five hundred guineas if you'll not put me in the well." So Jack put down the chist and took the five hundred guineas that the Old Passenger poked out. Jack jest tuk hit and went on. Old Passenger didn't have sense enough to say if you'll let me out. So some people come along and heard the Old Passenger a hollerin' and they run back to a house and said they was a talkin' chist up the road. They let the Old Passenger out.

Jack went on home and he had him a load of money. So his brothers said, "Jack, where'd you git all that money?" "Sold my cowhide, how'd you think I'd get hit?" So the brothers run out and shot some big fine horses and skun 'em. And they didn't give 'em time to dry or nothin! They jest sewed 'em up and started. So the flies just got after them and they drug 'em around and nobody wouldn't let 'em come in with old green flies. So they come home and says, "Jack, we're agoin' to kill you. You can have your choice. You can be shot, hung, or drown." He said, "Well, I reckon you kin jest drown me." So they sewed 'im up in a sheet and Jack walked with 'em about a mile down to the river. So when they got down there they poked Jack in but they didn't have no string to tie him. Their conscious was so guilty over killin' their brother neither one of them wanted to go back to the house to git a string. "Well, ye can both go back," says Jack, "I'll not leave." So while Jack was a layin' there a man come up the road with a big immense sheep drove. "Stranger, what are you doin' here?"—"I'm fixin' to fly to heaven," says Jack. "In a few minutes two little angels ul come and fly up to heaven with me." So the man said, "I'm old now and if you'll let me go to heaven in your place I'll give you my sheep drove." So Jack says, "All right," and he jumped out and drove his sheep up the road a bit and then he come back and holped the old man git in the sheet. He saw his brothers acomin' and he hide in the thicket. So they come on down and tied up the sheet and throwed hit in the river. So then Jack started to holler, "Sheep! Sheep! Open up the gates and let me in." "Where'd ye git them sheep?" says his brothers. "Got 'em in the river. Where did you think I got 'em?"— "Oh, Jack, you reckon we could git a sheep drove?"—"I reckon so, but I'm not agoin' to fix up your sheets. You'll have to yourselves. I'll throw you in. I could have got a lot more if you'd throwed me out in the river farther. So they throwed one of the brothers and he begin to kick about. "What's he doin' that fur?" says the other. "Oh, he's gathering his sheep."—"Oh, Jack, hurry up and throw me in fore he gits 'em all. Throw me farther." So Jack threwed him in and then he driv his sheep drove home and when I left there Jack was rich.

*Known as "The Heifer Hide" by Maud Long, R.M. Ward, Miles Ward, Stanley Hicks. Type 1535, The Rich and the Poor Peasant; 1737, The Parson in the Sack to Heaven.*

*Motif K1571, Trickster discovers adultery: Food goes to husband. K1574, Trickster as sham-magician buys chest containing hidden paramour. Bolte & Polivka, LXI.*

# Part III

# Jane Hicks Gentry's Songs

# The Songs

The manuscripts for Jane Gentry's songs were obtained on microfilm from the Houghton Library, Harvard University Library. Cecil Sharp's original manuscript collection is in the Clare College Library at Cambridge University, where he studied. He told Harvard professor George Lyman Kittredge that he wanted a set to go to Francis Child's college (Harvard University). This was arranged after Sharp's death by his literary executor, Maud Karpeles.

John Forbes, formerly a member of the music department of Berea College and now head librarian at Baker University, Baldwin, Kansas, transcribed Jane Gentry's tunes from the Sharp manuscripts. He also transcribed Maud Long's tunes from Library of Congress tapes, and I recorded the texts. Sharp's handwriting and notation were not always easy to interpret. Maud Karpeles's texts were carefully typed. We have tried to record both tune and text as accurately as possible. What may appear to be a typographical error may very well be Sharp's spelling or his interpretation of what Jane Gentry sang. Where Karpeles enclosed words in parentheses, I have retained those, for they seem to indicate that she had some question about either what Mrs. Gentry said or what she herself had written down hurriedly as the singer sang.

I have included all of the manuscripts attributed to Jane Gentry, since even scraps of songs may have some value. Some have only a tune or a tune and one verse. I feel certain that Mrs. Gentry sang some of those songs, but because he had collected multiple versions elsewhere, Sharp, who was primarily a musicologist, saved only the tune. He published forty of her songs and ballads in *English Folk-Songs from the Southern Appalachians*. By publishing all of the Gentry manuscripts here, we get a better sense of the range of her material.

Some of the ballads and songs are incomplete. "The Bloody Warning" is clearly an abbreviated version of "The Silver Dagger." One wonders if singers do not reach back in memory for songs they believe the collector would like but that they have not sung in a long time. Sharp said that he had printed them as he took them down without editing and without adornment. It seems important to present the songs here as they were transcribed. Where Sharp listed more than one title we have included all of them.

Ballad lovers and scholars will not be surprised by the irregularity of the stanzas and lines. In "Fair Annie," for example, there are stanzas with three, four, and five lines. Since they do not sing from a printed page, ballad singers are not concerned with time signatures and note values. Jane Gentry, like most traditional singers, measured out the words differently from one singing to the next, from one verse to the next. She had the shape of the tune in her memory and did not feel compelled to match words with notes. Sharp spoke of the habit of dwelling arbitrarily upon certain notes of the melody, generally the weaker accents, which he found common among singers in the Southern Appalachians. This tends to disguise the rhythm and break up the monotony of the phrases, and the resulting improvisation and freedom Sharp found pleasing. He believed that the changes made by singers are often inventive and lead to the development of new songs. On occasion he made note of changes in successive repetitions of the tune. In his notes on Mrs. Gentry's "Pretty Peggy O," Sharp mentioned that it seemed to have been a characteristic of hers to repeat the first phrase, that the first phrase often doubled where the lines were irregular.

The references to Sharp, Child, Bronson, Laws, and Newell are intended to aid students of folksong who are interested in knowing more about the songs. This may seem outmoded, but until there is a better system of identifying traditional songs, these sources are useful.

**Date:** The date on each song is the date Cecil Sharp collected the song.

**Numbers:** Sharp notated the tunes while Maud Karpeles took down the texts. The tunes are numbered 1 to 4977 and the texts are numbered 1 to 1019. The four-digit numbers following the date are Sharp's tune numbers.

**Child:** The ballads that can be found in Francis J. Child's collection *The English and Scottish Popular Ballads* (1882-1898; rpt. New York: Dover, 1965) are so designated, with the number assigned to them by Child.

**Bronson:** The ballads that can be found in Bertrand H. Bronson's *Traditional Tunes of the Child Ballads* 4 vols. (Princeton: Princeton Univ. Press, 1959), are so designated, with the number of the volume in which they appear.

**Laws:** Broadside ballads in Malcolm G. Laws Jr., *American Balladry from British Broadsides* (Philadelphia: American Folklore Society, 1957) are indicated with the letter and number designation used in that volume.

**Newell:** Some of the children's games and songs refer to William Wells Newell's *Games and Songs of American Children* (1883; rpt. New York: Dover, 1963) and the number indicated in that book.

# A Note on the Song Transcriptions

Transcribing folk songs from tapes works on at least two levels for me. First is the mechanical aspect of getting the right notes as far as possible, putting in the most noticeable grace notes and other addenda, and finally producing a reasonably aesthetic whole, useful to student, singer, and scholar alike.

The second level, perhaps more important to me, concerns the essence of the performer. For the performer is such an equal part of this recreation through song that listening and transcribing give unique insights into the quality and personality of the performer. Context plays a significant role: when, where, and under what circumstances did the recorded performance take place?

Jane Gentry sang her materials for Cecil Sharp, a pioneering giant in folk song and folk dance, who worked primarily in this country and in the British Isles. Although his approach to this work has been modified by collectors over the years, we must realize the importance of the corpus of materials he left to us that might otherwise have been lost.

Maud Gentry Long is a different matter. She was a music teacher and thus more conscious of musical accuracy than some traditional singers might be. Much of the material presented here was recorded by Duncan Emrich at the Library of Congress. This setting can be intimidating but did not seem to affect Maud in the least. To me, she sang as a grandmother sings to her grandchildren, passing on this vast, beautiful treasure for a later generation to select from and learn.

Betty Smith has been a patient, kind, and very accurate proofreader and provided all the words of the texts.

John Forbes
Baker University

# 1. THE FALSE KNIGHT IN THE ROAD

Sept 12, 1916 (3426)

Where are you go-ing? says the knight in the road. I'm a-go-ing to my school said the child as he stood. He stood and he stood, he well tho't on he stood, I'm a-go-ing to my school, said the child as he stood.

What are you eating? says the knight in the road.
I'm a-eating bread and cheese, said the child as he stood.

I wish'd you was in the sea, etc.
A good boat under me, etc.

I wish'd you was in the well, etc.
And you that deep in hell, etc.

*Child 3; Bronson vol. 1.*

# 2. THE TWO SISTERS

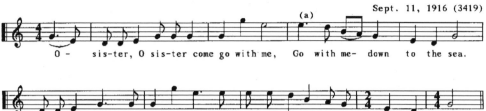

O - sis-ter, O sis-ter come go with me, Go with me- down to the sea.

Ju-ry flower gent the rose-ber-ry, The ju-ry hangs o - ver the rose - ber - ry

We'll take it and we'll make harp strings.

She picked her up all in her strong arms
And threwed her sister into the sea.
  Jury flower gent the rose-berry,
  The jury hangs over the rose-berry.

O sister, O sister, give me your glove
And you may have my own true love.

O sister, O sister, I'll not give you my
    glove
And I will have your own true love.

O sister, O sister, give me your hand
And you may have my house and land.

O sister, O sister, I'll not give you my hand
And I will have your house and land.

O the farmer's wife was sitting on a rock
Tying and a-sewing of a black silk knot.

O farmer, O farmer, run here and see,
What's this a-floating here by me.

It's no fish and it's no swan,
For the water's drowned a gay lady.

The farmer run with his great hook
And hooked this fair lady out of the sea.

O what will we do with her finger so
    small?
We'll take them and we'll make harp
    screws.

O what will we do with her hair so long?
We'll take it and we'll make harp strings.

O the farmer was hung by the gallows so
    high,
And the sister was burned by the stake
    close by.

*Child 10; Bronson vol. 1.*

# 3. EDWARD

August 26, 1916 (3316)

How come that blood on- your shirt sleeve? Pray son now tell to-

me. It is the blood of the old grey-hound that run young fox for me.

It is too pale for that old greyhound,
Pray, son, now tell to me.
It is the blood of the old grey mare
That ploughed that corn for me.

It is too pale for that old gray mare,
Pray, son, now tell to me.
It is the blood of my youngest brother
That hoed that corn for me.

What did you fall out about?
Pray, son, now tell to me.
Because he cut yon holly bush
Which might have made a tree.

O what will you tell to your father dear
When he comes home from town?
I'll set my foot in yonder ship,
And sail the ocean round.

O what will you do with your three little
    babes?
Pray, son, now tell to me.
I'll leave them here in the care of you
For to keep you company.

O what will you do with your sweet little
    wife?
Pray, son, now tell to me.
I'll set her foot in yonder ship
To keep me company.

O what will you do with your house and
    land?
Pray, son, now tell to me.
I'll leave it here in the care of you,
For to set my children free.

*Child 13; Bronson vol. 1.*

# 4. THE THREE RAVENS

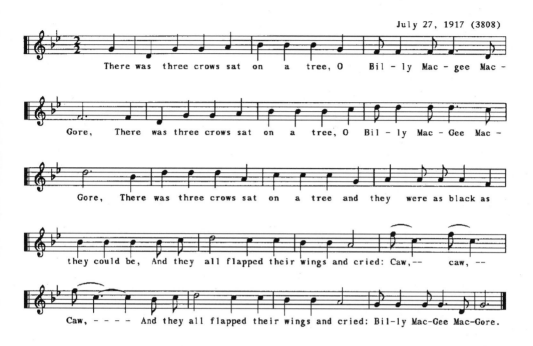

July 27, 1917 (3808)

There was three crows sat on a tree, O Bil - ly Mac - gee Mac -
Gore, There was three crows sat on a tree, O Bil - ly Mac - Gee Mac -
Gore, There was three crows sat on a tree and they were as black as
they could be, And they all flapped their wings and cried: Caw, -- caw, --
Caw, - - - - And they all flapped their wings and cried: Bil-ly Mac-Gee Mac-Gore.

Said one old crow unto his mate:
What will we do for grub to eat?

We'll perch ourselves on his back-bone,
And pick his eyes out one by one.

There is a dead horse on yonders plain,
Just by some cruel butcher's slain.

*Child 26; Bronson 2*

# 5. LORD BATEMAN
# (YOUNG BEICHAN)

August 24, 1916 (3309)

Lord Bee - ham to Glas - gow's gone. The Turks took him a

pris - on - er.

*Child 53; Bronson vol. 1.*

# 6. CHERRY TREE CAROL

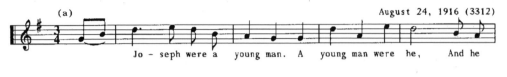

August 24, 1916 (3312)

Jo - seph were a young man. A young man were he, And he
court-ed Vir-gin Ma - ry, The Queen of Gal-i-lee.

Mary and Joseph
Were a-walking one day.
Here is apples and cherries
A-plenty to behold.

Mary spoke to Joseph
So meek and so mild:
Joseph, gather me some cherries,
For I am with child.

Joseph flew in angry,
In angry he flew,
Saying, Let the father of your baby
Gather cherries for you.

The Lord spoke down from Heaven,
These words he did say:
Bow you low down, you cherry tree,
While Mary gathers some.

The cherry tree bowed down,
It was low on the ground,
And Mary gathered cherries,
While Joseph stood around.

Then Joseph took Mary
All on his right knee:
Pray tell me little baby
When your birthday shall be.

On the fifth day of January
My birthday shall be,
When the stars and the elements
Shall tremble with fear.

Then Joseph took Mary
All on his left knee,
Saying: Lord have mercy upon me
For what I have done.

*Child 54; Bronson vol. 2.*

# 7. FAIR ANNIE

August 24, 1916 (3300)

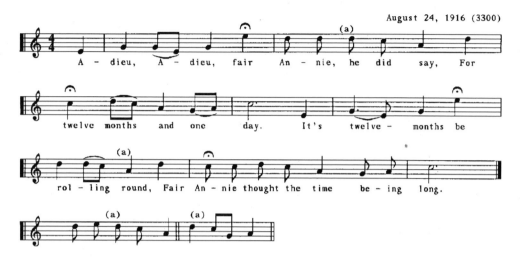

A - dieu, A - dieu, fair An - nie, he did say, For twelve months and one day. It's twelve - months be rol - ling round, Fair An - nie thought the time be - ing long.

She took her spy glass in her hands
And out of doors she went.
She looked to the East, she looked to the
    West
She looked both (to the) North and South
And looked all under the sun.

She thought she saw Lord Thomas a-coming,
All bringing his new briden home.
She called her own seven sons:
I think I see your father a-coming
And bringing your step-mother home.

Come down, come down, dear mother,
    they did say,
Some clothing to put on.
Saying: All of his merry, merry, merry maids
Might as well to come as one.

Fair Annie she had a silken towel
Hanging on a silver pin,
And she wiped out her watery eyes
As she walked out and in.

The rest of them drunk ale, beer and wine,
But fair Annie she drunk cold well water
To keep her spirits alive.

There is a fair lady in our house,
Before tomorrow morning she'll be dead.
We will call to our waiting maids
And have her taken out of town.

A word or two, Lord Thomas, she did say
Before I go away.
I wish my sons was seven greyhounds
And I was a fox on the hill,
And they might have longer (more) breath
    than I
That they might worry me down.

It's who is your father dear and who is
    your mother,
And who is your brother dear
And who is your sister?

It's King Henry he's my father dear,
Queen Chatry's my own mother,
Prince (Quince) Dudley he's my brother dear
And fair Annie she's my own sister.

If King Henry he's your own father dear,
Queen Chatry your own mother,
Quince Dudley your brother dear,
I'll ensure I'm your own sister.

We have seven ships all on the sea,
They're loaded to the brim,
And five of them I'll give to you
And two will carry me home.
And we'll have Lord Thomas burned.

*Child 62; Bronson vol. 2.*

# 8. YOUNG HUNTING
## (LOVING HENRY)

August 25, 1916 (3313)

Come in, come in, my pret-ty lit-tle boy, And stay this night with

me; For I have got of the ver-y best and I will give it up to

thee, I will give it up to thee.

I can't come in, I won't come in
And stay this night with thee.
For I have a wife in old Scotchee
This night a-looking for me.

She did have a little penknife
It was both keen and sharp,
She give him a deathlike blow
And pierced him through the heart.

She picked him up all in her arms,
Being very active and strong,
And she throwed him into an old dry well
About sixty feet.

One day she was setting in her father's
  parlour door,
Thinking of no harm,
She saw a bird and a pretty little bird
All among the leaves so green.

Come down, come down, my pretty little
  bird,
And parley on my knee.
I'm afeard you'd rob me of my life
As you did the poor Scotchee.

I wish I had my bow and arrow,
My arrow and my string;
I'd shoot you through your tender little
  heart,
For you never no more could sing.

I wish you had your bow and arrow,
Your arrow and your string;
I'd fly away to the Heavens so high,
Where I could for ever more sing.

*Child 68; Bronson vol. 2.*

# 9. LORD THOMAS AND FAIR ELEANOR

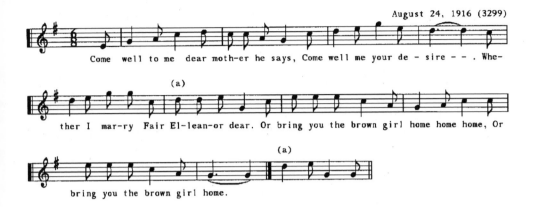

August 24, 1916 (3299)

Come well to me dear moth-er he says, Come well me your de - sire - - . Whether I mar-ry Fair El-lean-or dear. Or bring you the brown girl home home home, Or
bring you the brown girl home.

*Child 73; Bronson vol. 2.*

# 9A. LORD THOMAS AND FAIR ELLINOR

Cecil Sharp collected only the tune and one verse of "Lord Thomas" from Jane Gentry. Maud Long recorded the following very complete ballad for Artus Moser in 1944:

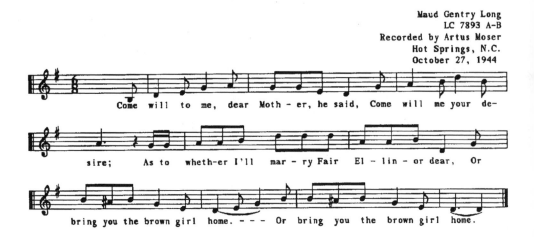

Maud Gentry Long
LC 7893 A-B
Recorded by Artus Moser
Hot Springs, N.C.
October 27, 1944

Come will to me, dear Moth - er, he said, Come will me your desire; As to wheth-er I'll mar - ry Fair El - lin - or dear, Or
bring you the brown girl home. - - - Or bring you the brown girl home.

The brown girl she has houses and land,
Fair Ellinor she has none.
A fore and blessing, my own dear son,
To bring me the brown girl home,
To bring me the brown girl home.

He dressed his playmates all in red,
Himself he dressed in blue.
They took him to be some lord or some
king,
Every town that he rode through,
Every town that he rode through.

He rode and he rode to Fair Ellinor's gate,
He dingled at the ring,
And none were as ready as Fair Ellinor
herself,
To arise and let him come in,
To arise and let him come in.

What news, what news, Lord Thomas, she
said,
What news have you brought to me?
No news, no news, no news at all.
Only, to ask you to my wed-ding,
Only, to ask you to my wed-ding.

Sad news, sad news, Lord Thomas, she
said,
Sad news you have brought to me.
For I had expected to be the bride,
And you the bridegroom for to be,
And you the bridegroom for to be.

Come will to me, dear Mother, she said,
Come will me your desire,
As to whether I go to Lord Thomas's
wedding,
Or dally at home with thee,
Or dally at home with thee.

Great many of your friends will be there,
And more of your foes,
A fore and blessing, my own dear daughter,
To dally at home with me,
To dally at home with me.

Great many of my friends will be there,
And more of my foes,
But be me dead or be me alive,
To Lord Thomas's wedding I'll go,
To Lord Thomas's wedding I'll go.

She dressed her playmates all in white,
Herself she dressed in green,
And every town that she rode through,
They took her to be some queen,
They took her to be some queen.

She rode and she rode to Lord Thomas's
    gate,
She dingled at the ring,
And none were as ready as Lord Thomas
    himself
To arise and let her come in,
To arise and let her come in.

He took her by her lily white hand,
He led her through chambers three;
He led her to his own fireside,
And there he sat down by she,
And there he sat down by she.

Is this your bride, Lord Thomas, she said,
Seems to me she looks wonderfully brown;
When you might have had as fair a lady,
As ever the sun shone on,
As ever the sun shone on.

Yes, this is my bride, Lord Thomas he said,
And, indeed she is wonderfully brown;
And I love the end of your little finger,
Bet-ter than her whole body,
Bet-ter than her whole body.

The brown girl had a little pen knife,
It was so keen and sharp;
She took and she stabbed Fair Ellinor dear,
And she gave her a death-ly blow,
And she gave her a death-ly blow.

It's are you sick, Lord Thomas he said,
Seems to me you look wonderfully pale;
Before your cheeks were as red as a rose,
But since your color has failed,
But since your color has failed.

It's are you blind, Lord Thomas, she said,
Or can't you very well see;
Oh, don't you see my own heart's blood,
Come trinkling down by thee,
Come trinkling down by thee.

Lord Thomas he had a two-edg-ed sword,
It was so keen and sharp;
He took and cut off the brown girl's head,
And he stove it against a tree,
And he stove it against a tree.

Go dig my grave, go dig my grave,
And dig it both wide and deep;
And place Fair Ellinor in my arms
And the brown girl at my feet,
And the brown girl at my feet.

*Child 73; Bronson vol. 2.*

# 10. WIFE OF USHER'S WELL

August 24, 1916 (3307)

Come in come in my two lit-tle babes, And eat and drink with

me. We will nei – ther eat sweet moth – er dear, Nor nei – ther drink of

wine. For yon-der stands our Sa – vior dear and to him we must join. And

to him we must join.

*Child 79; Bronson vol. 2.*

# 11. LITTLE MUSGRAVE AND LADY BARNARD

August 24, 1916 (3297)

The first come down was a ra-ven white, And the next come down was a-

pol-ly. And the next come down was Lord Thom - as' - s wife And

she was the fair-est of them all, all, And she was the fair-est of them all.

*The first phrase was often repeated when a stanza had extra lines.*

Little Matthy Groves was a-standing by,
She placed her eyes on him,
Saying: You're the darling of my heart
And the darling of my life,
And the darling of my life.

It's you no home, no place to lie,
Go home with me this night.
I think by the rings you wear on your
    fingers
You are Lord Thomas's wife,
You are Lord Thomas's wife.

True I am Lord Thomas's wife,
Lord Thomas is not at home.
The little foot-page was a-standing by,
These words heareth he,
And he licked to his heels and run.

He run, he run to the broken down bridge
He bent to his breast and swum,
He swum, he swum to the other, other
    side,
And he buckled up his shoes and he run.

He run, he run to Lord Thomas's gate,
And he dingled at the ring and it rung,
And he dingled at the ring and it rung.
What news, what news, my little foot-
    page,
What news you've brought to me?
Little Matthy Groves is at your house
In the bed with the gay lady.

If that be a lie you've brought to me,
And a lie I expect it to be,
If there is e'er a green tree in these whole
    worlds
A hangman you shall be.

If that be the truth you've brought to me,
And the truth I don't expect it to be,
You may wed my youngest daughter
And you may have all I've got.

Lord Thomas's wife raised up about half a
    doze asleep.
Lay still, lay still, little Matthy Groves
    says,
Lay still, I tell to thee,
For it's nothing but your father's little
    shepherd boy
A-driving the wolves from the sheep.

When little Matthy Groves did wake
Lord Thomas was at his feet.
Rise up, rise up, Lord Thomas he says,
And put your clothing on,
For it never shall be known in Old England
That I slew a naked man.

How can I rise up, he says
When I am afeard for my life?
For you have two good broad-edged swords
And I have not so much as a knife.

True, I have two good broad swords,
They cost me deep in the purse.
But you may have the very best one
And you may have the first lick.

The very first lick that Matthy Groves
     struck,
He struck him across the head,
The very next lick Lord Thomas he struck
And it killed little Matthy Groves dead.

He took his gay lady by the hand,
And he led her up and down.
He says: How do you like my blankets,
And how do you like my sheets?

Well enough your blankets,
And well enough your sheets.
But much better do I love little Matthy
     Groves
Within my arms asleep.

He took his gay lady by the hand
And he pulled her on his knee,
And with the very best sword that he did
     have
He split her head into twain (twine).

*Child 81; Bronson vol. 2.*

# 12. BARBARA ALLEN

August 25, 1916 (3325)

*Child 84; Bronson vol. 2.*

# 12A. BARBARA ALLEN

Cecil Sharp collected only the tune for "Barbara Allen" from Jane Gentry. Maud Long recorded the following version for the Library of Congress in 1947.

Maud Gentry Long
LC 9150 B2
Recorded by Duncan Emrich
Washington, D.C. 1947

So earl-y, earl-y in the spring, When green buds they were swell-ing, There was a young - - man tak-en down sick, love - sick for Bar-bry Al-len. -

He sent his servant down to town
Where Barbry she was dwelling,
My master's sick, lovesick for you
If your name is Barbry Allen.

So slow-ly, slow-ly she put on,
And slow-ly went unto him,
When she was there, made this remark:
Young man I think you're dying.

It's yes I'm sick and very sick,
And death is dealing with me,
And none the better will I be
Till I get Barbry Allen.

It's if you're sick and very sick,
And death is dealing with you,
It's none the better will you be
If you wait for Barbry Allen.

For don't you remember in yonders town
Where we were all a-drinking,
You drank a health to the ladies all around
But you slighted Barbry Allen.

It's yes I remember in yonders town
Where we were all a-drinking,
I drank a health to the ladies all around
And 'twas all for Barbry Allen.

He turned his pale face to the wall,
His back he turned unto them,
Adieu, adieu to my kindred all,
Be kind to Barbry Allen.

She had not gone one mile from the town
When she heard the death bells ringing.
And as they rang, to her they sang:
Hard hearted Barbry Allen.

She looked to the east, she looked to the
    west,
She saw the cold corpse coming,
Oh, put him down, oh, put him down,
And let me look upon him.

The more she looked, the more she wept,
Til she bursted out in crying,
She cried and cried until she died,
Hard hearted Barbry Allen.

He was buried in the old churchyard,
And she was buried beside him,
And out of his grave sprang a bright red
    rose,
And out of hers a briar.

They grew and they grew to the old church
    tower,
And they could not grow any higher,
They lapped and tied in a true love's knot,
And the rose ran 'round the briar.

*Child 84; Bronson vol. 2.*

# 13. LAMKIN (FALSE LAMKIN)

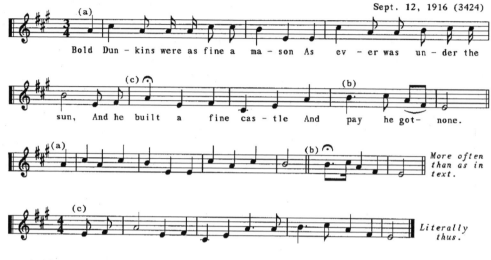

Sept. 12, 1916 (3424)

Bold Dun-kins were as fine a ma-son As ev-er was un-der the

sun, And he built a fine cas-tle And pay he got-none.

*More often than as in text.*

*Literally thus.*

But bold Dunkins crept in
By way of the back door,
And persuaded the nurse
To help him get her down.

We'll pick her baby Johnny
With the silver spade.
And the blood from the head
To the foot-board did run.

Bewore, ye fair lady,
You must come to your dearest one
How can I get to him
At this time of night
When there's no fire burning,
Nor no candle alight.

You've got five golden mantles
As bright as the (or, any) sun.
Bewore ye fair lady,
You must come by the light of one.

She was a-coming downstairs
A-thinking no harm,
When bold Dunkins was ready
To take her in his arms.

O spare my life Dunkins,
Just one half of an hour,
And you may have as much gold and silver
As endel [sic] in the streets.

*Mrs G. could not remember the rest of the
ballad, but she said the maid was sent to
warn the lady's husband of the murder
and she does so by saying that Dunkins
has killed a doe and a swan.*

*Child 93; Bronson vol. 2.*

## 14. JOHNNY SCOTT (JOHNNIE SCOT)

When John-ny Scott saw this big broad let-ter, It caused him for to

smile, – But the ve-ry first line that he did read, The tears run down for a –

while. But the ve-ry first line that he did read, The tears run down for a –

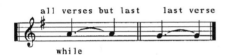

all verses but last    last verse

while

Away to old England I must go,
King Edwards has sent for me,
Away to old England I must go,
King Edwards has sent for me.

Up spoke young Jimmie Scott himself,
As he sat by his knees,
Five hundred of my best brave men
Shall bear you company.

The very first town that they rode through,
The drums, the fifes they played;
The very next town that they rode
    through,
The drums they beat all around.

They rode, they rode to King Edwards's
    gate,
They dingled at the ring;
But who did spy but his own sweetheart,
And her footspade (footpage) a-peeping
    down.

I can't come down, dear Johnnie, she says,
For Poppy has scolded me.
I'm forced to wear a ball (bow) and chain
Instead of the ivory.

Is this young Jimmy Scott himself,
Or Jimmy, Scotland's king,
Or is the father of that bastard child
From Scotland just come in.

I'm not young Jimmy Scott,
Nor Jimmy, Scotland's king,
But I am young Johnnie Scot himself,
From Scotland just come in.

There is a taveren in our town
That's killed more lords (lads) than one,
And before the sun rises tomorrow
    morning
A dead man you shall be.

The taveren flew over young Johnnie's
    head
As swift as any bird;
He pierced the taveren to the heart
With the point of his broad sword.

He whipped King Edwards and all his men,
And the king he liked to have him swung.
I'll make your girl my gay lady
And her child the heir of my land.

*Child 99 (Johnie Scot); Bronson vol. 2.*

# 15. GIPSY LADDIE

Sept. 16, 1916 (3448)

When Lord Thom - as    he  came  home en - quir - ing  for his la - dy, The an - swer that  they made  to  him, She's gone with the Gip-sy Dav - ie.    All  a  lip - to   tal-ly bon-ey, hair, hair,    All a lip - to  lad - die.

It's will you forsake your house and land
And will you forsake your baby
And will you forsake your own wedded
    lord
And go with the Gipsy Davy?
       All a lipto tally boney, hair, hair,
       All a lipto laddy.

I'll forsake my house and land,
And I'll forsake my baby,
And I'll forsake my own wedded lord
And go with the Gipsy Davy.

The night before last I lay on a feather bed,
Lord Thomas he lay with me.
Last night I lay on a cold straw bed
And with the calves a-bawling all around
    me.

*Child 200; Bronson vol. 3.*

# 16. WALY, WALY

Sept. 14, 1916 (3456)

As I walked out one morn - ing in May, A - gath - er - ing flow-ers
all so gay  I  gath - ered white and I  gath - ered blue  But
lit-tle did I know what  love  can  do.

Seven ships all on the sea,
Heavy loaded as they can be,
Deep in love as I have been,
But little do I care if they sink or swim.

*Child 204; Bronson vol. 3.*

# 17. GEORDIE

Sept. 14, 1916 (3451)

As I went o - ver Lon-don's Bridge One morn - ing bright and

ear-ly, I saw a maid for - bide the way La - ment-ing for poor

Char-lie.

It's Charlie's never robbed the king's high
    court,
Nor he's never murdered any,
But he stole sixteen of his milk white
    steeds
And sold them in old Virginia.

Go saddle me my milk white steed,
The brown one ain't so speedy,
And I'll ride away to the king's high court
Enquiring for poor Charlie.

She rode, she rode to the king's high court
Enquiring for poor Charlie.
Fair lady you have come too late,
For he's condemned already.

It's Charlie's never robbed the king's high
    court,
Nor he's never murdered any
But he stole sixteen of his milk white
    steeds
And sold them in old Virginia.

It's will you promise me she said,
O promise me, I beg thee,
To hang him by a white silk cord
That never has hung any.

*Child 209; Bronson vol. 3.*

# 18. THE DAEMON LOVER

It's I could have married the king's
  daughter fair,
And she would have married me,
But I refused a thousand weight of gold,
And 'twas all for the love of thee.

If you could have married the king's
  daughter fair,
I'm sure you are to blame,
For I am married to a house carpenter
And I think he's a nice young man.

It's won't you forsake your house carpenter
And go along with me?
I will take you to where the grass grows
  green
On the banks of sweet Willie.

She pick-ed up her sweet little babe
And kisses give it three,
Saying: Stay at home, mother's sweet little
  babe,
And keep your papee company.

She hadn't been on sea three days,
Not more than a week, I'm sure,
Till she fainted away in her true love's
  arms,
And she fainted for to rise no more.

It's are you weeping for my gold, he says,
Or are you weeping for my store,
Or are you weeping for your house
  carpenter,
That you never shall see any more?

It's I'm not a-weeping for your gold, she
  says,
And I'm not a-weeping for your store,
But I am a-weeping for my sweet little
  babe
That I never shall see any more.

She hadn't been dead but about three days,
Not more I will ensure,
Till there come a leak in her true love's
  ship
And it sunk for to rise no more.

*Child 243; Bronson vol. 3.*

# 19. THE GREY COCK

August 26, 1916 (3315)

All on one summer's eve-ning when the fev-er were a-dawn-ing I-heard a fair maid make a mourn. She was a-weep-ing for her fath-er and a griev-ing for her moth-er, And a-think-ing all on her true love John. At last John-ny came and he found the doors all shut And he ding-led so low at the ring. Then this fair maid she rose and she hur-ried on her clothes to make haste- to let John come in.

All around the waist he caught her and
   unto the bed he brought her,
And they lay there a-talking awhile.
She says: O you feathered fowls, O you
   pretty feathered fowls,
Don't you crow till 'tis almost day.
And your comb it shall be of the pure ivory
And your wings of the bright silveree
   (silver gray).
But him a-being young, he crowed very
   soon,
He crowed two long hours before day.
And she sent her love away, for she
   thought 'twas almost day,
And 'twas all by the light of the moon.

It's when will you be back, dear Johnny,
When will you be back to see me.
When the seventh moon is done and
   passed
And shines on yonder lea
And you know that will never be.
What a foolish girl was I when I thought
   he was as true
As the rocks that grow to the ground.
But since I do find he has altered in his
   mind,
It's better to live single than bound.

*Child 248; Bronson vol. 4.*

# 20. OLD WICHET (OUR GOODMAN)

Sept. 16, 1916 (3484)

She beats me, she bangs me, It is her hearts de-light To beat me with the
pok-ing stick when I come home at night. Old wo-man, old wo-man, what
means all of this? Hor-ses in the sta-bles where my mules ought to be.
You old fool, you blind fool, it's fool can't you see? It's noth-ing but some
milk cows your mam-my sent to me. Miles I have trav-eled, ten
thou-sand miles or more, Sad-dles on a milk cow I nev-er saw be-fore.

Old woman, etc.
Boots on the floor where my boots ought
    to be.
You old fool, etc.
It's nothing but a churn, sir, your mammy
    sent to me.
Miles I have traveled, etc.
Heels on a churn, sir, I never saw before.

Old woman, etc.
A hat on a table where my hat ought to be.
You old fool, etc.
It's nothing but a nightcap your mammy
    sent to me.
Miles I have traveled, etc.
Fur round a nightcap I never saw before.

Old woman, etc.
A man in the bed where I ought to be.
You old fool, etc.
It's nothing but a baby your mammy sent
    to me.
Miles I have traveled, etc.
Hair on a baby's face I never saw before.

*Child 274; Bronson vol. 4.*

# 21. THE GOLDEN VANITY

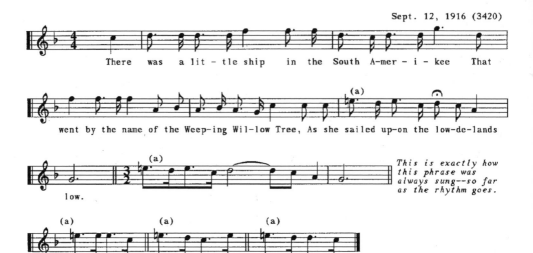

Sept. 12, 1916 (3420)

There was a lit-tle ship in the South A-mer-i-kee That went by the name of the Weep-ing Wil-low Tree, As she sailed up-on the low-de-lands low.

*This is exactly how this phrase was always sung--so far as the rhythm goes.*

There was another ship in the North
    Amerikee,
She went by the name of the golden
    silveree,
As she sailed upon the lowdelands deep.

O captain, O captain, what'll you give to
    me
If I'll go and sink the ship of the Weeping
    Willow Tree,
As she sailed upon the lowdelands deep?

I will give (to) you gold and I'll give to you
    a fee,
Give to you my daughter and married you
    shall be,
As we sailed upon the lowdelands deep.

He bent to his breast and away swum he,
He swum and he sunk the ship of the
    Weeping Willow Tree,
As they sailed upon the lowdelands deep.

He bent to his breast and back swum he,
Back to the ship of the golden silveree,
As they sailed upon the lowdelands deep.

O captain, O captain, pray take me on
    board,
For I have been just as good as my word,
I sunk her in the lowdelands deep.

I know that you've been just as good as
    your word,
But never more will I take you on board,
As we sailed upon the lowdelands deep.

If it wasn't for the love that I have for your
    girl,
I'd do unto you as I did unto them,
I'd sink you in the lowdelands deep.

But he turned on his back and down went
    he,
Down, down, down to the bottom of the
    sea,
As they sailed upon the lowdelands deep.

*Child 286; Bronson vol. 4.*

# 22. BRUTON TOWN (IN SEAPORT TOWN)

Sept. 16, 1916 (3447)

In Sea - port Town there was a merch-ant. He had two sons and a daught-er dear. A - mong them were a prince-y boy – Who was their daught-ers dear-est dear.

*Laws M32.*

# 23. SHOOTING OF HIS DEAR

*Evidently part of the tune only, though Mrs. Gentry seemed sure
this was how her mother sang it.*

He throwed down his gun
And to her he run.
He hugged her, he kissed her
Till he found she was dead.

Then dropping her down
To his uncle's he run.
Good woe and good lasses
I've killed poor Polly Bam.

O uncle, O uncle, what shall I do,
For woe and good lasses,
I've killed poor Polly Bam
Her white apron over her shoulder
But good woe and good lasses,
It was poor Polly Bam

Stay in your own country
And don't run away.
. . . . . . . . . .

The day before trial
The ladies all appeared in a row.
Polly Bam 'peared among them
Like a fountain of snow.

Don't hang Jimmy Danels
For he's not to blame.
My white apron over my shoulder
He took me for a swan,
But good woe and good lasses,
It was me, poor Polly Bam.


*Laws O36*

# 24. THE LADY AND THE DRAGOON

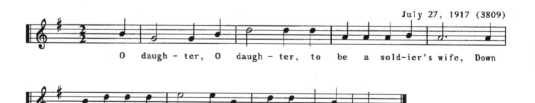

*Bronson vol. 1; Laws M27.*

## 25. EDWIN (EDWARD) IN THE LOWLANDS LOW

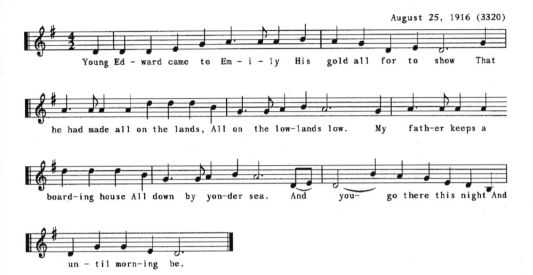

August 25, 1916 (3320)

Young Ed - ward came to Em - i - ly His gold all for to show That

he had made all on the lands, All on the low-lands low. My fath-er keeps a

board-ing house All down by yon-der sea. And you go there this night And

un - til morn-ing be.

Young Emily in her chamber,
She dreamed an awful dream.
She dreamed she saw young Edward's
    blood
Go flowing like the stream.
She rose so early in the morning
And dressed herself although
For to go and see young Edward
Who ploughed the lowlands low.

O father, where's that stranger
Came here last night to dwell?
His body's in the ocean
And you no tales must tell.
O father, O father, you'll die a public show
For the murdering of young Edward
Who ploughed the lowlands low.

Away then to some councillor
To let the deed be known.
The jury found him guilty
His trial to come on.
On trial they found him guilty
And hanged was to be
For the murdering of young Edward
Who ploughed the lowlands low.

The fish that's in the ocean
Swims over young Edward's breast,
While his body's in the ocean
I hope his soul's at rest,
For his name it was young Edward
Who ploughed the lowlands low.

*Laws M34.*

# 26. THE GREEN BED

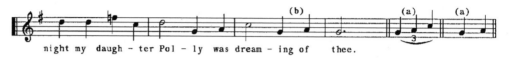

O what for luck, dear Johnny?
No for luck says he,
I lost my ship and cargo
All on the raging sea.

Go bring your daughter Polly
And set her down by me.
We'll drunk a melancholy
And married we will be.

My daughter's busy
And can't come in to thee,
Except you wait an hour,
It's one, two and three.

O Johnny being drowsy,
He dropped down his head.
He called for a candle
To light him to bed.

My beds they are full
And has been all the week,
And now for your lodging
Out of doors you may seek,

It's bring here your reckoning book,
Johnny he did say,
And let me pay my reckoning bill
Before I go away.

'Twas then forty guineas
Polly did behold,
And out of his pockets
Drawed handfuls of gold.

The old woman she vowed,
And she vowed in a tusk,
Saying: what she had said
Had been through a joke.

My green beds they are empty
And has been all this week,
Awaiting for you and daughter Polly
To take a pleasant sleep.

It's you and your daughter Polly
Both deserves to be burned,
And before I lodge here
I would lodge in a barn.

Be careful of your money, boys,
And lay it up in store,
For when you have no money, boys,
You're turned out of doors.

*Laws K36.*

## 27. THE THREE BUTCHERS

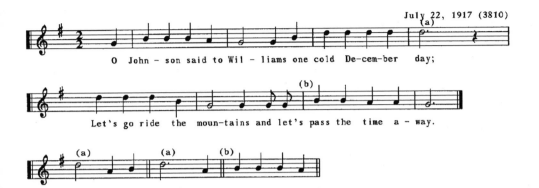

July 22, 1917 (3810)

O John – son said to Wil – liams one cold De–cem–ber day;

Let's go ride the moun–tains and let's pass the time a – way.

*Laws L4.*

# 28. JACK WENT A-SAILING

August 24, 1916 (3305)

Jack went a-sail-ing With troub-le on his mind, To leave his na-tive coun-try And his dar-ling dear be-hind. Sing ree and sing low, so fare you well my dear

She dressed herself in men's array,
And apparel she put on;
Unto the field of battle
She marched her men along.
        Sing ree and sing low,
        So fare you well my dear.

Your cheeks too red and rosy,
Your fingers too neat and small,
And your waist too slim and slender
To face a cannon ball.

My cheeks are red and rosy,
My fingers neat and small,
But it never makes me tremble
To face a cannon ball.

The battle being ended,
She rode the circle round,
And through the dead and dying,
Her darling dear she found.

She picked him up all in her arms,
And carried him down to town,
And sent for a London doctor
To heal his bleeding wounds.

This couple they got married,
So well they did agree;
This couple they got married,
And why not you and me?

*Laws N7.*

# 29. JOHN (GEORGE) RILEY

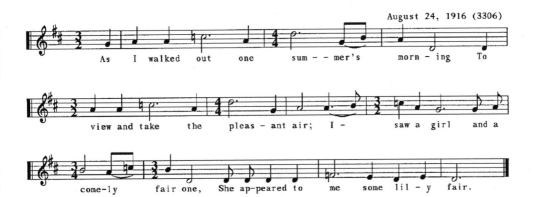

August 24, 1916 (3306)

As I walked out one sum - - mer's morn - ing To view and take the pleas - ant air; I - saw a girl and a come-ly fair one, She ap-peared to me some lil - y fair.

Said I: Kind Miss, don't you want to marry,
O won't you be a merchant's wife?
She said: No, kind Sir, I'd rather tarry,
I'd rather lead a single life.

What makes you differ?
O what makes you differ from all other
    womenkind?
For you are young and you are useful
And now to marry I do incline.

It's no, kind Sir, if I may please to tell you,
I could have been married full four years
    ago
Unto the man, the man they call George
    Riley,
The cause of all my overthrow.

It's when he found that her love was loyal,
Kisses he gave her by two, three, five, four;
I am the man you call George Riley,
The cause of all your overthrow.

Come, let us marry, love, no longer tarry,
We'll lay up riches in great store.
We'll sail the ocean high o'er promotion,
For upon my vow I'll leave you no more.

*Laws N37.*

# 30. JOHNNY DIALS

August 26, 1916 (3318)

Last Fri - day- eve - ning it hap-pened but late, When me and my
John-ny was a-bout to take a flight, My wait-ing maid was a-stand-ing by, these
words hear-ed she, She run to my moth - er and told up - on me.

She kindled up his clothes and bid him to
  be gone,
How slowly and slily he moved along.
By young Samuel Moor they forced me to
  ride,
Took six double horsemen to ride by my
  side.

As soon as the minister he entered the
  door,
My ear-bobs they bursted and fell to the
  floor;
In sixty-five pieces my stay-laces flew;
I thought in my soul my poor heart would
  break in two.

Behind my oldest brother they carried me
  safely home,
And through my mother's chamber and
  into my own room,
And by my own bedside I throwed myself
  down,
How sore, sick and wounded my poor body
  I found.

She called to her old mother: Pray do shut
  the door,
By this time tomorrow let in Samuel
  Moor.
He never shall enjoy me nor call me his
  bride,
For by this time tomorrow it's I will be
  dead.

Up spoke her old father with the water in
  his eyes:
As we found it no better, we'll send for
  Johnny Dials.
It's no use in sending, for the journey it is
  far,
And by this time tomorrow it's I'll be dead.

So farewell cruel father and likewise
  mother too,
And the last words she said was Farewell
  to Johnny Dials.

*Laws M2.*

# 31. MY BOY BILLY

How old is she, Billy boy, Billy boy,
How old is she, charming Billy?
She's a hundred like and nine
And I hope she will be mine.
She's a young girl, etc.

How tall is she, etc.
She's as tall as any pine
And as slim as a pumpkin vine.
She's a young girl, etc.

Can she make a chicken pie, etc.
She can make a chicken pie
Till it make the preachers cry.
She's a young girl, etc.

Can she roll a boat ashore, etc.
She can roll a boat ashore
And make her own door.
She's a young girl, etc.

*Parody of "Lord Randal"; Child 12;*
*Bronson vol. 1.*

# 32. PRETTY PEGGY O

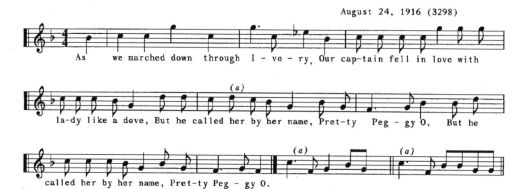

August 24, 1916 (3298)

As we marched down through I-vo-ry, Our cap-tain fell in love with
la-dy like a dove, But he called her by her name, Pret-ty Peg — gy O, But he
called her by her name, Pret-ty Peg — gy O.

*As in previous song first phrase often doubled where lines irregular.*
*It seems to have been a characteristic of Mrs. Gentry to repeat*
*first phrase; and in one instance (see No. 3317) she counters [?]*
*what is usually a ABBA tune into an AABA.*

It's will you marry me, Pretty Peggy O,
It's will you marry me, Pretty Peggy O?
You may dress in your silks and ride the
    buggy high,
Just as grand as any in the country O,
Just as grand as any in the country O.

It's William is the man I do adore,
But I'm afeard my mother would be angry
    O.
What would your mother think to hear the
    chingles dank
And the soldiers marching on the floor O,
And the soldiers marching on the floor O?

Come trip you downstairs, Pretty Peggy O,
Come trip you downstairs, Pretty Peggy O,
Come trip you downstairs and roach back
    your yellow hair,
Take the last farewell of your little
    William O,
Take the last farewell of your little
    William O.

# 33. SHEFFIELD APPRENTICE

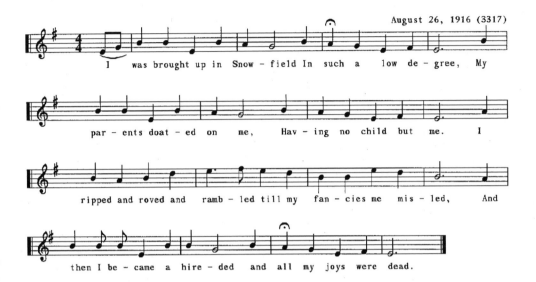

August 26, 1916 (3317)

I was brought up in Snow - field In such a low de - gree, My
par - ents doat - ed on me, Hav - ing no child but me. I
ripped and roved and ramb - led till my fan - cies me mis - led, And
then I be - came a hire - ded and all my joys were dead.

*Laws O39.*

# 34. THE BROKEN TOKEN

A pret-ty fair maid all in her gard - en, A gay young sold-er come a-
rid - ing by. He stepped up to this- hon - oured la - dy Say-ing:
O kind Miss, can't you fan - cy me?

August 25, 1916 (3324)

You're not a man of noble honour,
You're not the man that I took you to be,
You're not a man of noble honour,
Or you would not impose on a poor girl
    like me.

I have a true love in the army,
He has been gone just seven years long,
And seven years more I'll wait upon him,
No man on earth shall enjoy me.

Perhaps he's in some watercourse
    drownded,
Perhaps he's in some battle-field slain,
Perhaps he's stole some fair girl and
    married,
If that's the case you'll never see him
    again.

Perhaps he's in some watercourse
    drownded,
Perhaps he's in some battle-field slain,
Perhaps he's stole some fair girl and
    married,
I'll love the girl that married him.

He pulled his hands all out of his pockets
And rings and diamonds two or three.
He took out a ring that she had give him.
She saw and fell down at his feet.

He picked her up and did embrace her
And kisses give her two or three,
Saying: This is your poor single soldier
Just returned to marry thee.

*Laws N42.*

# 35. THE BRISK YOUNG LOVER
## (BUTCHER BOY)

August 25, 1916 (3322)

In Lon-don Cit-y- where I did dwell, There's a butch-er's boy and I loved him well. I loved him till he broke my heart, And now with me he will not stay.

There is a house in yonders town
Where my love goes and sits him down.
He takes a strange girl on his knee
And tells her what he won't tell me.

That troubles me and the reason why
Is because she has more gold than I,
But her gold will melt and her silver will
    fly,
But constant love will never die.

She went upstairs to make her bed
And not a word to her mother said.
When her mother come in, she says to her:
    My Nellie Dear.
O mother, O mother, you don't know
The grief and sorrow, pain and woe.

When her old father he came home
Enquiring for his Nellie dear,
He run upstairs and the door he broke
And there she's hanging by a rope.

He took his knife and he cut her down
And in her bosom this letter was found.
It's take this letter and read these lines,
For this is the last you'll read of mine.

Must I go bound, must I go free,
Must I love a young man that won't love
    me?
O no, O no, that never shall be,
Till apples grow on an orange tree.

*Laws P24.*

# 36. THE REJECTED LOVER
## (ONCE I COURTED A PRETTY LITTLE GIRL)

August 25, 1916 (3323)

O once I cour-ted a pret-ty lit-tle girl And I loved her as my

life. I'd free-ly give my heart and hand To have made- her my

wife, O to have made her my wife.

I took her by the hand
And I led her to the door.
I kindly asked this pretty little girl
To kiss me once more,
O to kiss me once more.

O who will shoe your feet, my love,
And who will glove your hands,
And who will kiss your ruby lips
When I'm in the far off land?

My father'll shoe my feet, my love,
My mother will glove my hand,
And you may kiss my ruby lips
When you come from far off land,

My being gone six long months,
It gave her room to complain,
And she wrote me a letter saying:
You can't come again.

One cold winter night when I was a-riding
And a-drinking of good wine
And a-thinking of that pretty little girl
That stole that heart of mine.

I wish I'd a-died when I was young,
Or never had a'been born,
For I never would have met her rosy
    cheeks,
Nor heard her flattering tongue.

*Laws P10.*

## 37. SWEET WILLIAM AND POLLY

August 24, 1916 (3304)

Sweet Wil-liam went to - Pol - ly to give her to un - der -stand That he had to go and leave - her To go to a for - eign land.

O stay at home, Sweet William,
O stay at home, said she,
O stay at home, Sweet William,
And do not go to sea.

My king doth give command, my love,
And I am bound to go;
If it was to save my own life,
I dare to answer No.

I'll cut my hair, love, paint my skin,
And men's apparel put on.
I will go with you, Sweet William
And sail on sea with you.

The men do lie bleeding there
And the bullets swiftly fly,
And the silver trumpets a-sounding
To drown the dismal cry.

O tell me of no death nor danger,
For God will be my guide,
And I value not no danger
When William's by my side.

O if I was to meet some pretty girl
All on the highway,
And was to take a like unto her,
What would my Polly say?

My Polly she'd be angry
Although I love her too.
I'd step aside, Sweet William,
That she might comfort you.

O my charming Polly,
These words has gained my heart,
And we will have a wedding
Before we ever part.

This couple they got married,
And William's gone on sea,
And Polly she's a-waiting
In their own coun-te-ree.

*Laws N8*

# 38. EARLY, EARLY IN THE SPRING

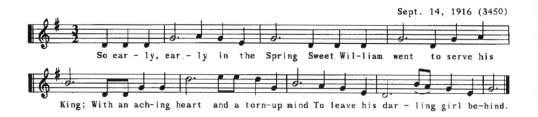

Sept. 14, 1916 (3450)

So ear-ly, ear.-ly in the Spring Sweet Wil-liam went to serve his King; With an ach-ing heart and a torn-up mind To leave his dar-ling girl be-hind.

# 39. THE DRUMMER AND HIS WIFE

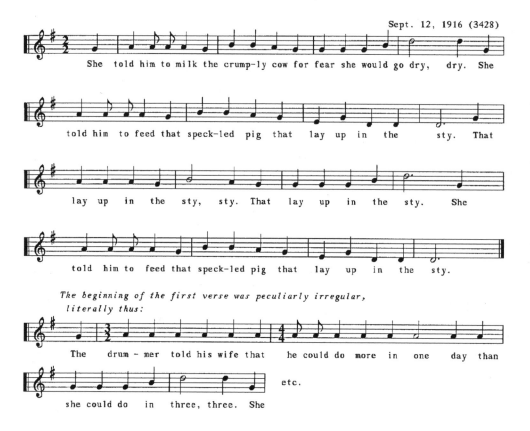

Sept. 12, 1916 (3428)

She told him to milk the crump-ly cow for fear she would go dry, dry. She told him to feed that speck-led pig that lay up in the sty. That lay up in the sty, sty. That lay up in the sty. She told him to feed that speck-led pig that lay up in the sty.

*The beginning of the first verse was peculiarly irregular, literally thus:*

The drum-mer told his wife that he could do more in one day than she could do in three, three. She

etc.

The drummer told his wife he could do
   more in one day
Than she could do in three, three.
She told him to take her place then
And she'd go to the plough.
    And she'd go to the plough, plough,
    And she'd go to the plough.
    She told him to take her place then
    And she'd go to the plough.

She told him to milk the crumply cow,
For fear she would go dry, dry.
She told him to feed that speckled pig
That lay up in the sty.

She told him to churn the churn of cream
That sat up in the frame,
She told him to watch the pot of fat,
Or it'd go up in flame.

She told him to feed that speckled hen,
For fear she would go stray, stray.
She told him to remember the spool of
  thread
That she spun was today.

The drummer went to milk the crumply
  cow
For fear she would go dry, dry.
She hoist her head and give a snort
And wouldn't let the drummer come a-
  nigh.

He went to feed the speckled pig
That lay up in the sty, sty.
He hit his head agin' the beam
And the blood come trinkling down.

He went to churn the churn of cream
That set up in the frame.
And he forgot the pot of fat
And it went up in the flame.

He went to feed the speckled hen
For fear she would go stray, stray.
And he forgot the spool of thread
She spun was to-day.

The drummer told his wife that she could
  do more in one day
Than he could do in three, three.
And if she'd only take her place again
He'd never grumble no more.

*The last two lines of each stanza are
  repeated ad lib. as in first stanza.*

*Laws Q1.*

## 40. ONCE I DID COURT (DON'T YOU REMEMBER)

August 24, 1916 (3303)

The first maid I court-ed was Ma - ry beau - ty bright, And

on her fix - ed my own heart's de-light. I court-ed her for love and

love was my in - tent, And she nev-er, nev-er more give me room to com-plain.

Her old father heard of me and his
  daughter,
To church together we did go.
He locked her up so late and so near
That I never, never more got the sight of
  my dear.

Away to the war I was forced to go,
To see whether I could forget my love or
  no;
When I got there it was all a-shining
  bright,
But I never, never more saw my own
  heart's delight.

I stayed there six months a-serving on my
  king,
And then I was ready to return back home
  again.
When her father saw me come he looked
  at me and cried,
Says: My daughter she loved you and for
  your sake she died.

I stood there like one that was slain,
Tears from my eyes like showers of rain.
My true love she's dead, she died in
  despair,
She lies in her grave and I wished that I
  was there.

*Laws M3.*

# 41. THE LITTLE MAUMIE

August 24, 1916 (3308)

As I went out ramb-ling For pleas-ure one day In

sweet rec - re - a - tion As the time passed a - way.

As I was a-musing
Myself on the grass,
O who did come here near me
But an Indian lass.

She came sat down by me
And took hold of my hand,
Saying: You look like a stranger,
Not one of our band.

But if you will follow
And go along with me
I'll teach you the language
Of the little Maumie.

Together we rambled,
Together we roamed,
Till we come to the river
Where the cokernuts grow.

And the fondest expression
She was heard to say:
Won't you leave your own country
And with me stay?

O no, my pretty fair maid,
It never can be,
For I have a sweetheart
In my own country.

And I'll not forsake her
For poverty,
For her heart is true
As the little Maumie's.

The last time I saw her,
It was down on the strand,
As the ship did pass by her
She waved her hand.

Saying: When you get home
To the girl that you love,
Please think of little Maumie
And the cokernut grove.

It's now I am back
With the girl that I love,
With friends and relations
Around me once more.

But all that around me
Not one do I see
Not one that I'll compare
With the little Maumie.

# 42. THE BLOODY WARNING

August 24, 1916 (3310)

Young men and maids, pray all at-ten-tion Un-to these few lines I'm a - going to write. A cer-tain young man that I may men-tion, He once did court a beau-ty bright.

He courted her both late and early,
He courted her both night and day,
He courted her till he gained her affection,
And drew his mind another way.

Saying: Single son, don't never have her,
For she's poor, she's poor, she's awful poor.
Her coal black eyes like stars are rolling,
Saying: True love, you have come too late.
It's won't you meet me on Mount Sion,
Where all your joys will be complete.

He pulled out a silver daggon (dagger),
He stove it thro' her lily white breast,
And these is the words she said as she
    staggered:
Farewell true love, I'm going to rest.

He picked up this bloody weepin (weapon),
He stole it through his aching heart.
This ought to be a bloody warning
Unto all true loves that has to part.

# 43. MY MOTHER SHE BID (SHE TOLD) ME

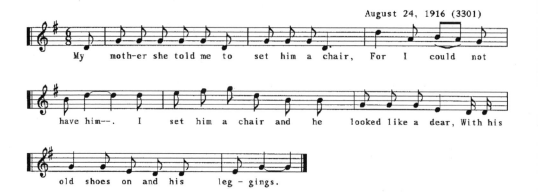

August 24, 1916 (3301)

My moth-er she told me to set him a chair, For I could not have him--. I set him a chair and he looked like a dear, With his old shoes on and his leg - gings.

My mother she told me to set him a stool,
  For I could not have him.
I set him a stool and he looked like a fool.
  With his old shoes on and his leggings.

My mother she told me to tell him to
  come back no more,
I told him to come back no more, but he
  hung in the door.

My mother told me to run him away.
I run him away, but he come back the next
  day.

My mother told me to ride him a path.
I rode him a path, then he went the road
  fast.

# 44. WAGONER'S LAD (MEETING IS A PLEASURE) (OLD SMOKEY)

August 25, 1916 (3319)

To the meet - ing, to the meet-ing, To the meet-ing goes I, For to meet my own true love, He'll come by and by.

I'll meet him in the meadow,
It is my delight.
I will set down and court him
From dark till daylight.

It's meeting is a pleasure
And parting is a grief,
And a false-hearted true lover
Is worse than a thief.

A thief can only rob you
And take all you've got,
And a false-hearted true lover
Can bring you to your grave.

Your grave it will hold you
And turn you to dust.
Just one man in fifty
That a poor girl can trust.

# 45. THE WAGGONER'S BOY (THE WAGONER'S LAD)

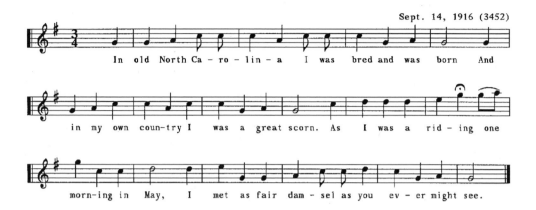

Sept. 14, 1916 (3452)

In old North Ca-ro-lin-a I was bred and was born And
in my own coun-try I was a great scorn. As I was a rid-ing one
morn-ing in May, I met as fair dam-sel as you ev-er might see.

I viewed her features and she pleased me
    well,
I forced all on her my mind for to tell.
She quickly consented my bride for to be,
But her parents wasn't willing for she to
    have me.

I am a poor girl and my fortune is bad,
And I've duly been courted by the
    waggoner lad.
I've duly been courted by night and by day,
But now he's a-loaded, he's going away.

Your horses is hungry, go feed them some hay,
Come set down beside me is all I can say.
My horses ain't hungry, they won't eat
    your hay,
So farewell, pretty Nancy, I've no time to stay.

Your horses is not geared up, nor your
    whip in your hand,
Come set down by me just at my
    command.
My horses is geared up, my whip in my
    hand,
So farewell, pretty Nancy, I've no time to
    stand.

I've duly been courted by day and by night,
I've duly been courted by the waggoner
    lad.
Now he's loading, he's going away.
But if ever I meet him I'll crown him with
    joy
And kiss the sweet lips of my waggoner
    boy.

# 46. IF I HAD A'KNOWN
# (COME ALL YE FAIR AND TENDER LADIES)

Sept. 12, 1916 (3425)

If I had a'known be-fore I'd a court-ed, I nev-er would have
court-ed none. I'd have locked my heart in a box of gold-en And a-
fast-ened it up with a sil-ver pin.

# 47. THE BIRD SONG

Sept. 12, 1916 (3430)

Says the Rob-in as he flew: When I was a young man I choosed two. If one did-n't love me the oth-er one would. And don't you think my no-tion's good?

Says the blackbird to the crow:
What makes white folks hate us so?
For ever since old Adam was born,
It's been our trade to pull up corn.

Hoots! says the owl with her head so
    white:
A lonesome day and a lonesome night.
Thought I heard some pretty girl say,
She'd court all night and sleep next day.

No, no, says the turtle dove,
That's no way for to gain his love.
If you want to gain his heart's delight,
Keep him awake both day and night.
One for the second and two for the go,
And I want another string to my bow, bow,
    bow.

# 48. ANYTHING

August 24, 1916 (3302)

Now gen-tle-men you must not think me wrong, I'm sure you asked me to sing a song, I asked you all what should I sing, And you said you'd like just an-y-thing.

I'll tell you how the gamblers do
That walk the streets both late and true:
Their bodies do totter and their eyes do
    swim,
And they're not fit for anything.

I'll tell you how the ladies do
That dress so fine to catch a beau;
Fine silk dress and a diamond ring
And think they're worth just anything.

184 • Jane Hicks Gentry's Songs

## 49. ONE DAY, ONE DAY

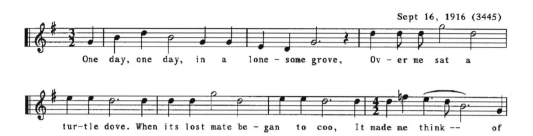

Sept 16, 1916 (3445)

One day, one day, in a lone - some grove, Ov - er me sat a

tur-tle dove. When its lost mate be - gan to coo, It made me think -- of

my love too.

My little dove you're not alone,
For I like you am left alone.
Once like you I had a maid,
But now like you I'm desolate.

*The remaining verses, which relate how
the family is carried off by consumption,
are modern.*

## 50. YOU WELL REMEMBER
## (I WENT TO CHURCH LAST SATURDAY)

Sept. 16, 1916 (3446)

I went to church last Sat - ur - day, My love came rid-ing

by, And I knew her love had changed by the roll - ing of her

eye. By the roll-ing of her eye, boys, by the roll-ing of her eye.

It's don't you remember
You once gave me your hand.
Your vowed if you married
That I might be the man.
That I might be the man, love,
That I might be the man.

But now you have proved false to me,
Go marry who you please.
While my poor heart is aching, love,
You're lying at your ease.
You're lying at your ease, love,
You're lying at your ease.

My love she is a fair maid,
She is proper, neat and small,
And besides that she's good-natured
And that's the best of all.
And that's the best of all, boys,
And that's the best of all.

## 51. THERE'S NOTHING TO BE GAINED BY ROVING

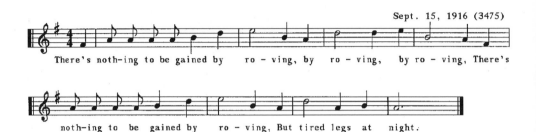

Sept. 15, 1916 (3475)

There's noth-ing to be gained by ro - ving, by ro - ving, by ro - ving, There's
noth-ing to be gained by ro - ving, But tired legs at night.

I'll stay with the girls till morning,
Till morning, till morning,
I'll stay with the girls till morning,
Almost till the break of day.

My mother she will scold me, etc.
For staying away all night.

My daddy he'll uphold me, etc.
And say that I've just done right.

## 52. THE JOHNSON BOYS

July 27, 1917 (3812)

The mount-ain boys are bur - ied in the ash-es, They don't know how to
court a maid. They'll turn their backs and hide their fa - ces, The
thoughts of a pret-ty girl will make them a - fraid.

But the Johnson boys are brave young fellows,
They know how for to court a maid.
They'll hug and kiss and call them honey.
Pitch in, boys, and don't be afraid.

## 53. HOW HARD IT IS TO LOVE

Sept. 12, 1916 (3423)

How hard it is to love and can't be loved a - gain. For

love it is a kill-ing thing and a hard dy - ing pain.

## 54. (O) GO AWAY WILLIE

Sept 14, 1916 (3449)

O- go a - way Wil - lie, And let me a - lone. For

I'm a poor strange girl and a long way from home.

My father's a preacher,
He's very well known
He preaches the gospel
Wherever he goes.

I'll build my love a castle
All on yon mountain high
Where the wild geese can see me
And hear my sad cry.

## 55. IF I HAD AS MANY WIVES

Sept. 14, 1916 (3454)

If I had as man-y wives as stars in the skies I would

be as old as Mo - ses. Turn a - round and kiss your love right quick But

mind don't burst your nos - es.

# 56. JACOB'S LADDER

Sept 15, 1916 (3470)

We'll - climb up Ja - cob's lad-der and its high-er up and high - - er, We'll climb up Ja-cob's lad-der, Hal-le-lu - - jah, hal - le - lu - jah- - - -. We'll climb up Ja - cob's lad - der and its high - er up and high - - er, We'll climb up Ja-cob's Lad - der, Hal - le - lu - jah

See the books of all ages,
There's ten thousand pages,
And we'll climb up Jacob's ladder,
Hallelujah, hallelujah.

See the green leaves a-shaking,
And the sinners' hearts are shaking,
And we'll climb up Jacob's ladder
Hallelujah, hallelujah.

# 57. JESUS BORN IN BETHANY

August 24, 1916 (3311)

Je-sus born in Beth-a-ny,     Je-sus born in     Beth-a-ny,     Je-sus born in
Beth-a-ny. And in the mang-er laid.     And in the mang-er     laid, - -
Je-sus born in Beth-a-ny     and     in a     mang-er laid.

The wise men came and worshipped him,
The wise men came and worshipped him,
The wise men came and worshipped him,
They was guided by the star,
They was guided by the star.
The wise men came and worshipped him,
They was guided by the star.

Judeas betrayed him.
And he give him to the Jews.

The Jews they crucified him
And they nailed him to the cross.

Joseph begged his body
And he laid it in the tomb.

But the tomb it could not hold it,
For it broke the bonds of death.

Mary came a-weeping,
Saying: You stole my lord away.

# 58. INDIAN METHODIST CONVERSION

Sept. 15, 1916 (3474)

In the dark woods poor In-dian lies. He looks up heav-en, he
sends up cries, Down on my knees so low.

Light-ning's a-bla-zing, thun-der's a-roll-ing. Come my lov-ing fath-er, I'm
on my jour-ney home. Glo - ry, glo - ry, glo - ry hal-le-lu-jah!
Come my lov-ing fa-ther, I'm on my jour-ney home.

*The word father is changed to mother, brother,*
*in subsequent verses.*

# 59. THE TREE IN THE WOOD

Sept. 12, 1916 (3431)

There was a tree all in the woods, Ve-ry nice and a hand-some tree The tree in the woods and the woods a - way - down in the val-ley a-way- down in the val-ley. And on that tree there was a limb, Ve-ry nice and a hand-some limb, And the limb on the tree and the tree in the woods and the woods a- way down in the val-ley. A - way- down in the val-ley.

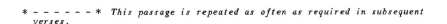

\* - - - - - - \* *This passage is repeated as often as required in subsequent verses.*

And on that tree there was a limb,
Very nice and a handsome limb,
And the limb on the tree,
And the tree in the woods,
And the woods away down in the valley,
Away down in the valley.

And on that limb there was a twig, etc.

And on that twig there was a nest, etc.

And in that nest there was an egg, etc.

And in that egg there was a bird, etc.

And on that bird there was a down, etc.

And on that down there was a feather
Very nice and a handsome feather,
And the feather on the down,
And the down on the bird,
And the bird in the egg,
And the egg in the nest,
And the nest on the twig,
And the twig on the limb,
And the limb on the tree,
And the tree in the woods,
And the woods away down in the valley,
Away down in the valley.

*Newell 46.*

# 60. THE FARM YARD

The hen went ka-ka-ka.

The hog went kru-si, kru-si.

The sheep went baa-baa-baa.

The cow went moo, moo, moo.

The calf went ma, ma, ma.

*This song can be extended at will by adding names and noises of any other animals.*

*Newell 48.*

# 61. I WHIPPED MY HORSE

Sept. 15, 1916 (3478)

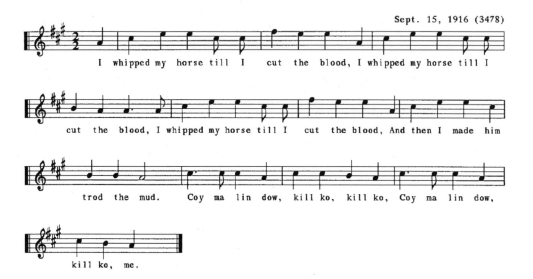

I whipped my horse till I cut the blood, I whipped my horse till I cut the blood, I whipped my horse till I cut the blood, And then I made him trod the mud. Coy ma lin dow, kill ko, kill ko, Coy ma lin dow, kill ko, me.

I fed my horse in a poplar trough
And there he caught the whooping cough.
    Coy ma lin dow, kill ko, kill ko,
    Coy ma lin dow, kill ko, me.

I fed my horse in a silver spoon,
And then he kicked it over the moon.

My old horse is dead and gone,
But he left his jaw-bones ploughing the
    corn.

# 62. THE FROG HE WOULD A-WOOING GO

September 15, 1916 (3477)

The frog went a - court-ing he did ride, Hm, Hm, The

frog went a-court-ing he did ride With the sword and pis - tol by his side, Hm,

Hm.

He rode up to Miss Mouse's door, Hm, hm,
He rode up to Miss Mouse's door
Where he never had been before, Hm, Hm.

He says: Miss Mouse, won't you marry
    me, Hm, Hm,
He says: Miss Mouse, won't you marry
    me.
No, not without Uncle Rat will agree, Hm,
    Hm.

Uncle Rat went a-running down to town,
    Hm, Hm,
Uncle Rat went a-running down to town,
To buy his niece a wedding gown, Hm,
    Hm.

The frog would laugh and shake his fat
    sides, Hm, Hm,
The frog would laugh and shake his fat
    sides
To think that mouse would be his bride,
    Hm, Hm.

O where will the wedding supper be, Hm,
    Hm,
O where will the wedding supper be?
Way down yonder in the hollow tree, Hm,
    Hm.

O what will the wedding supper be, Hm,
    hm,
O what will the wedding supper be?
Three green beans and a black eyed pea,
    Hm, Hm.

The first come in was a bumble bee, Hm,
    Hm,
The first come in was a bumble bee
With his fiddle on his knee, Hm, Hm.

The next come in was an old fat goose,
    Hm, hm.
The next come in was an old fat goose,
He began to fiddle and she got loose, Hm,
    Hm.

The next come in was the old tom cat,
    Hm, Hm,
The next come in was the old tom cat.
He says: I'll put a stop to that, Hm, Hm.

The goose she then flew up on the wall,
    Hm, Hm.
The goose she then flew up on the wall,
And then she got an awful fall, Hm, Hm.

The goose she then flew up on the wall,
    Hm, Hm,
The goose she then flew up on the wall,
And old Tom cat put a stop to it all, Hm,
    Hm.

## 63. THE HIGHER UP THE CHERRY TREE

July 27, 1917 (3811)

The high - er up the cher - ry tree, The rip - er grows the ber - ry; The soon - er a young man courts a girl, The soon - er they will mar - ry.

I went over to my love's house,
But I'm going back no more,
For my foot slipped and I went down
And my head went under the floor.

## 64. REAP BOYS REAP

Sept. 14, 1916 (3455)

It rains and it hails and it's cold stor - my weath - er. In comes the land - lord a - drink - ing of his ci - der. Reap boys Reap and I'll be the bind - er. Lost my true love and where shall I find her.

## 65. EH, LOR! MISS MOLLY

Sept. 14, 1916 (3453)

Eh, lor Miss Mol - ly. Take a walk with me. Down in yon-der gar-den where those pret - ty lil - lies be. Sweet pret-ty, pret - ty ros - es. Straw-ber-ries on the vine. So rise you up go choose the one that's suit - a - ble to your mind.

## 66. COCK ROBIN

Sept. 12, 1916 (3429)

Who killed Bo Rob-in O? Me, said the spar-row, with my lit-tle teen-ty ar - row I killed Bo Rob - in.

Who saw him die?
Me, says the fly,
With my little teenty eye
I saw him die.

Who catched his blood O?
Me, says the fish,
With my little silver dish
I catched his blood O.

Who dug his grave O?
Me, says the jade,
With my little teenty spade
I dug his grave O.

Who hauled him there O?
Me, says the bull,
Just as hard as I could pull,
I hauled him there O.

Who preached his funeral O?
Me, says the swallow,
Just as hard as I could holloa,
And I preached his funeral O.

Who covered him up O?
Me, says the crow,
With my little teenty hoe
I covered him up O.

## 67. THREE LITTLE MICE

Sept. 12, 1916 (3632)

Three lit-tle mice set down to spin, down to spin, down to spin,

**8 times**

Three lit-tle mice set down to spin, Hi - O, Hi - O Hi - O.

(last time) (a) (a)

got no mouse, Me - ow - oo Me - ow - oo

Pussy crept along and she peeped in, etc.

O what are you doing my fine little man, etc.

We're making coats for gentlemen, etc.

May I come in and bite your thread, etc.

O no Miss Pussy, you needn't do that, etc.

For we don't want to see any bad old cat, etc.

For a long time ago we heard you said,
Heard you said, heard you said,
A long time ago we heard you said,
That you meant to bite off our heads.

So, O Miss Pussy, she got no mouse,
Got no mouse, got no mouse,
O, Miss Pussy, got no mouse,
Me-ow-oo.

*Mrs. Gentry accompanied this song with
actions, i.e., spinning in the first verse,
creeping in the second, listening, sewing, etc.,
etc. At the words Hi-O, she made an upward
spiral movement with her right hand.*

## 68. BABY'S BALL

Sept. 12, 1916 (3433)

Here's a ball for ba - by, Big and soft and round.

Here is ba - by's ham - mer, O how she can pound.

Here is baby's soldiers
Standing in a row.
Here is baby's music
Clapping, clapping so.

Here is baby's trumpet
Too, too, too, too, too.
Here is the way that baby
Plays her peek-a-boo.

Here's baby's big umbrella,
Keeps the baby dry.
Here is baby's cradle,
Rock the baby by.

# 69. SING SAID THE MOTHER (OVER IN THE MEADOWS)

Sept. 15, 1916 (3476)

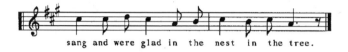

Ov-er in the mead-ows in the nest in the tree Lived an old mo-ther bir-dy and her

lit-tle bird-ies three. Sing, said the mo-ther, We sing said the three. So they

sang and were glad in the nest in the tree.

Over in the meadows in the sand in the
    sun
Lived an old mother toadie and her little
    toadie one.
Hop, said the mother. We hop, said the
    one.
So they hopped and were glad in the sand
    in the sun.

Over in the meadows in a sly little den
Lived an old mother spider and her little
    spiders ten.
Spin, said the mother. We spin, said the
    ten.
So they spun and caught flies in the sly
    little den.

# 70. WE'RE MARCHING ROUND AND ROUND (SINGING GAME)

Sept. 15, 1916 (3469)

We're march-ing round and round and it's two at a time. We're

march-ing round and round and it's two at a time. We're cling-ing to each

oth - er like grapes to the vine. Our com-pan-y's in - creas - ing the

crown we will win. Our com-pan-y's in - creas - ing the crown we will

win. So rise you up my old love to bring a-noth-er in.

Newell 162.

# 71. JENNIE JENKINS

Maud Gentry Long
LC 7923 A-1
Recorded by Artus Moser
Hot Springs, N.C. April, 1946

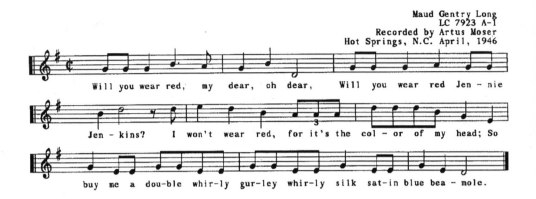

Will you wear red, my dear, oh dear, Will you wear red Jen - nie Jen - kins? I won't wear red, for it's the col - or of my head; So buy me a dou-ble whir-ly gur-ley whir-ly silk sat-in blue bea - mole.

Will you wear yellow, my dear, oh dear,
Will you wear yellow, Jennie Jenkins?
I won't wear yellow, for it'd plague my
    feller;
So buy me a double whirly gurley whirly
    silk satin blue beamole.

Will you wear green . . .
For I'd be ashamed to be seen . . . .

Will you wear black . . .
For it's the color of my back . . . .

Will you wear white . . .
For I'd be out of sight . . . .

Will you wear brown . . .
For it's the color of the ground . . . .

Will you wear blue, my dear, oh dear,
Will you wear blue, Jennie Jenkins?
I will wear blue, for it's the color of my
    shoe;
So buy me a double whirly gurley whirly
    silk satin blue beamole.

*Newell 11.*

*Jennie Jenkins was the only song Jane
deliberately taught her daughter Maud
Long. The rest were "caught."*

# Appendix A

# Song Listings in the Sharp and Bronson Collections

Note: All the songs of Jane Gentry and Maud Gentry Long [MGL] reprinted in this book are listed here, arranged according to Sharp's edition.

| | | Sharp number[1] | Bronson listing[2] |
|---|---|---|---|
| **Traditional Ballads** | | | |
| 1. | False Knight in the Road | 2B | 1: 3, 6 |
| 2. | The Two Sisters | 5A | 1: 10, 91 |
| 3. | Edward | 8A | |
| 4. | The Three Ravens | | 1: 26, 7 |
| 5. | Lord Bateman (Young Beichan) | | 1: 53, 103 |
| 6. | Cherry Tree Carol | 15B | 2: 54, 17 |
| 7. | Fair Annie | 16 | 2: 62, 4 |
| 8. | Young Hunting (Loving Henry) | 18A | 2: 68, 35 |
| 9. | Lord Thomas and Fair Eleanor | 19E | 2: 73, 5 |
| 9A. | Lord Thomas and Fair Ellinor [MGL] | | |
| 10. | The Wife of Usher's Well | 22E | 2: 79, 47 |
| 11. | Little Musgrave and Lady Barnard | 23B | 2: 81, 18 |
| 12. | Barbara Allen | | 2: 84, 54 |
| 12A. | Barbara Allen [MGL] | | |
| 13. | Lamkin (False Lamkin) | 27A | 2: 93, 11 |
| 14. | Johnny Scott (Johnnie Scot) | 29A | 2: 99, 2 |
| 15. | Gipsy Laddie | 33D | 3: 200, 26 |
| 16. | Waly, Waly | | |
| 17. | Geordie | 34B | 3: 209, 31 |
| 18. | The Daemon Lover | 35H | 3: 243, 7 |
| 19. | The Grey Cock | 36 | 4: 248, 6 |
| 20. | Old Wichet (Our Goodman) | 38A | 4: 274, 55 |
| 21. | The Golden Vanity | 41A | 4: 286, 94 |

|  |  | Sharp number[1] | Bronson listing[2] |
|---|---|---|---|
| **Broadsides and Other Ballads** | | | |
| 22. | Bruton Town (In Seaport Town) | 48D | |
| 23. | Shooting of His Dear | 50A | |
| 24. | The Lady and the Dragoon | | 1: 7, App. 1 |
| 25. | Edwin (Edward) in the Lowlands Low | 56A | |
| 26. | The Green Bed | 58A | |
| 27. | The Three Butchers | | |
| 28. | Jack Went A-Sailing | 65A | |
| 29. | John (George) Riley | 82A | |
| 30. | Johnny Dials | 83A | |
| 31. | My Boy Billy (Lord Randal) | 89A | 1: 12, App. 22 |
| 32. | Pretty Peggy O | 95B | |
| 33. | Sheffield Apprentice | 97B | |
| 34. | The Broken Token | 98B | |
| 35. | The Brisk Young Lover (Butcher Boy) | 101B | |
| 36. | The Rejected Lover (Once I Courted a Pretty Little Girl) | 109A | |
| 37. | Sweet William and Polly | 121A | |
| 38. | Early, Early In the Spring | 125D | |
| 39. | The Drummer and His Wife | 188A | |
| 40. | Once I Did Court | | |
| 41. | The Little Maumie | | |
| 42. | The Bloody Warning | | |
| **Lyrics and Songs** | | | |
| 43. | My Mother She Bid (She Told) Me | 108A | |
| 44. | Wagoner's Lad (Meeting Is a Pleasure, Old Smokey) | 117D | |
| 45. | The Waggoner's Boy (The Wagoner's Lad) | | |
| 46. | If I Had A'Known (Come All Ye Fair and Tender Ladies) | 118E | |
| 47. | The Bird Song | 215A | |
| 48. | Anything | | |
| 49. | One Day, One Day | | |
| 50. | You Well Remember (I Went To Church Last Saturday) | | |
| 51. | There's Nothing To Be Gained by Roving | | |
| 52. | The Johnson Boys | | |
| 53. | How Hard It Is To Love | | |
| 54. | (O) Go Away Willie | | |
| 55. | If I Had As Many Wives | | |
| **Religious Songs** | | | |
| 56. | Jacob's Ladder | 212 | |
| 57. | Jesus Born in Bethany | | |

| | | Sharp number | Bronson listing |
|---|---|---|---|
| 58. | Indian Methodist Conversion | | |

**Children's Songs and Playparty Games**

| | | | |
|---|---|---|---|
| 59. | The Tree in the Wood | 206A | |
| 60. | The Farm Yard | 218 | |
| 61. | I Whipped My Horse | 219 | |
| 62. | The Frog He Would A-Wooing Go | 220 | |
| 63. | The Higher Up the Cherry Tree | 268 | |
| 64. | Reap, Boys, Reap | 271 | |
| 65. | Eh, Lor! Miss Molly | | |
| 66. | Cock Robin | | |
| 67. | Three Little Mice | | |
| 68. | Baby's Ball | | |
| 69. | Sing Said the Mother (Over in the Meadow) | | |
| 70. | We're Marching Round and Round: Singing Game | | |
| 71. | Jennie Jenkins [MGL] | | |

1. Listing in Cecil Sharp, *English Folk Songs from the Southern Appalachians*.
2. Listing in Bertrand Harris Bronson, *Traditional Tunes of the Child Ballads*. Numbers are for Bronson volume number, ballad number, and version; e.g., 1: 3, 6 means volume 1, Child ballad 3, version 6.

# Appendix B

# Discography of
# Maud Gentry Long

Archive of Folk Culture, Library of Congress

AFS-L 14. *Anglo-American Songs and Ballads*
  The Cherry Tree
  Fiddle-I-Fee
AFS-L 21. *Anglo-American Songs and Ballads*
  The Broken Token
  The False Knight Upon the Road
  Jackie's Gone A-Sailing
  Sweet William
  My Grandmother Green
AFS-L 47. *Jack Tales*
  Jack and the Drill
  Jack and the Sop Doll
  Jack and the Bull
AFS-L 48. *Jack Tales*
  Jack and the Giants' New Ground
  Jack and the Varmints

# Notes

## 1. An Introduction

1. Manly Wade Wellman, *The Kingdom of Madison* (Chapel Hill: Univ. of North Carolina Press, 1973), p. 3.

2. Irving Bacheller, "My Lost Novel," in *From Stores of Memory* (New York: Farrar & Rinehart, 1938), p. 210.

3. Irving Bacheller, "The Happiest Person I Ever Knew," *American Magazine*, March 1924, p. 7.

4. Eugenia Elliott, personal interview, August 14, 1994, Hot Springs, N.C. This story concerns Elliott's grandfather's visit to Dorland Institute.

5. Bacheller, "The Happiest Person," p. 7.

6. Arnold Toynbee, "Scotland, Ulster, and Appalachia." in *A Study of History*, vol. 2: *The Geneses of Civilization* (London: Oxford Univ. Press, 1935), p. 312.

7. Maud Karpeles, *Cecil Sharp* (Chicago: Univ. of Chicago Press, 1967), p. 146.

8. Ibid., pp. 148-49.

9. Bacheller, "My Lost Novel," pp. 212-14.

10. Elliott interview.

## 2. The Hickses and the Harmons

1. Genealogical information was obtained from *The Hicks Families of Western North Carolina* compiled by John Henry Hicks, Mattie Hicks, and Barnabas B. Hicks (Boone, N.C.: Minor's Printing, 1991); *The Harmon Family* compiled by Terry Harmon (Boone, N.C.: Minor's Publishing, 1984); John Preston Arthur's *History of Watauga County, North Carolina* (Richmond: Everett Waddey, 1915); John Preston Arthur's *Western North Carolina: A History from 1730 to 1913* (Raleigh, N.C.: Edwards and Broughton, 1914); Sanna Gaffney, ed., *The Heritage of Watauga County, North Carolina*, vol. 1 (Winston Salem. N.C.: Hunter, 1984); William Elsey Connelley's *The Founding of Harman's Station* (New York: Torch Press, 1910); census and vital statistics records; World Family Tree; family records; and oral history.

2. Arthur, *Western North Carolina*, p. 354.

3. Arthur, *History of Watauga County*, p. 212.

4. Hicks, Hicks, and Hicks, *Hicks Families*, p. 22.

5. John P. Hale, *Trans-Allegheny Pioneers* (Raleigh, N.C.: Derreth, 1971), pp. 16-35; *Encyclopedia of Virginia* (New York: Somerset, 1992), p. 229.

6. Connelley, *Founding of Harman's Station*, pp. 22-91; *Kentucky: A Guide to the Bluegrass State* (1939; rpt. New York,: Harcourt, Brace, 1973; Lexington: Univ. Press of Kentucky, 1996 [as *The WPA Guide to Kentucky*]), p. 240.

7. Harmon, *Harmon Family*, pp. 16-17.

8. Ibid., p. 23.

9. Hicks, Hicks, and Hicks, *Hicks Families*, p. 27.

10. Gaffney, *Heritage of Watauga County*, 1:369.

11. Harmon, *Harmon Family*, p. 72.

12. Ibid., pp. 40-41.

13. Horton Cooper, *A History of Avery County* (Asheville, N.C.: Biltmore Press, 1964), p. 17.

14. Hicks, Hicks, and Hicks, *Hicks Families*, p. 44.

15. Arthur, *History of Watauga County*, pp. 202-3.

16. Hicks, Hicks, and Hicks, *Hicks Families*, p. 46.

17. Ibid., p. 42.

18. Duncan Emrich, *Folklore on the American Land* (Boston: Little, Brown, 1972), pp. 339-40. In a letter to Duncan Emrich at the Library of Congress, Maud Gentry Long stated that Ransom Hicks was "a minister and Federal soldier" at the time her mother was born.

19. Eugene Hicks, personal interview, March 6, 1992, Hot Springs, N.C. Eugene Hicks, grandson of Uncle Doc, purchased the hotel property and reopened the springs in the spring of 1991.

20. Hicks, Hicks, and Hicks, *Hicks Families*, p. 186.

21. Isabel Gordon Carter, "Mountain White Folk-Lore: Tales from the Southern Blue Ridge," *Journal of American Folklore* 38 (July-Sept. 1925): 365-66.

22. Richard Chase, *The Jack Tales* (Boston: Hougton Mifflin, 1943), p. ix.

23. Harmon, *Harmon Family*, pp. 38-39.

## 3. From Watauga to Madison

1. Rev. Andrew Graves, "Madison County Main Route to Tennessee in 1795," *Asheville Citizen-Times*, Jan. 26, 1969.

2. Chase, *Jack Tales*, p. ix.

3. Bacheller, "My Lost Novel," p. 202.

4. Christian Reid (Frances C. Tiernan), *The Land of the Sky* (New York: D. Appleton, 1892), pp. 43-45.

5. Ibid., pp. 34-35, 46-47. Wilma Dykeman, *The French Broad* (Knoxville: Univ. of Tennessee Press, 1955), p. 144.

6. For a full account of the Shelton Laurel massacre see Phillip Shaw Paludan, *Victims* (Knoxville: Univ. of Tennessee Press, 1981).

7. William T. Moore, personal interview, Aug. 29, 1985, Meadow Fork, Madison County, N.C.

8. Hicks, Hicks, and Hicks, *Hicks Families*, p. 52.

9. Irving Bacheller, "Left Behind," *Collier's*, Oct. 30, 1915, p. 18.

10. Ibid.

11. Lena Penland Purkey, *Home in Madison County*, (Johnson City: East Tennessee State Univ., 1975), p. 26.

12. Bacheller, "My Lost Novel," p. 206.

13. Ibid., p. 203.

14. Eugenia Elliott, personal interview, Aug. 14, 1994, Hot Springs, N.C. When Mrs. Elliott was a student at Dorland Institute, Mrs. Gentry spelled words for the students using the syllabic technique.

15. Irving Bacheller, "The Quest for Happiness," in *Opinions of a Cheerful Yankee* (Indianapolis: Bobbs Merrill, 1926), p. 17.

16. Irving Bacheller, "The Happiest Person," p. 7.

17. Ibid.

18. Bacheller, "Left Behind," p. 19.

19. Jeannette Armstrong, daughter of Emily Gentry Byford, San Luis Obispo, Calif., to the author, April 21, 1989. Bill Moore's account of Ransom's death agrees with Armstrong's (interview, Aug. 29, 1985).

## 4. Plantin' and Hoein' on Meadow Fork

1. Muriel Miller Dressler, "Mountain Sarvis," *Appalachia* (Charleston, W.V.: MHS Publications, 1977), p. 44.

2. Bacheller, "My Lost Novel," p. 211.

3. Warren Wilson, "The Lower Standard of Living," *Mountain Life and Work*, Jan. 1933, p.10.

4. Bacheller, "The Happiest Person," p. 7.

5. Bacheller, "My Lost Novel," p. 211.

6. Jane Long Douglas, personal interview, Oct. 8, 1985, Athens, Ga.

7. Bacheller, "The Quest for Happiness," p.15.

8. Bacheller, "My Lost Novel," p. 207.

9. Ibid., pp. 208-9.

10. Bacheller, "The Happiest Person," p. 7.

11. Irving Bacheller, "Left Behind," p. 19.

12. Nathan Hicks, personal interview, Aug. 1, 1992, Hot Springs, N.C.

13. John Parris, "Roaming the Mountains," *Asheville Citizen Times*, Jan. 1993, from "Random Thoughts of a Mountaineer" by State Superior Court Judge Felix E. Alley of Jackson County, N.C.

14. Courtesy of Jane Douglas.

15. Jeannette Armstrong to the author, March 2, 1989.

16. Hicks, personal interview, Aug. 1, 1992, Hot Springs, N.C.

17. Betty Rolfe, personal interview, Oct. 19, 1987, Hot Springs, N.C. This story was also told by Eugenia Elliott, Mary Kestler Clyde, Irving Bacheller, Jeannette Armstrong, and Lalla Bailey.

18. Eugenia Elliott, personal interview, Aug. 14, 1994, Hot Springs, N.C.

19. C.A. Bowlick, "Roots, Herbs Were Once Big Money Crop," *Asheville Citizen-Times*, Jan. 26, 1969.

20. Armstrong to author, March 2, 1989.

21. Armstrong to author, Sept. 22, 1985.

22. Jeannette Armstrong, personal interview, Oct. 11, 1994, San Luis Obispo, Calif.

23. Bacheller, "Quest for Happiness," p. 18.

24. Armstrong to author, March 2, 1989.

25. Nola Jane Gentry Yrjana to the author, Feb. 26, 1989.

## 5. Moving to Town

1. Karpeles, *Cecil Sharp*, p. 153.

2. John C. Campbell, *The Southern Highlander and His Homeland* (1921; rpt. Lexington: Univ. Press of Kentucky, 1969), p. 260.

3. Henry D. Shapiro, *Appalachia on Our Mind* (Chapel Hill: Univ. of North Carolina Press, 1978), pp. 32-34.

4. Jan Davidson, introduction to new edition, Frances Louisa Goodrich, *Mountain Homespun* (1931; rpt. Knoxville: Univ. of Tennessee Press, 1989), pp. 16-17.

5. Christian Reid (Frances C. Tiernan), *The Land of the Sky* (New York: D. Appleton, 1892), p. 48.

6. Purkey, *Home in Madison County*, p. 114.

7. F.A. Sondley, *A History of Buncombe County*, vol. 2 (Asheville, N.C.: The Advocate, 1930), pp. 587-96, 609.

8. Paint Rock is a high rock along the French Broad River streaked with color from which it takes its name. Folklore has it that Indians painted it, but it seems certain that minerals in the rock are responsible for the vivid color.

9. Pamphlet, *Hot and Warm Springs Hotel*, Warm Springs, N.C., March 1, 1883.

10. William T. Moore, personal interview, Aug. 29, 1985, Meadow Fork, Madison County, N.C.

11. Ledger from the Hot and Warm Springs Hotel, 1882, courtesy of Mary Barden, New Bern, N.C.

12. Jacqueline Burgin Painter, *The Season of Dorland-Bell* (Asheville, N.C.: Biltmore Press, 1987), pp. 11-12.

13. Jinsie Underwood, *This is Madison County* (Mars Hill, N.C.: Bicentennial Commission, 1974), p. 43.

14. Ina W. Van Noppen and John J. Van Noppen, *Western North Carolina since the Civil War* (Boone, N.C.: Appalachian Consortium Press, 1973), p. 160.

15. "Appalachia Calling . . . From a Small Mountain Village to the Great Northwest," *Mountaineer Times* 3 (Summer 1988): pp. 18-20.

16. Pat Roberts, personal interview, July 31, 1994, Marshall, N.C. Roberts was a student at Asheville Normal School when Mrs. Gentry spent a weekend there and gave a program for the students. At age ninety-one she is still active in Republican Party politics.

17. Van Noppen and Van Noppen, *Western North Carolina*, p. 160.

18. Jeannette Armstrong to author, March 17, 1988.

19. Bacheller, "Left Behind," p. 19.

20. Eugenia Elliott, personal interview, Aug. 14, 1994, Hot Springs, N.C.

21. Elizabeth Dotterer, lecture, Sept. 29, 1987, Jesuit Residence, Hot Springs, N.C.

22. Ibid.; Della Hazel Moore, *Hot Springs of North Carolina* (Asheville, N.C.: Biltmore Press, 1992), p. 100.

23. Elliott interview.

24. Elizabeth Dotterer, personal interview, Jan. 25, 1988, Hot Springs, N.C.

25. Dorothy Gentry, personal interview, Oct. 21, 1985, Hot Springs, N.C.

26. Elliott interview.

27. Nola Jane Gentry Yrjana, personal interview, Sept. 20, 1990, Fairbanks, Alaska.

28. Moore interview.

29. Dotterer lecture.

30. Yrjana to author, Dec. 2, 1988.

31. Sharon Baker, personal interview. Dec., 1993, Hot Springs, N.C. Ms. Baker is a teacher in Madison County and a former student of Maud Long's.

32. Yrjana to author, Feb. 27, 1988.

## 6. The Writer Meets the Storyteller

1. Dorland-Bell Papers, Warren Wilson College, Swannanoa, N.C.

2. Irving Bacheller, untitled manuscript, St. Lawrence University Library, Canton, N.Y.

3. Isabel Gordon Carter, "White Mountain Riddles," *Journal of American Folklore* 47 (Jan. 1934): 78.

4. Bacheller, untitled manuscript.

5. Charles E. Samuels, "Irving Bacheller: A Critical Biography," Ph.D. diss., St. Lawrence University, 1942, pp. 288-89, 229-30.

6. A.J. Hanna, *A Bibliography of the Writings of Irving Bacheller* (Winter Park, Fla: Rollins College, 1939), p. 19.

7. William Dean Howells, author and contemporary of Irving Bacheller, book review, published in Irving Bacheller, *Darrel of the Blessed Isles* (Boston: Lothrop, 1903).

8. Bacheller, "My Lost Novel," pp. 200-201.

9. Pat Roberts, personal interview, July 31, 1994, Marshall, N.C.

10. Jeannette Armstrong to the author, March 12, 1988.

11. Mary Kestler Clyde. "Gentle Jane's Recital," in *Flashbacks to Dawn: Eyeopeners in Preparatory School, Circa 1914-1922* (New York: Vantage Press, 1983), p. 61

12. Ibid.

13. Jeannette Armstrong to author, Sept. 22, 1985.

14. Bacheller, "Left Behind," p. 37.

15. Bacheller, "My Lost Novel," p. 201.

16. Book reviews in *Darrel of the Blessed Isles*.

17. Clarence Hurd Gaines, "Irving Bacheller: An Attempt at Interpretation," in Hanna, *Bibliography of the Writings of Irving Bacheller*, p. 12.

18. Samuels, "Irving Bacheller," pp. 267-89.

19. Ibid., p. iv.

20. Ibid., pp. 184-86.

21. Nola Jane Gentry Yrjana to author, Feb. 27, 1988.

22. Irving Bacheller to Maud Long, June 17, 1942, courtesy of Jane Long Douglas.

### 7. Old Counce, Jane, and the Jack Tales

1. Hicks, Hicks, and Hicks, *The Hicks Families*, p. 180.

2. Cheryl Oxford, "The Storyteller as Craftsman: Stanley Hicks Telling 'Jack and the Bull,'" *North Carolina Folklore Journal* 36, no. 2 (1989): 75.

3. Thomas G. Burton, *Some Ballad Folks* (Johnson City: East Tennessee State Univ., 1978) , p. 19.

4. Harmon, *The Harmon Family*, p. 82.

5. Yrjana to author, Feb. 26, 1988.

6. Stith Thompson, *The Folktale* (New York: Holt Rinehart & Winston, 1946), p. 8.

7. Maud Long, Library of Congress Recording 9159 B1, B2, LC 47, recorded by Duncan Emrich, Washington, D.C., 1947.

8. C. Paige Gutierrez, "The Jack Tale: A Definition of a Folk Tale Sub-Genre," *North Carolina Folklore Journal* 26, no. 2 (Sept. 1978): 85-110. This volume of the journal is called the "Jack Tale Issue" and is given entirely to Jack tales and articles about them.

9. Bacheller, "My Lost Novel," p. 214-19.

10. E. Henry Mellinger, *Folk-Songs of the Southern Highlands* (New York: J.J. Augustin, 1933), p. 153.

11. Maud Gentry Long, "Old Fire Dragaman," Library of Congress Recording 9162 A, B, LC/AFS, recorded by Duncan Emrich, Washington, D.C., 1947.

12. Richard Chase, *Grandfather Tales* (Boston: Houghton Mifflin, 1948), p. vii.

13. Chase, *Jack Tales*, p. xi.

14. Carter, "Mountain White Folk-Lore," p. 360.

15. Ibid., p. 362.

### 8. Balladry

1. The results of John C. Campbell's research for the Russell Sage Foundation are contained in *The Southern Highlander and His Homeland*, completed by Olive Dame Campbell from his notes after her husband's death. It was first published in 1921 by the Russell Sage Foundation and republished in 1969 by the University Press of Kentucky.

2. Olive Dame Campbell, *The Life and Work of John Charles Campbell, September 15, 1868-May 2, 1919* (Madison: Wisconsin College Printing, 1968), p. 140.

3. Ibid., pp. 140-41

4. Davidson, introduction to Goodrich, *Mountain Homespun*.

5. Campbell, *Life and Work of John Charles Campbell*, pp. 297, 375.

6. Ibid., p. 419.

7. Ibid., p. 231.

8. In 1988 Douglas Day, folklorist at the John C. Campbell Folk School in Brasstown, North Carolina, searched for Olive Dame Campbell's original manuscripts, believing that there were sixty or so ballads. They were not in the school's archives or with the Campbell papers in the Southern Historical Collection at the University of North Carolina in Chapel Hill. In the Sharp collection there were about sixty ballads which Sharp had taken down from Olive Campbell's singing. At the Ralph Vaughn Williams Memorial Library at the Cecil Sharp House in London, Day discovered copies of Olive Campbell's entire collection- -more than 250 ballads and songs collected in Kentucky, Tennessee, and Georgia between 1907 and 1914. The tunes were missing, but copies of the texts were recovered. Betty Nance Smith and Douglas Day, Folk School Song Book (Brasstown: John C. Campbell Folk School, 1991), pp. iv-v. Karpeles, *Cecil Sharp*, pp. 130-31.

9. H.M. Belden, Missouri folk song scholar, book review in *Sewanee Review* (1917):

253-55. Francis James Child, *The English and Scottish Popular Ballads*, 5 vols. (Boston and New York: Houghton Mifflin, 1882-1898; rpt., New York: Dover, 1965). This collection of 305 traditional English and Scottish ballads with many versions and variants was done by Child, a Harvard English professor, in the last part of the nineteenth century.

10. David E. Whisnant, *All That Is Native and Fine: The Politics of Culture in an American Region* (Chapel Hill: Univ. of North Carolina Press, 1983), pp. 124-25.

11. Archie Green, "A Folklorist's Creed and Folksinger's Gift," *Appalachian Journal* 7, no. 1-2 (1979-80): 40.

12. *Asheville-Citizen Times*, January 26, 1969.

13. Campbell, *Life and Work of John Charles Campbell*, p. 487.

14. Karpeles, *Cecil Sharp*, p. 143.

15. John C. Campbell to Frances Goodrich, Aug. 7, 1916, in Campbell, *Life and Work of John Charles Campbell*, p. 409.

16. Karpeles, *Cecil Sharp*, p. 145.

17. Campbell, *Life and Work of John Charles Campbell*, pp. 490-91.

18. Ibid., p. 487.

19. John C. Campbell to Goodrich, Aug. 7, 1916, ibid., p. 490.

20. Cecil Sharp, Diary, Vaughn Williams Memorial Library, Cecil Sharp House, London.

21. Pat Roberts, personal interview, July 31, 1994, Marshall, N.C.

22. John C. Campbell to John Glenn, Russell Sage Foundation, in Campbell, *Life and Work of John Charles Campbell*, p. 494.

23. Cecil Sharp to John C. Campbell, Sept. 12, 1916, ibid., p. 496.

24. Cecil Sharp to Professor C. Alphonso Smith, Sept. 17, 1916, in Arthur Kyle Davis Jr., *Traditional Ballads of Virginia* (1929; rpt., Charlottesville: Univ. Press of Virginia, 1969), p. 40.

25. Cecil Sharp, *English Folk Songs from the Southern Appalachians* (1932; rpt., London: Oxford Univ. Press, 1973), p. xxv.

26. Jane Gentry to Cecil Sharp, June 16, 1917, Cecil Sharp Collection, Vaughn Williams Memorial Library.

27. Elizabeth Dotterer, lecture, Sept. 29, 1987, Jesuit Residence, Hot Springs, N.C.

28. Berzilla Wallin, comments in author's class at Mars Hill College. Wallin was seventeen years old when Sharp came to Sodom, the name used by local residents. Davidson, introduction to *Mountain Homespun*, p. 4. This community was known as Sodom until 1901, when the post office name was changed to Revere. Frances Goodrich had expressed dismay at a name with such evil connotations.

29. Cecil Sharp to Olive Dame Campbell, Aug. 15, 1916, in Campbell, *Life and Work of John Charles Campbell*, p. 492

30. Sharp, *English Folk Songs*, p. xxiii.

31. Cecil Sharp to Olive Dame Campbell, Sept. 28, 1916, in Campbell, *Life and Work of John Charles Campbell*, p. 500.

32. C. Alphonso Smith, "Ballads Surviving in the U.S," *Musical Quarterly* 2, no. 1 (Jan. 1916): 129.

33. *Asheville Citizen-Times*, June 28, 1936.

34. Elizabeth Dotterer, personal interview, Jan. 25, 1988, Hot Springs, N.C.

35. William T. Moore, personal interview, Aug. 29, 1985, Meadow Fork, Madison County, N.C.

### 9. The Songs She Sang

1. Frances Dunham, "Genealogy of Madison County Sheltons," unpublished manuscript sent to author, Sept. 24, 1993.

2. William B. Shelton, "The Sheltons of Shelton Laurel," March 20, 1963, unpublished manuscript.

3. Burton, *Some Ballad Folks*.

4. R.P. Harriss, "Miss Gentry Collecting Folk Songs of Mountains Just Like Her Mother," Durham, Jan. 22 (no year), newspaper clipping in Bascom Lamar Lunsford Scrapbook, Appalachian Room, Mars Hill College, Mars Hill, N.C.

5. Sharp, *English Folk Songs*, p. xxix.

6. Ibid., p. xxx-xxxi.

7. Ibid., p. xxvii.

8. Bertrand H. Bronson, *The Traditional Tunes of the Child Ballads*, 4 vols. (Princeton: Princeton Univ. Press, 1959), 1: xxii.

9. Cecil Sharp to Phillips Barry, Nov. 20, 1917, Houghton Library, Harvard University.

10. John Forbes to author, March 1, 1989.

11. Maud Karpeles, *Introduction to English Folk Song* (London: Oxford University Press, 1973), p. 30.

12. Joan Baez, Vanguard Recording VRS 9094, vol. 2.

13. Cecil Sharp manuscript 3424/215, "Lamkin," collected from Jane Gentry Sept. 12, 1916.

14. Maud Long, Library of Congress recording ML 7889 A, recorded by Artus Moser, 1944.

15. James Watt Raine, *The Land of Saddle-Bags* (1924; rpt., Detroit: Singing Tree Press, 1969; Lexington: Univ. Press of Kentucky, 1997), pp 119-20. Bronson, *Traditional Tunes*, 3: 212.

16. James Watt Raine, "Mountain Ballads for Social Singing," manuscripts and documents, Special Collections, Berea College Library, Berea, Ky.

17. Child, *English and Scottish Popular Ballads*, 5 vols. (Boston and New York: Houghton Mifflin, 1882-1898; rpt., New York: Dover, 1965). p. 377, Johnie Scot. The 305 ballads in this collection are often referred to by the number given in this collection; thus Johnie Scot is Child 99.

## 10. Riddles and Rhymes

1. Maud Gentry Long, Library of Congress tape, recorded by Artus Moser, Oct. 21, 1944.

2. Maud Gentry Long, Library of Congress tape 9153 A1, recorded by Duncan Emrich, 1947.

3. Ibid., tape 9153 B5.

4. Dorothy Hartley, *Lost Country Life* (New York: Pantheon, 1980), in Anne Warner, *Traditional American Folk Songs from the Anne and Frank Warner Collection* (Syracuse: Syracuse Univ. Press, 1984), p. 204.

5. Evelyn Kendrick Wells, *The Ballad Tree* (New York: Ronald Press, 1950), p. 295.

6. Maud Gentry Long, Library of Congress tape 7905 A, recorded by Artus Moser, Oct. 27, 1944.

7. Ibid., tape 7905 B.

8. Hazel Moore, personal interview, Nov. 1994, Hot Springs, N.C.

9. H.B. Parks, "Follow the Drinking Gourd," in *The Treasury of Southern Folklore*, ed. B.A. Botkin (New York: Bonanza Books, 1980), pp. 476-77.

10. Yrjana to author, Feb. 26, 1988.

11. Yrjana, personal interview, Sept. 29, 1990, Fairbanks, Alaska. Dorothy (Mrs. James) Gentry, personal interview, Aug. 27, 1992, Hot Springs, N.C.

12. Carter, "Mountain White Riddles," pp. 76-80.

13. Maud Gentry Long, Library of Congress tape 9153 A2, recorded by Duncan Emrich, 1947.

14. Ibid.

15. Maud Clay Gibbs to author, Nov. 14, 1989. I have been unable to find the song "Dixie Dan."

16. Carole Honstead, "The Developmental Theory of Jean Piaget" in *Early Childhood Education Rediscovered* (New York: Holt Rinehart & Winston, 1968), p. 133.

17. Yrjana to author, Feb. 26, 1988.

18. Sharon Baker, personal interview, Dec. 1993, Hot Springs, N.C.

19. Bacheller, "My Lost Novel," pp. 217-19.

## 11. Time Passes

1. "Appalachia Calling . . . From a Small Mountain Village to the Great Northwest," *Mountaineer Times* 3 (Summer 1988): 18-20.

2. On weaving in the mountains, see Goodrich, *Mountain Homespun*. Elmeda Walker of Flag Pond, Tennessee (just across the North Carolina state line) was a master weaver. She and her two sisters were prolific weavers of coverlets, counterpanes, and plain cloth (Goodrich, p. 24). Josephine (Josie) Mast of Valle Cruces, Watauga County, North Carolina, along with her two sisters, supported a mail-order business with their expert weaving. A piece of Josephine's weaving was a gift to President Woodrow Wilson's daughter, Jesse, on her wedding day. The blue colors in the weaving did not match Jesse's bedroom, so the room was redecorated to match the weaving. Josephine was the granddaughter of Susan Harman Mast, who was the daughter of Cutliff Harman and sister of Andrew (Council Harmon's father) (Harmon, *Harmon Family*, p. 100)

3. Jeannette Armstrong to author, March 12, 1988. A "Pine Burr" coverlet draft attributed to "Mrs. Gentry" has been found in Francis Goodrich's notebook "Sources." Courtesy of Barbara Miller, Pisgah Forest, N.C., a member of the Southern Highland Handicraft Guild.

4. Eugenia Elliott, personal interview, Aug. 14, 1994, Hot Springs, N.C.

5. Lalla Bailey, tape recording, Gentry family reunion, 1980, courtesy of Phyllis Davies and Jeannette Armstrong.

6. Sunnybank registers, courtesy of Jane Long Douglas.

7. Jeannette Armstrong to author, April 12, 1993.

8. Maud Clay Gibbs to author, Nov. 14, 1989.

9. Elizabeth Dotterer, lecture, Sept. 29, 1987, Jesuit Residence, Hot Springs, N.C.

10. Brochure published by the Board of National Missions, Presbyterian Church, courtesy of Nancy Lippard, Hot Springs, N.C.

11. Bobbie Shuping told this story at a Gentry family reunion in Hot Springs in 1980 and confirmed it by telephone Dec. 1, 1994.

## 12. Epilogue

1. For the development of American music from traditional to commercial see Bill Malone, *Country Music USA* (Austin: Univ. of Texas Press, 1968).

2. R.P. Harriss, "Miss Gentry Collecting Folk Songs." Bessie Copeland McCastlain, personal interview, Aug. 31, 1996, Lake Junaluska, N.C.

3. Joan Moser, telephone interview, June 16, 1993, Swannanoa, N.C.

4. Jane Long Douglas, personal interview, Oct. 8, 1985, Athens, Ga.

5. Duncan Emrich to Maud Long, Oct. 22, 1954, Archive of Folk Song, Library of Congress.

6. Rae Korson to Maud Long, June 10, 1957, Archive of Folk Song, Library of Congress.

7. "Woman of the Week," *Asheville Citizen*, March 4, 1963.

# Bibliography

Arthur, John Preston. *History of Watauga County*. Richmond: Everett Waddey, 1915.

_____. *Western North Carolina: A History from 1730 to 1913*. Raleigh, N.C.: Edwards and Broughton, 1914.

Bacheller, Irving. *From Stores of Memory*. New York: Farrar & Rinehart, 1938.

_____."The Happiest Person I Ever Knew," *American Magazine*, March 1924.

_____. "Left Behind," *Collier's*, Oct. 30, 1915.

_____. *Opinions of a Cheerful Yankee*. Indianapolis: Bobbs Merrill, 1926.

Botkin, B.A. *A Treasury of Southern Folklore*. New York: Crown, 1944.

Bronson, Bertrand H. *The Traditional Tunes of the Child Ballads*. 4 vols. Princeton: Princeton Univ. Press, 1959.

Burton, Thomas. *Some Ballad Folks*. Johnson City: East Tennessee State Univ., 1978.

Campbell, John C. *The Southern Highlander and His Homeland*. 1921; reprint, Lexington: Univ. Press of Kentucky, 1969.

Campbell, Olive Dame. *The Life and Work of John Charles Campbell September 15, 1868-May 2, 1919*. Madison: Wisconsin College Printing Co., 1968.

Carter, Isabel Gordon. "Mountain White Folk-Lore: Tales from the Southern Blue Ridge." *Journal of American Folklore* 38 (July-Sept. 1925): 340-70.

_____. "White Mountain Riddles." *Journal of American Folklore* 47
(January 1934): 76-80.

Chase, Richard, ed. *American Folk Tales and Songs*. New York: New American Library, 1956.

_____. *Grandfather Tales*. Boston: Houghton Mifflin, 1948.

_____. *The Jack Tales*. Boston: Houghton Mifflin, 1943.

Child, Francis James. *The English and Scottish Popular Ballads*. 5 vols. Boston and New York: Houghton Mifflin, 1882-1898; reprint, New York: Dover, 1965.

Clyde, Mary Kestler. *Flashbacks to Dawn: Eyeopeners in Preparatory School, Circa 1914-1922*. New York: Vantage Press, 1983.

Connelley, William Elsey. *The Founding of Harman's Station*. New York: Torch Press, 1910.

Davis, Arthur Kyle. *Traditional Ballads of Virginia*. Charlottesville: Univ. Press of Virginia, 1929; reprint, 1969.

Dressler, Muriel Miller. *Appalachia.* Charleston, W.V.: MHS Publications, 1977.

Dykeman, Wilma. *The French Broad.* Knoxville: Univ. of Tennessee Press, 1955.

Emrich, Duncan. *Folklore on the American Land.* Boston: Little, Brown , 1972.

Gaffney, Sanna, ed. *Heritage of Watauga County, North Carolina,* vol. 1, 1984. Winston Salem. N.C.: Hunter, 1984.

Goodrich, Frances Louisa. *Mountain Homespun.* Knoxville: Univ. of Tennessee Press, 1989. [A facsimile of the original published in 1931, with a new introduction by Jan Davidson.]

Hale, John P. *Trans-Allegheny Pioneers.* Raleigh, N. C.: Derreth Printing, 1971.

Hanna, A.J. *A Bibliography of the Writings of Irving Bacheller.* Winter Park, Fla.: Rollins College, 1939.

Harmon, Terry. *The Harmon Family.* Boone, N.C.: Minor's Publishing, 1984.

Hicks, John Henry, Mattie Hicks, and Barnabas B. Hicks. *The Hicks Families of Western North Carolina.* Boone, N.C.: Minor's Printing, 1991.

Jones, Loyal. *Appalachian Values.* Ashland, Ky.: Jesse Stuart Foundation, 1994.

Karpeles, Maud. *Cecil Sharp.* Chicago: Univ. of Chicago Press, 1967.

_____. *Introduction to English Folk Song.* London: Oxford Univ. Press, 1973.

*Kentucky: A Guide to the Bluegrass State.* 1939. Reprint, New York: Harcourt Brace, 1973; Lexington: Univ. Press of Kentucky, 1996 [as *The WPA Guide to Kentucky*].

Laws, G. Malcolm, Jr. *American Balladry from British Broadsides.* Philadelphia: American Folklore Society, 1957.

Malone, Bill C. *Country Music U.S.A.* Austin: Univ. of Texas Press, 1968.

Mellinger, E. Henry. *Folk-Songs of the Southern Highlands.* New York: J.J. Augustin, 1933.

Miles, Emma Bell. *The Spirit of the Mountains.* 1905; reprint, Knoxville: Univ. of Tennessee Press, 1975.

Moore, Della Hazel. *Hot Springs of North Carolina.* Asheville, N.C.: Biltmore Press, 1992.

Newell, William Wells. *Games and Songs of American Children.* 1883; reprint, New York: Dover, 1963.

*North Carolina Folklore Journal.* Vols. 22, no. 1; 26, no. 2; 31, no. 1; 34, nos. 1, 2; 36, no. 2; 38, no. 2.

Painter, Jacqueline Burgin. *The German Invasion of Western North Carolina.* Asheville, N.C.: Biltmore Press, 1992.

_____. *The Season of Dorland-Bell.* Asheville, N.C.: Biltmore Press, 1987.

Paludan, Phillip Shaw. *Victims.* Knoxville: Univ. of Tennessee Press, 1981.

Perdue, Charles, ed. *Outwitting the Devil.* Santa Fe, N.M.: Ancient Press, 1987.

Purkey, Lena Penland. *Home in Madison County.* Johnson City: East Tennessee State University, 1975.

Raine, James Watt. *The Land of Saddle-Bags.* 1924; reprint, Detroit: Singing Tree Press, 1969; Lexington: Univ. Press of Kentucky, 1997.

Reid, Christian (Frances C. Tiernan). *The Land of the Sky.* New York: D. Appleton, 1892.

Samuels, Charles E. "Irving Bacheller: A Critical Biography." Ph.D. diss., Syracuse University, 1952.

Shapiro, Henry D. *Appalachia on Our Mind.* Chapel Hill: Univ. of North Carolina Press, 1978.

Sharp, Cecil. *English Folk Songs from the Southern Appalachians*. 1932; reprint, London: Oxford Univ. Press, 1973.

_____, and Maud Karpeles. *Eighty English Folk Songs from the Southern Appalachians*. Cambridge: MIT Press, 1968.

Sondley, F.A. *History of Buncombe County*, vol. 2. Asheville, N.C.: Advocate, 1930.

Thompson, Stith. *The Folktale*. New York: Holt, Rinehart & Winston, 1946.

_____. *Motif-Index of Folk-Literature*. Bloomington: Indiana Univ. Press, 1966.

Trotter, William R. *Bushwhackers: The Civil War in North Carolina: The Mountains*. Winston-Salem, N.C.: John F. Blair, 1988.

Underwood, Jinsie. *This Is Madison County*. Mars Hill, N.C.: Bicentennial Commission, 1974.

Van Noppen, Ina W., and John J. Van Noppen. *Western North Carolina Since the Civil War*. Boone, N.C.: Appalachian Consortium Press, 1973.

Warner, Anne. *Traditional American Folk Songs from the Anne and Frank Warner Collection*. Syracuse: Syracuse Univ. Press, 1984.

Wellman, Manley Wade. *The Kingdom of Madison*. Chapel Hill: Univ. of North Carolina Press, 1973.

Wells, Evelyn Kendrick. *The Ballad Tree*. New York: Ronald Press, 1950.

Whisnant, David E. *All That Is Native and Fine: The Politics of Culture in an American Region*. Chapel Hill: Univ. of North Carolina Press, 1983.

White, Newman Ivey, ed. *The Frank C. Brown Collection of North Carolina Folklore*, vols. 2-5. Durham, N.C.: Duke Univ. Press, 1952.

# Index

language, 82; changes in successive repetitions, 138
"ballets," 72
Banner Elk, 18
"Barbara Allen," 76, 78, 81, 152, 153, 199; Olive Campbell, 65; Emma Hensley, 68; Jane Gentry, 69; Ellie Johnson, 75; common ballad, 75
barn raisings, 25
Barry, Philips, 79, 99
Battle of New Orleans, 18
Beech Creek, N.C., 16, 17
Beech Mountain, N.C., 16, 17, 58, 63, 77; singers from, 75
Belden, H.M., 99
Bell Institute, 94
Berea College, 82, 137
Big Falls of Elk, Cranberry Settlement, 18
Big Laurel, N.C., 66, 68, 74
Big Rich Mountain, 87
Big Ridge, N.C., 16, 17
"Billy Boy." See "My Boy Billy"
"Billy McGee McGore" ("The Three Ravens"), 78, 143, 199
"Bird Song, The," 78, 184, 200
"Black Is the Color of My True Love's Hair" (sung by Lizzie Roberts), 70
Black Mountains, 23
Blackwell, J. Lawton (Jack), 95
"Bloody Warning, The" ("The Silver Dagger"), 69, 137, 181, 200
"Blue Danube Waltz," 47
Blue Mountain Room (White House), 93
boarders, 46, 47
boarding house, Gentry, 44, 94; cost of lodging and meal, 46; cooking, 95-96
Bolte, Johannes, 106
Boone, Daniel, 14
Boone, N.C., 15, 19, 20, 93
Botkin, B.A.: The Treasury of Southern Folklore, 101
Bridge Street, Hot Springs, 87, 93
"Brisk Young Lover, The" ("Butcher Boy"), 69, 78, 175, 200
British tradition, 71
broadside ballads, 72, 138, 200
Brockway, Howard, 99
"Broken Token, The," 69, 74, 78, 80, 101, 174, 200; as "The Soldier's Return," 81; recording (MGL), 202
Bronson, Bertrand H., 67, 78, 79; "Gypsy Laddie," 82; The Traditional Tunes of the Child Ballads, 99, 138
Broughton State Hospital, 29
Brown, Frank C., 99
"Bruton Town" ("In Seaport Town"), 80, 163, 200
Buchanan, Annabel Morris, 100, 102
Buckeye, N.C., 16, 17
Buncombe Turnpike, 23, 42
Burnsville, N.C., 23

Burton, Thomas G., Some Ballad Folks, 75
Byford, Enoch Virgil, 92-93
Byford, Virgil (son of Emily), 93

Cades Cove, Tenn., 57
calculating time, 18
Calfee, Dr., 44; and Asheville Normal School, 72
"Calling Now for Me," 83
Cambridge University, 137
Campbell, John C., 66, 67, 68, 80; on illiteracy and education, 40; social survey, 65, 207 n 8.1
Campbell, Olive Dame, 65; collecting, 66, 67, 68, 70; manuscripts, 207 n 8.8
cane mill, 17
cante-fable, 61, 121-22
cantilever bridge, 19
Carmen, N.C., 68, 74
Carolina Special (train), 45-46
Carter family (A.P., Sara, and Maybelle), 100
Carter, Isabel Gordon, 21, 51, 57, 64, 94, 99; "Mountain White Folk-lore: Tales from the Southern Blue Ridge," 4, 106; "Mountain White Riddles," 88
Caswell County, N.C., 12
Catholic church, 48
Charlotte (ship), 14
Chase, Richard, 102; Jack Tales, 58, 63, 90; recording Maud, 100 Cherokee Indians, 14, 41
"Cherry Tree Carol," 69, 74, 76, 79-80, 81, 101, 144, 199; "The Cherry Tree" (recording, MGL), 202
Chickamauga Indians, 13
Child, Francis James, 67, 137; The English and Scottish Popular Ballads, 138
Child ballads, 70, 75, 78, 138
children's songs, 75, 78, 201; Laurel singers, 79, 138
Christie, William: Traditional Ballad Airs, 78
Civil War, 20, 23, 25, 40, 42
Clay (Rolfe), Betty (dau. of Mae), 37, 93, 102
Clay (Rolfe), Lalla Mae (dau. of Mae), 93, 102
Clay, Luther, 93
Clay, Margaret (dau. of Mae), 93
Clay (Gibbs), Maud (dau of Mae), 78, 93, 97; and "Dixie Dan" (game), 89
Clay (Shuping), R.L. (Bobbie) (dau. of Mae), 93
Clinton, Ill., 16
Clyde, Mary Kestler, 37, 78, 100
"Cock Robin," 78, 195, 201
Collier's, 53-54
Combs, Josiah, 99
"Come All Ye Fair and Tender Ladies," 77. See also "If I Had A'Known"
commercial music, 100; recordings, 101
Confederate government, and death benefits, 17

Kincaid, Bradley, 100
Kittredge, George Lyman, 67, 137
Knoxville, Tenn., 22, 41, 42; Mae attended
  school in, 93
Korson, Rae: Archive of Folk Song, 101

"Lady and the Dragoon, The," 164, 200
"Lamkin" ("False Lamkin," "Long
  Lamkin"), 70, 71, 75, 78, 81, 154, 199
Lance Hotel, 71
Lance sisters, 48
land, buying, 22, 31, 72
Land of Saddle-Bags, The (James Watt
  Raine), 82
Langdon, William Chauncy, 66
"Laurel Country," 65, 66, 67, 68
Laurel River, 23, 25
Lawless, Ray: Folksingers and Folksongs
  in America, 101
Laws, Malcolm G., Jr.: American Balladry
  from British Broadsides, 138
Lawson, Pete, 45
Lawson Suttles place, 31
Lawton J. Blackwell Elementary and High
  School, Alaska, 95
"Lazy Jack and His Calf Skin," 59, 62, 106,
  132-34. See also "Jack and the Heifer
  Hide"
Leach, MacEdward: The Ballad Book, 100
leather britches, 36
Lenoir, N.C., 20
Lewis, Leo, 66
Library of Congress, 5, 58, 63, 64, 84, 139;
  tapes, 79; recording, 81; Archive of Folk
  Song, 99; recording Maud, 100-101;
  tapes, 137
Lincoln, Mass., 40, 67
Little Creek, Madison County, N.C., 22
"Little Dicky Wigbun," 62, 107, 121-22;
  cante-fable, 61
"Little Maumie, The," 69, 180, 200
"Little Musgrave and Lady Barnard"
  ("Little Mattie Groves"), 69, 75, 76, 78,
  80, 151-152, 199
Lomax, John, 99
London Company, 12
Long, Grover Cleveland, 95, 97
Long, Maud Gentry. See Gentry, Lillie
  Bertha Maud
"Long Lamkin." See "Lamkin"
looms, 47, 93; and Emily, 27
"Lord Bateman" ("Young Beichan"), 74,
  76, 143, 199
"Lord Thomas and Fair Eleanor (Ellinor),"
  69, 73, 74, 75, 76, 78, 147, 199
"Lord Thomas and Fair Ellinor," 148-49,
  199
Lover's Leap, 41
lullabies, 86
Lunsford, Bascom Lamar, 4, 77, 99
Lyda, Dave, 92

Lyda, Mae (dau. of Nora), 92
Lynch, N.C., 25, 31

Macon, Uncle Dave, 100
Madison County, N.C., 4, 22, 23, 26, 59,
  66, 72, 74, 93; "Bloody Madison," 25;
  tobacco growing, 39; schools, hospital,
  43; Cecil Sharp in, 65; 66; flood, 67;
  singers, 75; other musicians, 99
Madison County Record, 26
manuscripts, 67, 207 n 8.8
map of Western North Carolina, 24
Maple Springs-Brushy Ridge area, 25
maple syrup, 17
Marchen (European fairy tales), 58
Marion, N.C., 94; textile mills, 49
Marks, Mrs. A.S., 98
Marshall, N.C., 23, 26, 31; tobacco
  warehouse, 39; flood, 67
Mast, John, 16
Mast, Josephine, 94, 210 n 11.2
Mast, Noah, 19
Mast, Susan Harmon, 16
Mathias, Louisa Katrina, 13
Matthews, Mary, 19
McCastlain, Bessie Copeland, 100
McGill, Josephine, 99
McNeil, W.K.: Southern Folk Ballads, 101-2
Meadow Fork of Spring Creek, 22, 23, 25,
  29, 31, 32, 39, 41, 44, 52, 63; Till
  Stamey's store, 36
"Meeting Is a Pleasure," 71, 182, 200
melodies, 77. See also tunes
Merrill, Charles, 55
Merrit, Charles, 49
missionaries, 66; Northern Protestant
  denominations, 40; Presbyterians, 41
missions, 67; Frances Goodrich, 66
molasses making, 25
Montezuma, N.C., 93
Moore, Jennie, 67
Moore, William (Bill), 25; m. Susan Reese,
  29; supplying hotel, 47-48; politics, 48;
  quoted, 73
Morgan, Thomas, 42
Moser, Artus, 81, 100, 101
Moses, Roy (son of Maggie), 93
Moses, Will, 93
Mount Mitchell, N.C., 23
Mountain Ballads for Social Singing
  (James Watt Raine), 82
"mountain friend of Dorland," 45
Mountain Homespun (Frances Louisa
  Goodrich), 210 n 11.2
Mountain Park Hotel, 42, 71, 75, 87, 92;
  supplies for dining room, 43, 47;
  internment camp, 47-48; burned, 48;
  flood, 67
mountain people, 32
mountain speech, 45
mountain ways, 45

222 • Index

radio, 75, 100
railroad service, 42
Raine, James Watt: *The Land of Saddle-Bags*, 82; *Mountain Ballads for Social Singing*, 82
Randolph County, N.C., 13
Rappahannock River, Va., 12
reading and writing: Jane, 6, 27; Goulder, 17; Hiram, 18; Ransom, 20; Doc and his sons, 36; Jane's children, 44
"Reap, Boys, Reap, 194, 201
recipes: leather britches, 36; scalloped apples and cheese, 95
recording machines, 73, 100
recordings, 75, 100
Rector, James E., 49
Reese, Harriett, 29, 49
Reese, Marion F., 29
Reese, Susan, 29
refrains, 62
Regis, Kundigunda, 11, 13
"Rejected Lover, The" (Once I Courted a Pretty Little Girl"), 69, 77, 81, 176, 200
religious songs, 201
repertoire, Jane's, 3, 64, 74-75, 78, 82, 83
"Revenoor Lady," 7-8
Revere (Sodom Laurel), 72
Reynolds, Henry, 42
Rice, Mrs. Tom, 74, 99
riddles, 51, 53, 88 -89, 94
Robbinsville, N.C., 95
Roberts, Harry, 70
Roberts, Lizzie, 70
Roberts, Pat, 52-53, 206 n 5.16
Robinson, Colonel, 14
Rogers, Jimmy, 100
Rolfe, Betty Clay. *See* Clay, Betty
Rosmond, 49
Rotary Club, Greeneville, Tenn., 97
Route 19 and 19E, 23
Rowan (now Randolph) County, N.C., 14
Rowland, Cyrena Harmon (Rene), 22
Rowland, Ellen Harmon (Ellie), 22
Rowland, Mike 22
Rowland, William, 22
Rumbough, Carrie, 42,45
Rumbough, Henry Thomas, 86
Rumbough, Col. James Henry, 42, 43, 45, 46, 48, 49, 87
Russell Sage Foundation, 66; Southern Highland Division, 65; and John Glenn, 69

Safford, Bessie, 48
Saluda Gap, 42
Sanders, Bud, 93
Sands, Mary, 74, 99
Scotia Seminary, 43
Scottish connection, 78
serviceberry ("sarvis") trees, 31, 32
Sevier, John, 13

Shafer, Lucy, 68
Shapiro, Henry, 41
Sharp, Cecil J., 6, 7, 10, 32, 40, 41, 49, 66, 69, 70, 75, 82, 94, 138; *English Folk Songs from the Southern Appalachians*, 4; musician, collector, 65; characteristics, 67; in "Laurel Country," 68; asthma, 68; singing communities, 71; British tradition, 71; religious songs, 71; letter from Jane Gentry, 71; method of collecting, 72; notation, 76; scales, 77; *Nursery Songs from the Appalachian Mountains*, 79; accuracy of notation, 79; musicologist, 137; dates songs collected, 138
Sharp-Campbell collection, 67, 79, 99; Campbell manuscripts, 207 n 8.8
Sharp manuscripts, 137
Shawnee Indians, 14
Shearin, Hubert, 99
sheep and cattle, 17; fleece, 5
"Sheffield Apprentice, The," 69, 74, 76, 173, 200
Shelton, Mandie, 66
Shelton, Roderick, descendants, 74
Shelton, William Riley, 74
Shelton Laurel, 74
Shelton Laurel massacre, 25
"Shooting of His Dear," 69, 164, 200
Shull's Mills, N.C., 23, 93
Shupe's Rockhouse, 15
Shuping, Bobbie Clay. *See* Clay, R.L. (Bobbie)
Shuping, Clay, 98
Shuping, Roy, 98
"Silver Dagger, The," 137. *See* "Bloody Warning, The"
Silvermine Creek, 70, 97
"Sing Said the Mother" ("Over in the Meadows"), 71, 79, 80, 197, 201
singing, community, 71
singing games, 71
slaves, 87
Smith, Ada: "Barbara Allen," 65
Smith, C. Alphonso, 7, 71, 72, 73; collecting, 99
Smith, Reed, 99
"snakin' the beds," 18
Snowbird Mountain, 95
soap making, 17
Sodom Laurel (Revere), 72
"Soldier, Soldier, Won't You Marry Me," 78, 79, 87, 101
"Soldier's Return, The." *See* "Broken Token, The"
*Some Ballad Folks* (Thomas G. Burton), 75
song collecting, 72; regional, 99
songs, Jane Gentry's, 137-38, 140-98
songs and ballads, 5, 45; of British origin, 65; modal, high quality, 68; variants, 78; emotion in, 79; how they were learned, 86. *See also* ballads